Contents at a Glance

W9-AHB-607

Table of Contents

About the Author

Craig James Johnston has been involved with technology since his high school days at Glenwood High in Durban, South Africa, when his school was given some Apple][Europluses. From that moment, technology captivated him, and he has owned, supported, evangelized, and written about it.

Craig has been involved in designing and supporting large-scale enterprise networks with integrated email and directory services since 1989. He has held many different IT-related positions in his career ranging from sales support engineer to mobile architect for a 40,000-smartphone infrastructure at a large bank.

You can see Craig's previously published work in his books *Professional BlackBerry*, and many books in the *My* series, covering devices from Apple, BlackBerry, HTC, Google, Motorola, and Samsung.

Craig also enjoys high-horsepower, high-speed vehicles and tries very hard to keep to the speed limit while driving them.

Originally from Durban, South Africa, Craig has lived in the United Kingdom, the San Francisco Bay Area, and New Jersey, where he now lives with his wife, Karen, and a couple of cats.

Craig would love to hear from you. Feel free to contact Craig about your experiences with *My Android Phone* at http://www.CraigsBooks.info.

All comments, suggestions, and feedback are welcome, including positive and negative.

Dedication

"I have noticed even people who claim everything is predestined, and that we can do nothing to change it, look before they cross the road."
—*Stephen Hawking*

Acknowledgments

I would like to express my deepest gratitude to the following people on the *My Android Phone* team who all worked extremely hard on this book:

Michelle Newcomb, my acquisitions editor who worked with me to give this project an edge as well as technical editors Vince Averello, Christian Kenyeres, and Chaim Krause, development editor Charlotte Kughen, project editor Lori Lyons, copy editor Karen Annett, compositor Gloria Schurick, indexer Cheryl Lenser, and proofreader Debbie Williams.

We Want to Hear from You!

As the reader of this book, *you* are our most important critic and commentator. We value your opinion and want to know what we're doing right, what we could do better, what areas you'd like to see us publish in, and any other words of wisdom you're willing to pass our way.

We welcome your comments. You can email or write to let us know what you did or didn't like about this book—as well as what we can do to make our books better.

Please note that we cannot help you with technical problems related to the topic of this book.

When you write, please be sure to include this book's title and author as well as your name and email address. We will carefully review your comments and share them with the author and editors who worked on the book.

Email: feedback@quepublishing.com

Mail: Que Publishing
         ATTN: Reader Feedback
         800 East 96th Street
         Indianapolis, IN 46240 USA

Reader Services

Visit our website and register this book at quepublishing.com/register for convenient access to any updates, downloads, or errata that might be available for this book.

In this chapter, you become familiar with the external features of a typical Android phone and the basics of getting started with the Android operating system. Topics include the following:

→ Your Android phone's external features
→ Fundamentals of Android 5.0 (Lollipop)
→ First-time setup
→ Synchronization software

Getting to Know Your Android Phone

You can start to get to know more about your Android phone by examining the external features, device features, and how Google's latest operating system—Android 5.0 (Lollipop)—works.

One important thing to remember about any Android phone bearing the Nexus name is that it is a pure Android phone with no wireless carrier or vendor modifications. This book refers to this unchanged version of Android, but where appropriate some vendor-specific information is included, too.

Your Android Phone's External Features

Becoming familiar with the external features of your Android phone is a good place to start because you will be using them often.

Front

Light sensor

Proximity sensor

Front camera

Touchscreen

Home button

Back button

Overview button

Proximity sensor Detects when you place your phone against your head to talk, which causes it to turn off the screen so that your ear doesn't inadvertently activate things on the screen.

Light sensor Normally placed near the front camera, it adjusts the brightness of the screen based on the brightness of the ambient light.

Front camera Front-facing camera that you can use for video chat, taking self-portraits, and even unlocking your Android phone using your face.

Touchscreen The Android phone has a screen that incorporates 10-finger capacitive touch. The exact physical dimensions, technology used, and resolution of the screen differ depending on which vendor makes and sells the phone.

Back button   Tap to go back one screen when using an application or menu. This virtual button is actually on the screen; however some vendors place a touch-sensitive Back button below the screen.

Overview button   Previously called the Recent Apps button, tap it to see a list of recently used apps and switch between them. This virtual button is actually on the screen. Some vendors, such as Samsung, HTC, and others, modify Android so that this virtual button is removed. These vendors normally require that you touch and hold the Home button to see recent apps or they have a dedicated Recent Apps/Overview button under the screen.

Home button   Tap to go to the Home screen. The application that you are using continues to run in the background. This virtual button is actually on the screen; however, some vendors, such as Samsung, HTC, and others, place an actual physical Home button below the screen.

Menu button   Some vendors, such as Samsung, HTC, and others, keep the Menu button even though it is a hold-over from a much older version of Android. Tap the Menu button to see a context-aware menu of options based on the screen or app you are using.

Button Placement

Google creates Android, and in older versions of Android, many devices that ran Android used physical buttons and even featured trackballs for navigation. More recent versions of Android have moved the physical buttons onto the screen as virtual buttons. Android also no longer has a Menu button (virtual or not), opting for a Menu icon in each app. However some vendors, such as Samsung, HTC, and others, have chosen to implement buttons using their own design. Samsung has chosen to keep the physical Home button on all its devices. Samsung (as well as some other vendors) also has kept the Back and Overview/Recent Apps buttons below the screen. Depending on the model of phone you own, you may have an Overview/Recent Apps button or a Menu button. These are some variations you might see.

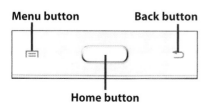

Menu button   **Back button**

Home button

Back button   **Home button**

Back

3.5mm headphone jack

Rear camera

LED Camera flash

Micro-USB port

Microphone

Microphone   Used for video and audio calls (using apps such as Skype or Google Talk) and recording video. The actual placement of this microphone differs between manufacturers. This microphone is also used for noise cancelling while you are on a phone call.

3.5 mm headphone jack   Used with third-party headsets so that you can enjoy music and talk on the phone. The actual placement of the headphone jack differs based on the manufacturer of the phone.

Micro-USB port   Used to synchronize your Android phone to your desktop computer and charge it. The placement of the Micro-USB port differs based on the manufacturer of the phone. Some manufacturers are starting to include a Micro-USB 3 port, which is slightly longer. Your Android phone's Micro-USB port may include technology that allows you to plug your phone directly into your TV to play content on it.

LED camera flash   Illuminates the area when you're taking photos or recording video. In this example the LED flash is contained in the ring around the camera; however, the vast majority of Android phones have an LED flash either alongside or under the camera.

Rear camera   Rear-facing camera. The exact lens type, sensor resolution, and aperture differ based on who makes and sells the phone.

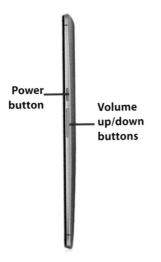

Power button

Volume up/down buttons

Power button   Press once to wake your Android phone. Press and hold for 1 second to reveal a menu of choices. Depending on the manufacturer of the phone, the choices enable you to put your Android phone into silent mode, airplane mode, or power it off completely. The location of the Power button differs based on the phone manufacturer.

Volume up/down buttons   Control the audio volume on calls and while playing audio and video. The location of the volume buttons differs based on the phone manufacturer.

Other Sensors and Radios

Your Android phone includes a Wi-Fi (WLAN) radio for connecting to your home or office networks or to Wi-Fi hotspots in airports, coffee shops, and even on planes. It also has a Bluetooth radio for connecting Bluetooth accessories such as headsets. Most Android phones include a Near Field Communications (NFC) radio for mobile payments and swapping information between other Android devices. On the sensor front, your Android phone probably has an accelerometer for detecting movement, a compass for directional awareness, a gyroscope for assisting with movement detection and gaming, a Global Positioning System (GPS) for detecting where you are on the planet, and, in some cases, a Hall Sensor for detecting a magnetic field. Finally, your Android phone will include radios for connecting to cellular voice and data networks. These could include GSM, GPRS, CDMA, WCDMA, and LTE.

First-Time Setup

Before setting up your new Android phone, it is advisable that you have a Google account. This is because your Android phone running Android is tightly integrated into Google and enables you to store your content in the Google Cloud, including any books and music you buy or movies you rent. If you do not already have a Google account, head to https://accounts.google.com on your desktop computer and sign up for one.

You Need Connectivity

You need to connect to a Wi-Fi network, or make sure that your Android phone can connect to the cellular data network, when using the following steps to set it up. It is recommended that you connect to a Wi-Fi network due to the amount of data that may be used after the phone finishes its setup and starts updating apps.

1. Press the Power button until you see the animation start playing.

2. Swipe up or down to change your location if needed.

3. Tap to start the setup process.

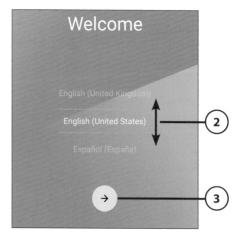

4. Select a Wi-Fi network to connect to. If you are not in range of a Wi-Fi network, or would rather use your cellular data, tap Skip, and continue with step 7.

5. Type in the Wi-Fi network password (if a password is required).

6. Tap Connect.

7. If you have another Android device (phone or smartphone) running Android 5.0 (Lollipop) and you want to transfer the data from it to your new phone, follow the instructions on this screen, or tap Skip to continue.

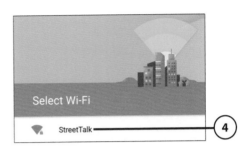

Select Wi-Fi

StreetTalk —————————————— ④

StreetTalk
Password
• • • • • • • • • • • —————————————— ⑤

☐ Show password

☐ Advanced options

CANCEL   CONNECT ——— ⑥

Tap & Go

Quickly copy any Google Accounts, backed up apps and data from your existing Android device. To copy:

1. Make sure your other device is on and ————— ⑦
unlocked.

2. Briefly place the two devices back-to-back until you hear a tone, then set aside.

Learn more

<   SKIP >

**Tap to skip
this step**

8. Enter your Gmail email address if you already have a Gmail account and tap Next.

9. Enter your Google account password.

10. Tap Next.

11. Tap to choose one of your other Android devices to restore data from, or choose Set Up as New Device to continue setting this phone up as a new Android phone.

12. Tap Next to continue.

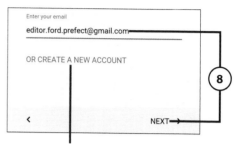

Enter your email

editor.ford.prefect@gmail.com

OR CREATE A NEW ACCOUNT

8

< NEXT →

Tap to get a Google account

Password

··········

9

Forgot password? · Privacy & Terms

< NEXT → **10**

Get your apps & data

Easily set up your new device by restoring from a backup of another device.

Backups include apps, app data, system settings and Wi-Fi passwords.

Restore from this backup

Set up as new device ▼ **11**

< NEXT > **12**

13. Check this box if you want to back up your phone's data so that it can be restored to a new Android phone or smartphone in the future.

14. Check this box if you are okay with Google collecting information about your geographic location at any time. Although Google keeps this information safe, if you are concerned about privacy rights, you should uncheck this box.

15. Check this box if you are okay with your phone scanning for Wi-Fi networks even if you have the Wi-Fi radio turned off. This helps improve location accuracy.

16. Check this box if you are okay letting Google collect diagnostic information about your phone and the apps running on it.

17. Tap Next to continue.

18. Choose whether you want to let Google use and store your location, and have access to your calendar and data so that it can allow you to use Google Now. Learn more about Google Now in Chapter 7.

19. Tap Next to complete your phone setup.

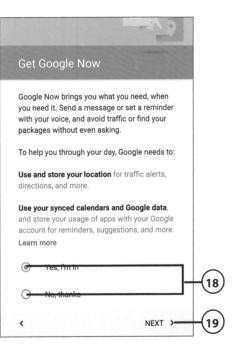

Extra Setup Steps for Some Phones

Many vendors that make Android phones modify them so that they include special services and features unique to their brand of phone—for example, separate app stores, special cloud services that provide backup and restore services, and other unique brand-only features. Normally, these features require that you have an account with the vendor itself in addition to having your Google account. Some phone vendors include extra apps such as Dropbox and use those services to back up your phone or store the pictures you take with the camera. During the phone setup, you might be asked to enter your vendor-specific account details (or create a new account) or participate in extra services such as Dropbox.

Fundamentals of Android 5.0 (Lollipop)

Your Android phone is run by an operating system called Android. This book covers the latest version of Android, called Android 5.0 (also called Android Lollipop). Some manufacturers of Android phones modify Android to provide a unique experience. For example Samsung's modifications are called TouchWiz, and HTC's modifications are called Sense UI. Where appropriate, this book covers these differences.

The Lock Screen

If you haven't used your Android phone for a while, the screen goes blank to conserve battery power. Here is how to interact with the Lock screen.

1. Press the Power button to wake up your Android phone. Some phones have a physical Home button (as discussed earlier), and in these instances, pressing the physical Home button also wakes up your phone.

2. Swipe up anywhere on the screen to unlock your phone.

Notifications

T-Mobile

2:25
Sunday, February 8

Craig Johnston   2:24 PM
Hi
editor.ford.prefect@gmail.com   52

USB debugging connected
Touch to disable USB debugging.

Charging (30 mins u til full

Swipe left to launch the Camera app

Swipe right to launch the Phone app

2

Ambient Display

Some Android phones include a feature called Ambient Display. If you tap the screen twice or pick up your phone, you see a dimmed version of the Lock screen showing your notifications. Tapping the screen while the Ambient Display is visible wakes up your phone fully, but if you just leave it or put it back down, the Ambient Display screen disappears. New notifications also briefly appear on-screen as they arrive.

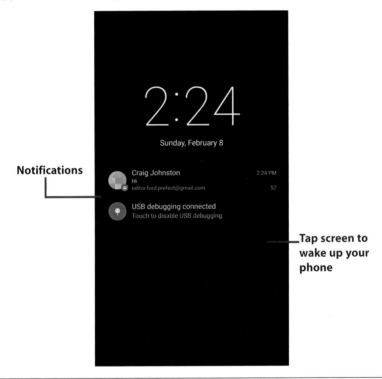

Notifications

Tap screen to wake up your phone

Lock Screen Differences

Some manufacturers modify Android to create their own experience, and one of the tweaks is how the Lock screen works. For example, on Samsung phones, you can swipe randomly in any direction to unlock the phone, and to launch the Phone or Camera apps, you drag the respective icons upward. HTC is another example. On its phones' Lock screens, you see a row of icons plus the Lock icon. To unlock the HTC phone, you drag the Lock icon upward. To launch apps, drag the App icon upward.

Talk to Your Phone While It's Sleeping

As long as it is plugged into power, you can speak to your phone and give it commands, even while it is sleeping. Just say "OK Google" to make your phone wake up and listen for commands. You can search your phone or the Internet, or give commands to send an email, add reminders, and many other things. To enable this feature, go to Settings, Language & Input, Voice Input, tap the cog icon to the right of Enhanced Google Services, tap "OK Google" Detection, and make sure that all three switches are in the on position.

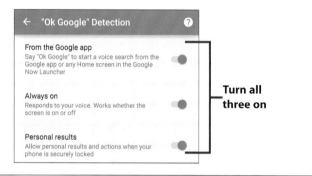

Work with Notifications on the Lock Screen

With Android 5.0 (Lollipop) you can work with notifications right on the Lock screen. Tapping a notification takes you straight to the app that created it. Read more about notifications later in this section.

Work with Android Settings on the Lock Screen

With Android 5.0 (Lollipop) you can work with settings (such as Airplane Mode, turning Wi-Fi on or off, and so on) right on the Lock screen. To work with settings, pull down the Quick Settings Bar by swiping down from the top of the screen with two fingers to view and change commonly used settings. Tap the Settings icon to see a full list of settings. Tap the User icon to log in as a different phone user, a guest phone user, or create a new phone user. Read more about phone users later in this chapter in the "Setting Up Multiple Users on Your Phone" section.

See all settings

Log in as a different user

Slide down the Quick Settings Bar

Answering a Call from the Lock Screen

If your phone is locked when a call comes in, you have three choices: Drag the phone icon right to answer the call, drag it left to reject the call, or drag it up to reject the call and send a preset text message (SMS) to the caller.

Reject with message

Reject

Answer

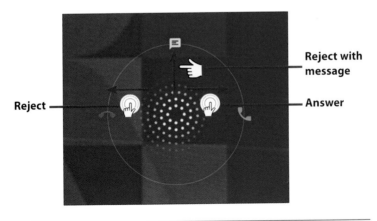

The Home Screen

After you unlock your Android phone, you are presented with the middle Home screen pane. Your Android phone typically has five Home screen panes. The Home screen panes contain application shortcuts, a Launcher icon, a Notification panel, shortcuts, a Favorites Tray, and widgets.

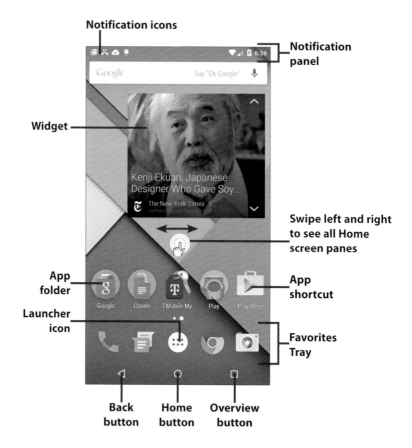

Notification panel The Notification panel shows information about Bluetooth, Wi-Fi, and cellular coverage, as well as the battery level and time. The Notification panel also serves as a place in which apps can alert or notify you using notification icons.

Notification icons Notification icons appear in the Notification panel when an app needs to alert or notify you of something. For example, the phone app can show the new email icon indicating that you have new unread emails.

Widgets   Widgets are mini apps that run right on the Home screen panes. They are specially designed to provide functionality and real-time information. An example of a widget is one that shows the current weather or provides search capability. You can move and resize widgets.

App shortcut   Tapping an app shortcut launches the associated app.

App folders   App folders are groups of apps that you can use to organize and declutter your screen.

Favorites Tray   The Favorites Tray is visible on all Home screen panes. You can drag apps to the Favorites Tray so that they are available no matter which Home screen pane you are looking at. You can rearrange and move apps in the Favorites Tray.

Launcher icon   Tap to show application icons for all applications that you have installed on your Android phone. The exact appearance and placement of the Launcher icon may differ on your phone, but it is usually an icon made up of a grid of dots or squares and may appear in the middle of the Favorites Tray or to the right.

>>>*Go Further*

WORKING WITH NOTIFICATIONS AND QUICK SETTINGS

To interact with notifications that appear in the Notification panel, place one finger above the top of the screen and swipe down to reveal the notifications. Swipe each individual notification off the screen to the left or right to clear them one by one. Using two fingers, drag down on a notification to expand it. You can also work with settings (such as Airplane Mode or turning Wi-Fi on or off). To work with settings, tap the Quick Settings Bar to view and change commonly used settings. Tap the Settings icon to see a full list of settings. If you want to get to Quick Settings right away, use two fingers and swipe down from the top of the screen. The Quick Settings Bar slides down with the notifications underneath it. Swiping down to see notifications and Quick Settings works on any screen and while running any app.

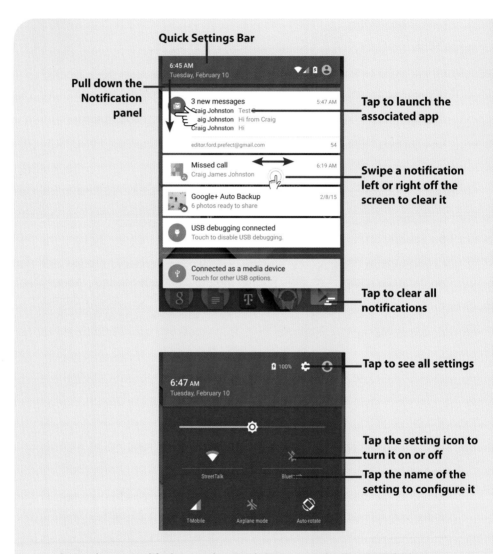

Quick Settings Bar

Pull down the Notification panel

Tap to launch the associated app

Swipe a notification left or right off the screen to clear it

Tap to clear all notifications

Tap to see all settings

Tap the setting icon to turn it on or off

Tap the name of the setting to configure it

Some phones modify the way that Quick Settings works. For example, on a Samsung phone, when you swipe down with two fingers you see a lot more Quick Settings icons. To control how many you see, tap the pencil icon. To configure a setting like Bluetooth, touch and hold the setting icon. Tap the icon to turn the setting on or off.

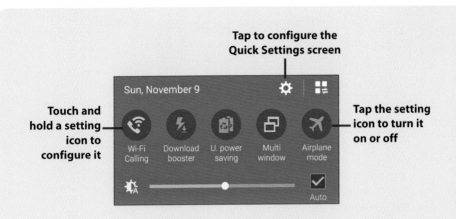

Tap to configure the
Quick Settings screen

Touch and
hold a setting
icon to
configure it

Tap the setting
icon to turn it
on or off

>>>Go Further

CREATING APP SHORTCUTS AND APP FOLDERS

Tap the Launcher icon to see all your apps. Touch and hold on the app you want to make a shortcut for. After the Home screen appears, drag the app shortcut to where you want it on the Home screen, drag it to an app folder to add it to the folder, or drag it left or right off the screen to move it between Home screen panes. If your Home screen panes are all full and there is no space for the app shortcut, keep dragging the icon to the right until you see an empty Home screen pane. This creates a new Home screen pane. Release the icon to place it.

Touch and
hold an
app icon

Earth

Drag between Home screen panes

Drag to where you want it and release it

To create a new app folder, simply drag one app shortcut onto another one. An app folder is created automatically. To name your new app folder, tap the folder to open it, and tap Unnamed Folder to enter your custom name.

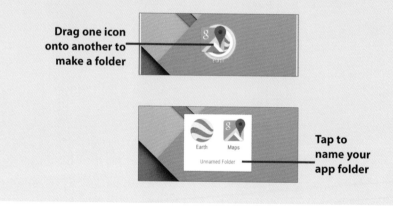

Drag one icon onto another to make a folder

Tap to name your app folder

The System Bar

Your Android phone running Android 5.0 (Lollipop) has no physical buttons. Instead it has an area of the screen set aside for virtual buttons. This area is called the System bar. The System bar includes the Back, Home, and Recent Apps virtual buttons.

My Phone Doesn't Have a System Bar

Although Google's Android operating system is designed to use virtual buttons in the System bar, some phone vendors have chosen to use physical and touch-sensitive buttons below the screen. Because the buttons are below the screen, there is no need to have a System bar. Refer to the "Button Placement" margin note earlier in this chapter for more information.

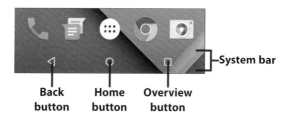

Back button   Home button   Overview button   —System bar

System bar   Reserved area of the screen where virtual buttons are displayed.

Back button   Tap to go back one screen in an app or back one step while navigating Android.

Home button   Tap to exit what you are doing and return to the Home screen. Your app continues to run in the background.

Overview button   Previously called the Recent Apps button, tap to see your recently used apps, switch between them, and close them.

The Leftmost Home Screen Pane

While on the Home screen view, if you keep swiping right until you see the leftmost Home screen pane, you are likely to find an app running there—typically Google Now (which is covered in Chapter 7, "Google Now and Navigation"). However, on some Android phones, instead of Google Now you might find an app called Flipboard (Samsung phones) or an app called Highlights (HTC phones).

Using Your Touchscreen

You mostly interact with your Android phone by touching the screen—what's known as making gestures on the screen. You can tap, touch and hold, swipe, pinch, unpinch, and double-tap.

Tap   To start an application, tap its icon. Tap a menu item to select it. Tap the letters of the onscreen keyboard to type.

Touch and hold   Touch and hold to interact with an object. For example, if you touch and hold a blank area of the Home screen, a menu pops up. If you touch and hold an icon, you can reposition it with your finger.

Drag   Dragging always starts with a touch and hold. For example, if you touch and hold the Notification panel, you can drag it down to read all the notification messages.

Swipe or slide   Swipe or slide the screen to scroll quickly. To swipe or slide, move your finger across the screen quickly. Be careful not to touch and hold before you swipe or you will reposition something. You can also swipe to clear notifications or close apps when viewing the recent apps.

Double-tap   Double-tapping is like double-clicking a mouse on a desktop computer. Tap the screen twice in quick succession. For example, you can double-tap a web page to zoom in to part of that page.

Pinch   To zoom in and out of images and pages, place your thumb and forefinger on the screen. Pinch them together to zoom out or spread them apart (unpinch) to zoom in. Applications such as Browser, Photos, and Maps support pinching.

Rotate the screen   If you rotate your Android phone from an upright position to being on its left or right side, the screen switches from portrait view to landscape view. Most applications honor the screen orientation. The Home screens and Launcher do not.

Using Your Keyboard

Your Android phone has a virtual (onscreen) keyboard for those times when you need to enter text. You might be a little wary of a keyboard that has no physical keys, but you will be pleasantly surprised at how well it works.

Most apps automatically show the keyboard when you need to enter text. If the keyboard does not appear, tap the area where you want to type and the keyboard slides up ready for use.

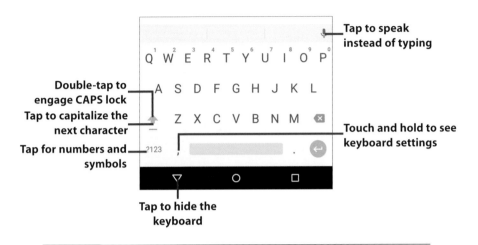

Tap to speak instead of typing

Double-tap to engage CAPS lock

Tap to capitalize the next character

Tap for numbers and symbols

Touch and hold to see keyboard settings

Tap to hide the keyboard

Keyboard Quick Tips

If you are typing an email address or a website address, the keyboard shows a button labeled .COM. If you tap it, you type .COM, but if you touch and hold it, you can choose between .EDU, .GOV, .ORG, and .NET. If you touch and hold the Return key, the cursor jumps to the next field. This is useful if you fill out forms on a website or move between fields in an app. If you touch and hold the comma key, you can change the language and keyboard settings. Some manufacturers of Android phones have moved the settings key to an adjacent key, sometimes combining it with the microphone key. The microphone key, used for dictation, that is normally on the top-right of the keyboard is moved to the bottom row of keys by some manufacturers.

Using the virtual keyboard as you type, your Android phone makes word suggestions. Think of this as similar to the spell checker you would see in a word processor. Your Android phone uses a dictionary of words to guess what you are typing. If the word you were going to type is highlighted, tap the space or period to select it. If you can see the word in the list but it is not highlighted, tap the word to select it.

List of suggested words

Tap to select an alternative suggested word

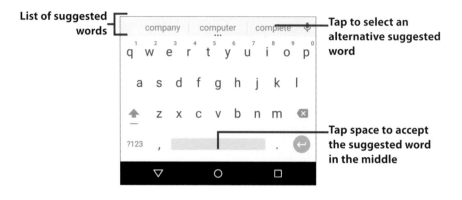

Tap space to accept the suggested word in the middle

Add Your Word

If you type a word that you know is correct, you can add it to your personal dictionary so that the next time you type it, your Android phone won't try to correct it. To do this, after you type the word, but before you tap space, you'll notice that your word is underlined. Tap the underlined word and your word appears in the middle of the suggested words area. Tap the word to add it to your personal dictionary. Tap it once more to complete the action.

First tap your word to add it to the dictionary

Next tap the word as it appears here

Tap your word again to complete the save

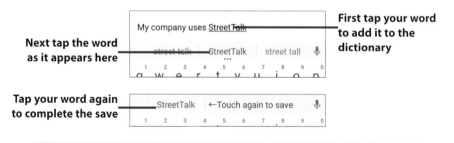

To make the next letter you type a capital letter, tap the Shift key. To make all letters capitals (or CAPS), double-tap the Shift key to engage CAPS Lock. Tap Shift again to disengage CAPS Lock.

To type numbers or symbols, tap the Symbols key.

When on the Numbers and Symbols screen, tap the Symbols key to see extra symbols. Tap the ABC key to return to the regular keyboard.

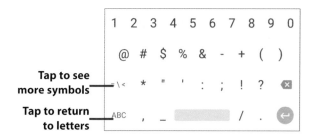

Tap to see more symbols

Tap to return to letters

To enter an accented character, touch and hold any vowel or the C, N, or S keys. A small window opens enabling you to select an accented or alternative character. Slide your finger over the accented character you want to use, and lift your finger to type it.

Touch and hold for accented characters

To reveal other alternative characters, tap and hold any other letter, number, or symbol.

___

Want a Larger Keyboard?
Turn your Android phone sideways to switch to a landscape keyboard. The landscape keyboard has larger keys and is easier to type on.

Landscape keyboard

>>>Go Further

SAMSUNG ONE-HANDED TYPING

Some Android phones are pretty large and unlike smaller phones that have
4-inch or 4.7-inch screens, you cannot comfortably type with one hand.
Samsung addresses this on the larger phones by enabling you to put the
keyboard into one-handed typing mode. This mode squashes the keyboard so
that you can type with one thumb. To enable one-handed mode, touch and
hold the microphone key (to the right of the Sym key), then tap the stacked
keyboard icon. Drag the shrunken keyboard anywhere on the screen where
it is comfortable for you to type with one hand. To exit one-handed mode,
touch and hold the microphone key (to the right of the Sym key), then tap the
stacked keyboard icon.

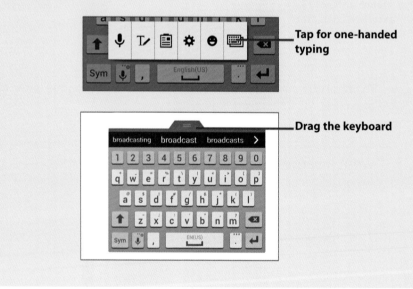

Tap for one-handed typing

Drag the keyboard

Dictation: Speak Instead of Typing

Your Android phone can turn your voice into text. It uses Google's speech recognition
service, which means that you must have a connection to the cellular network or a Wi-Fi
network to use it.

1. Tap the microphone key. Some manufacturers of Android phones have moved the microphone key to the bottom row on the keyboard.

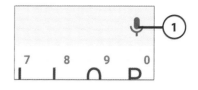

2. Wait until you see Speak Now, and then start saying what you want to be typed. You can speak the punctuation by saying "comma," "question mark," "exclamation mark," or "exclamation point."

3. Stop speaking to finish dictation.

Tap to select a different dictation language

Tap to cancel voice dictation

Swipe to Type

Instead of typing on the keyboard in the traditional way by touching each letter individually, you can swipe over the letters in one continuous movement. This is called Gesture Typing. It is enabled by default; to use it, just start swiping your finger over the letters of the word you want to type. As you swipe your finger, you see a trail following your finger. Lift your finger after each word. To add a space, swipe over the space bar or just start the next word and let the keyboard add the space for you. To type a double letter (as in the word "pool"), loop around that letter on the keyboard.

Samsung Writing Instead of Typing

Some larger Android phones, such as the Samsung Galaxy Note 4, come with a stylus. Samsung calls their stylus the S Pen. Instead of typing on the keyboard, you can use handwriting recognition to write. To enable Handwriting mode, pull out the S Pen from its holder and tap the Back key to dismiss the Air Command window. Then hover the S Pen over the screen in the text area until you see the handwriting icon. Tap the icon with your S Pen. Any text you have typed appears to be in handwriting. Now write in your own handwriting on the screen and it is turned into text. Tap Done to return to typing.

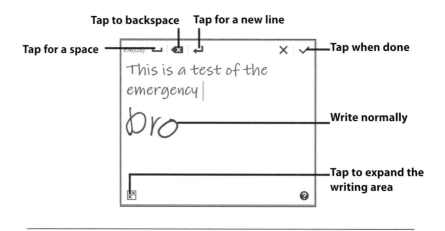

Tap to start Handwriting mode

Tap to backspace   **Tap for a new line**

Tap for a space   **Tap when done**

Write normally

Tap to expand the writing area

Edit Text

After you enter text, you can edit it by cutting, copying, or pasting the text. Here is how to select and copy text and then paste over a word with the copied text.

1. While you are typing, tap and hold a word you want to copy. The word highlights in blue, and you see end markers on either side of the word.

2. Slide the blue end markers until you have selected all the text you want to copy. In this example, just one word has been highlighted.

3. Tap to copy the text. You can also cut the text. This example demonstrates copying text.

4. Touch and hold the word you want to paste over.

5. Tap the word Paste or tap the paste icon.

Tap to select all text   **Tap to cut the text**

Text selection   3

To

First email on my new phone   1

Hi Craig.   2

I'm enjoying my new portable so far.
What are you doing for dinner tomorrow night?
I'd like to show it to you.

Ford.

5

Text selection

To

First email on my new phone

Hi Craig.   PASTE   REPLACE...

I'm enjoying my new portable so far.   4
What are you doing for dinner tomorrow night?
I'd like to show it to you.

Ford.

Simpler Copy/Paste

You might want to just copy some text and paste it somewhere else, instead of pasting it over a word. To do this, after you have copied the text, tap once in the text area, and move the single blue marker to where you want to paste the text. Tap the blue marker again, and tap Paste.

Move marker to the desired location

Hi Craig.   PASTE   **Tap to paste**

I'm enjoying my new so far.
What are you doing for dinner tomorrow night?   **Tap marker to see actions**
I'd like to show it to you.

Ford.

Menus

Your Android phone has two types of menus: app menus and context menus. Let's go over what each one does.

Most applications have a Menu icon, which enables you to make changes or take actions within that application. The Menu icon should always appear in the top-right corner of an app; however, it can sometimes appear in the System bar next to the Recent Apps button or elsewhere in the app. Remember that some phones have a physical Menu button below the screen and might not have the onscreen Menu icon.

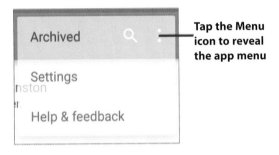

Tap the Menu icon to reveal the app menu

A context menu applies to an item on the screen. If you touch and hold something on the screen (in this example, a link on a web page), a context menu appears. The items on the context menu are based on the type of object you tapped.

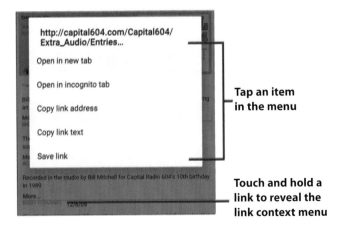

Tap an item in the menu

Touch and hold a link to reveal the link context menu

Switch Between Apps

Your Android phone has an icon called the Overview icon. This icon is always on the System bar at the bottom of your screen. You can use this icon to switch between apps, close apps, and force them to quit if they have stopped responding. The Overview screen also allows you to switch between different Chrome web browser tabs and close them.

1. Tap the Overview icon.

Where Is My Overview Button?

The Overview icon/button may be a physical button on your phone positioned below the screen. Phones without the Overview button normally require that you double-tap the Home button to see the Overview screen. Sometimes the Overview button is called the Recent Apps button.

2. Scroll up and down the list of recent apps and Chrome browser tabs.

3. Swipe an app or Chrome browser tab left or right off the screen to close it.

4. Touch and hold an app's icon to reveal the app's information screen. If you touch and hold the icon of a Chrome browser tab, you see the Chrome app info.

5. Tap to force an app to close if it has stopped responding.

Tapping the X icon also closes the app

Chrome web browser tabs are included

Run Multiple Apps on the Screen at the Same Time (Samsung Only)

Some larger Samsung phones have a feature called Multi Window that allows certain apps to run on the same screen at the same time. They can either run in a split-screen configuration, in multiple separate small windows, or a combination of both.

Make Sure Multi Window Is Enabled

Before you start this section, make sure that Multi Window is enabled in the Quick Settings.

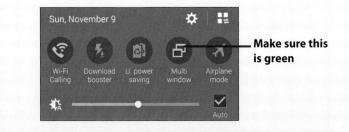

Two Apps Together on a Split-Screen

This section describes how to run two apps at the same time in a split-screen configuration.

1. Touch and hold the Back button to see apps that support Multi Window.

2. Drag an app onto the screen and release it. Since this is the first app you are choosing, it fills the screen.

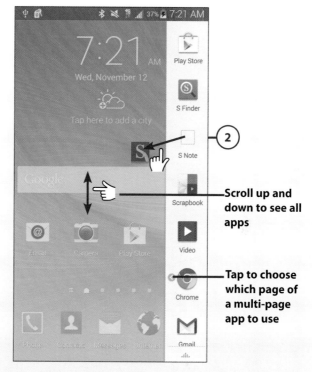

Some Apps Want To Be Popups

When you drag an app onto the screen in step 2, the app might want to be a pop-up app. Pop-up apps start by running in a small separate window on the screen instead of either filling the top or bottom of the screen. Unfortunately it is not clear which apps always want to start in pop-up mode, and which always start in split-screen mode. The next section covers pop-up apps.

**App wants to
start as a popup**

Multi-Page Apps

Some of the app icons have a small left arrow next to them. This indicates that
the app is already running and has multiple pages open. An example of this is
a web browser like Chrome. You may have many different websites open each
in their own tabs. If you tap the little arrow, you can choose which open pages
you want to drag onto the multi-window screen.

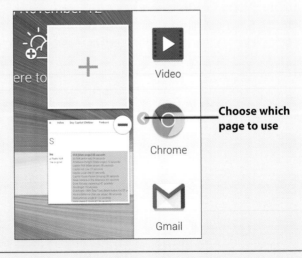

**Choose which
page to use**

It's Not All Good

Not All Apps Support Multi Window

Apps must be specially written to take advantage of Multi Window mode. This means that you might not see the apps you are looking for until the developer updates the app to support Samsung's Multi Window mode.

3. Drag another app to either the top or bottom half of the screen and release it. If the multi-window pane on the right of the screen disappears before you complete step 3, touch and hold the Back button to see the pane again.

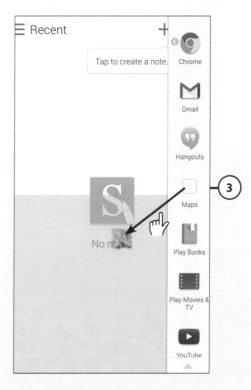

4. Drag the circle up or down to give more or less room to each app.

5. Tap the circle to reveal extra Multi Window features.

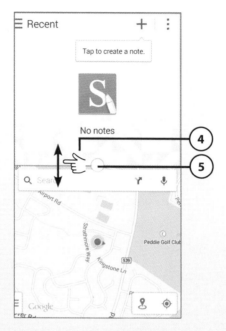

6. Tap to swap the position of the apps on the screen.

7. Tap to enable dragging content between windows (like text or images).

8. Tap to minimize the selected app to a small draggable circle on the screen

9. Tap to maximize the selected app to full screen.

10. Tap to close the app in the selected window.

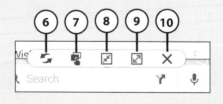

>>>Go Further

MINIMIZED APPS

When you choose to minimize an app as seen in step 8, the app shrinks to a small circle on the screen. You can drag the minimized app anywhere on the screen. If you touch and hold the app, a trash can icon appears allowing you to close the app. If you tap the minimized app it enlarges to a pop-up window instead of maximizing back to its original window in the split-screen. You can then continue working on the app in its small window. Minimized apps continue to be shown no matter what screen you are on and what app you are running.

Minimized apps

App in a pop-up window

More Than One App in Each Window

When you use Multi Window, the screen is split into two windows—one at the top and one at the bottom. You can drag an app to either the top or bottom window. You can actually drag more than one app into each window. Follow steps 1 through 3 from the "Two Apps Together on a Split Screen" task, and simply drag the new app on top of the one that's already there. The only downside to this is that you can only work with the last app that was dragged to the window. Even though the previous apps are there and running, you cannot switch to them. Your only course of action is to close the app on top and continue working on the previous app in the same window.

>>>Go Further

PRESETTING PAIRS OF APPS

You can create preset pairs of apps. This enables you to quickly open two apps on the screen without first dragging them onto the screen manually each time you open Multi Window. To do this, open the two apps that you want to work with (if you have more than one app in each window, only the one visible is added to the pair). Tap the Multi Window up arrow and tap Create. A new icon is added to the list of multi-window apps with the name of both apps. In the future when you open the Multi Window list, your preset app pairs are right at the top.

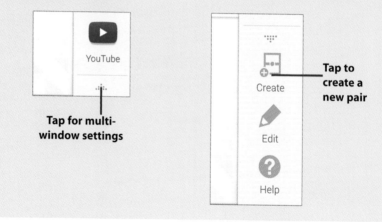

Tap for multi-window settings

Tap to create a new pair

Setting Up Multiple Users on Your Phone

Your Android phone may have the capability to support multiple users. This enables you to share your phone among co-workers, family members, or friends, with each person having his own unique login, apps, photos, videos, and settings. Your phone can support up to eight users. Some phone vendors do not support this option.

Add a New Phone User

A phone user can have their own apps, photos, videos, wallpapers, and do anything on the phone with the exception of removing other users and factory resetting the phone. To add other users, the original owner of the phone must be logged in and needs to use the following steps. The user being added should also be present at the time the new user profile is created.

1. Pull down the Quick Settings Bar, and tap the User icon.

2. Tap Add User.

3. Tap OK. Your phone switches to the Lock screen, which is ready for you to start the new user process.

Add new user?

When you add a new user, that person needs to set up their space.

Any user can update apps for all other users.

CANCEL   OK

4. Swipe the Lock icon upward to unlock your phone.

5. Hand the phone to the person who will be setting up her account. She can now follow the steps in the "First-Time Setup" section earlier in this chapter.

How to Switch Between Phone Users

To switch between phone users, pull down the Quick Settings Bar on the Lock
screen, Home screen, or while running any app, and tap the User icon. Tap the
user you want to switch to.

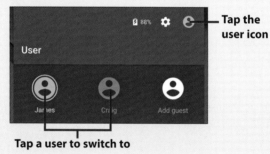

Add a Phone Guest User

A phone guest user can use the phone like a regular user, however their information is
not permanently saved. There can only be one guest account, and it can either be reused
by the same guest or wiped for a new guest.

1. Pull down the Quick Settings Bar, and tap the User icon.

2. Tap Add Guest.

3. Hand the phone to the guest. No setup is required.

Continue as a Guest or Start Over

If you previously added a guest user and allowed someone to use it, the guest account remains untouched until your guest wants to use it again. If the same person wants to continue where he left off, when he switches to the guest user he is asked to either start over or continue. If he taps continue, the guest session continues where it left off. However if you are allowing a new person to use the guest user, she must tap Start Over to wipe the previous guest session and start fresh.

Welcome back, guest!

Do you want to continue your session?

Tap to start as a new guest —— START OVER   YES, CONTINUE —— Tap to continue as the previous guest

>>>Go Further

LET YOUR CHILDREN USE YOUR PHONE SAFELY

When you add a new user, the user has his own Google account and full access to all apps that he installs while he is logged in to the phone. A restricted profile is a copy of your own login profile, but the apps and content are restricted. You can imagine using restricted profiles for your children who might not have their own Google accounts and who should not have access to all apps. By creating a restricted profile, you can decide which apps and content the person may access, but you don't have to worry about having to set up a whole new user on your phone. Restricted profiles appear like new users, but they actually function under your user account with restrictions in place. To add a restricted profile, go into Settings, tap Users, tap Add User or Profile, and tap Restricted Profile. If you haven't already set a screen lock, you are asked to set one now. This is to protect your account so nobody can switch to it from a restricted profile. After you set your screen lock, you set up the restricted profile. Please note that as of the writing of this book, there appears to be a bug preventing you from adding restricted profiles on Android phones; however, the feature does currently work on Android tablets. Google will likely fix this bug soon.

Name the restricted profile

Choose which apps and content the restricted profile has access to

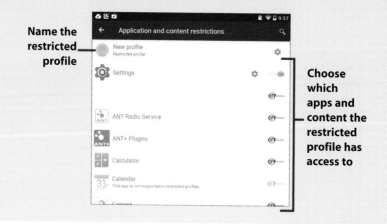

Installing Synchronization Software

Because your Android phone is tightly integrated with Google and its services, all media that you purchase on your phone is stored in the Google Cloud and accessible anywhere and anytime. However, you might have a lot of music on your computer that you need to copy to your Google cloud, so you need to install the Google Music Manager software or the Android File Transfer app for your Mac to copy any file back and forth.

Install Android File Transfer (Apple Mac OS X)

You need only the Android File Transfer app when using an Android phone on an Apple Mac running OS X, and only if you think you want to drag files to and from your phone using Finder.

1. From your Mac, browse to http://www.android.com/filetransfer/ and download the Android File Transfer app.

2. Click the downloads icon to reveal your downloaded files.

3. Double-click the androidfiletransfer.dmg file in your Safari Downloads.

4. Drag the green Android to the Applications shortcut to install the app.

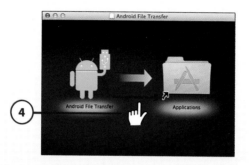

Install Google Music Manager (Apple Mac)

Don't install Google Music Manager unless you plan to upload files from your computer to the Google Music cloud.

1. Visit https://play.google.com/music/listen#manager_pl from your desktop web browser, and log in to your Google account if prompted.

2. Click to download Music Manager.

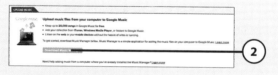

3. Click the downloads icon to reveal your downloaded files.

4. Double-click the musicmanager.dmg file in your Safari Downloads.

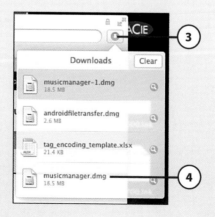

5. Drag the Music Manager icon to the Applications shortcut to install the app.

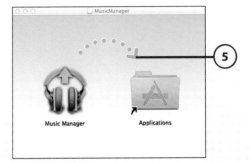

6. Double-click the Music Manager icon in the Applications folder.

7. Skip to the "Configure Music Manager" section later in the chapter to complete the installation.

Install Google Music Manager (Windows)

Don't install Google Music Manager unless you plan to upload files from your computer to the Google Music cloud.

1. Visit https://music.google.com/music/listen#manager_pl from your desktop web browser, and log in to your Google account if prompted.

2. Click to download Music Manager.

3. Double-click the musicmanagerinstaller app in your Downloads folder and then follow the steps in the next section.

Configure Music Manager (Windows and Apple Mac)

1. Click Continue.

2. Enter your Google (Gmail) email address.

3. Enter your Google (Gmail) password.

4. Click Continue.

5. Choose where you keep your music.

6. Click Continue.

7. Choose whether to upload all your music or just some of your playlists. Remember that you can upload only 50,000 songs for free. Skip to step 12 if you choose to upload all music.

8. Check if you want to also upload podcasts.

9. Click Continue.

10. Select one or more playlists of music.

11. Click Continue.

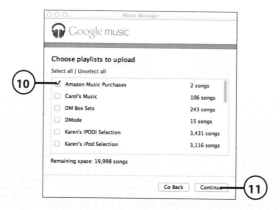

12. Choose whether you want to automatically upload any new music that is added to your computer.

13. Click Continue and your files start uploading.

14. Click Close.

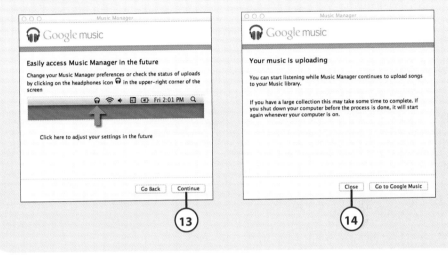

>>>Go Further
OTHER SYNC SOFTWARE

Manufacturers of Android phones may provide their own synchronization software that's specific to their brand of phone. For example, HTC provides software called HTC Sync Manager. You can download it from http://www.htc.com/us/support/software/htc-sync-manager.aspx.

Samsung provides its own software called Kies. You can download it from http://www.samsung.com/us/kies/

Freeing Up Memory

If you have installed a Secure Digital card (SD card) then you have the ability to move media and parts of some apps to the SD card to free up memory on your Android phone.

Move Apps

Not all apps support being moved to the SD card (external memory), and even apps that do support this feature only move part of themselves to the SD card.

1. Touch and hold an app you want to move to the SD card

2. Drag the app to the App Info icon.

3. Tap Move to SD card.

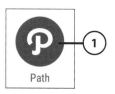

Path

STORAGE	
Total	29.36MB
Application	29.36MB
SD card app	0.00B
Data	0.00B
SD card data	0.00B
Move to SD card	Clear data

>>>Go Further

MOVE DOCUMENTS AND MEDIA

You can also move documents, media, and other file types from your Android phone's main memory to an SD card using a third-party file manager. Search the Google Play Store for "my files" or "file manager," and you can download and use a file manager to move files between your phone's main memory and external memory. Some Android phones come with file manager apps preinstalled. For example, Samsung phones come with the My Files file manager, and HTC phones come with the File Manager app.

Show the keypad

Craig James Johnston

Mobile   00:08

Turn your
current
call into a
conference
call

In this chapter, you find out how to make and take phone calls and send instant messages on your Android phone. Topics include the following:

→ Making phone calls
→ Making conference calls
→ Sending and receiving text messages
→ Sending and receiving multimedia messages

Phone, SMS, and MMS

As a cellular phone, your Android phone includes powerful features that enable you to make phone calls swiftly and easily. Using your Android phone, you can also send both text messages and multimedia messages with the Messenger app.

Using the Phone App

With the Phone app, you can quickly make and receive calls across the cellular network. When you need to talk to more than one other person, you can turn your current call into a conference call.

Make a Call

The Phone app contains three tabs that enable you to make calls in various ways and to track the calls you receive.

1. On the Home screen, tap Phone.

2. Tap to search for contacts and places nearby to call. This only works if you have enabled this feature. See how to enable it in the section "Configure the Phone App," step 21, later in this chapter.

3. Tap to use your voice to search for contacts and places nearby to call.

4. Tap the most recent call to dial the number. The most recent call may be the last incoming call, the last outgoing call, or the last missed call.

5. Tap to see all recent incoming and outgoing calls.

6. Tap to see all of your contacts.

7. Tap the Keypad icon to manually type the numbers to call.

8. Tap the Speed Dial tab, and tap the icon for someone you have setup as a speed dial.

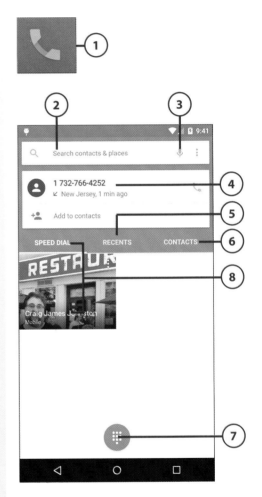

Dial by Typing Search Terms

Find a contact or nearby place to call by typing a contact name or place name.

1. Type the name of the person you want to call, or the name of the nearby place you want to call. Contacts are pulled from your phone's Contacts app, whereas the nearby places are gathered in real time based on where you are.

2. Tap the contact you want to call. If the contact has more than one phone number, such as mobile and home numbers, tap the particular number you want to call.

3. Tap one of the discovered nearby places to call the main number.

Tap to return to the main Phone app screen

Dial by Speaking Search Terms

Find a contact or nearby place to call by speaking a contact name or place name.

1. When the green Microphone icon appears, speak the name of the person or the name of the nearby place you want to call. Contacts are pulled from your phone's Contacts app, whereas the nearby places are gathered in real time based on where you are.

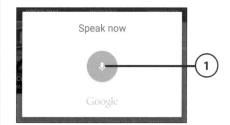

2. Tap the contact you want to call. If the contact has more than one phone number, such as mobile and home numbers, tap the particular number you want to call.

3. Tap one of the discovered nearby places to call the main number.

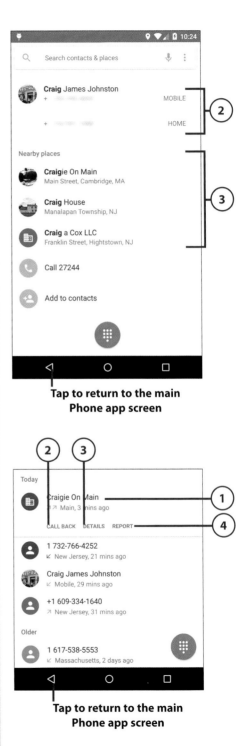

Tap to return to the main Phone app screen

Dial by Using the Recents Tab

All incoming, outgoing, and missed calls are shown on the Recents tab. You can call a listed number, see the call details, and report an incorrect number to Google.

1. Tap a recent call to see the options.

2. Tap to call the contact or business back.

3. Tap to see details of your recent calls to and from this number. While viewing the call details, you can delete the specific recent call entry and even edit the phone number before you call it back.

4. Tap to report to Google that the number for a business is incorrect.

Tap to return to the main Phone app screen

Dial by Using the Keypad

If you need to call a number that isn't in Contacts, you can dial a number using the keypad.

1. Type the phone number to call using the keypad and tap the green Phone icon to place the call.

2. Tap to backspace if you make a mistake.

3. As you type a number, the Phone app displays any contacts with numbers that match what you are typing. If you see the contact you want to call, tap it to call.

4. Tap to place the call when you've finished typing the number or you've selected a contact name.

Arthur Dent
+44 604 555-1212

Add to contacts

Tap to add a two-second pause or a wait

604

Tap to return to the main Phone app screen

>>>Go Further

WHAT ARE PAUSES AND WAITS?

While using the keypad to make a call, you can add a two-second pause or a wait between numbers. A two-second pause, indicated by a comma, simply pauses for two seconds before continuing with the rest of the numbers in the phone number. You can add multiple, consecutive two-second pauses to increase the pause time. This is useful, for example, if you are dialing a number that requires that you enter an extension number after being connected. A wait, indicated by a semicolon, makes the Phone app stop and wait until you tap the screen to continue with the rest of the phone number. This is useful if you are not sure how long the wait time is between dialing a business and entering the person's extension, or it can be useful when using calling cards. You can use two-second pauses and waits when entering phone numbers into Contacts, too.

>>>Go Further
PHONE APP VARIATIONS

Some manufacturers of Android phones modify the Phone app to make it fit in with their other phone style changes or to add vendor-specific functionality. For example, on HTC phones you can swipe left and right to move between call history, the keypad, favorite contacts, people (HTC's name for contacts), and groups of contacts. On Samsung phones, you have to tap each tab to switch between the keypad, call logs, favorite contacts, and the full list of contacts.

Swipe left and right through the tabs

Tap to switch tabs

Tap to speak a call command

Dial from a Contact Entry

If you have a contact entry for the person you want to dial, you can start from that contact entry.

1. Tap the Contacts tab in the Phone app.

2. Tap the contact to display the contact's details.

3. Tap the number you want to call.

Use the search bar to find contacts quickly

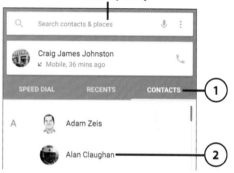

Starting a Call from the Contacts App

Instead of launching the Phone app and then tapping the Contacts tab to go to the Contacts app, you can start a call directly from the Contacts app. Tap Contacts on the Home screen or the Apps screen to launch the Contacts app, tap the contact to display his or her details, and then tap one of the contact's numbers to call the person.

Tap to send a text message to the number shown

Using Other Apps During a Call

During a call, you can use most other apps freely, but you cannot play music or video. You can take photos with the Camera app, but you cannot shoot videos. To switch to another app, either use the Overview (Recent Apps) list or press the Home button and use the Apps screen as usual. While you are using another app, your Android phone displays a Phone icon (and on some Android phones a green bar) at the top of the screen to remind you that you are in a call. Pull down the Notification panel to control the call or return to it. On Samsung phones, you also see an in-call pop-up window. You can drag the in-call pop-up window anywhere on the screen, and tap it to return to the in-progress call.

Indicates call is in progress

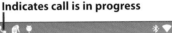

Tap to return to your call

Tap to hang up the call

>>>Go Further

DRAGGING AND DROPPING ITEMS TO CALLERS ON SAMSUNG PHONES

With a call in progress on Samsung phones, you can drag and drop text and images to the person you are talking to. Text is sent as a text (SMS) message, and images are sent as multimedia (MMS) messages. Tap the Minimize icon to minimize the call window. While the call window is minimized, you can drag it around the screen if you need to. Open the app you want to drag the content from—for example, images from the Gallery app. Drag the content to the green area within the minimized call window to send it.

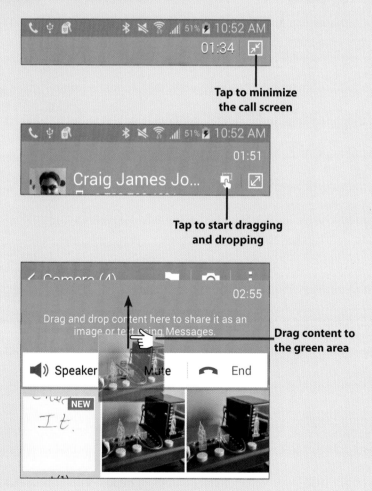

Tap to minimize
the call screen

Tap to start dragging
and dropping

Drag content to
the green area

Receive a Call

When someone phones your Android phone, you can accept the call, reject it, or reject it and send a text message.

Accept a Call

1. When the phone rings, look at the contact name (if it is available) or the phone number (if it is not) and decide whether to take the call.

2. Drag the gray Phone icon to the blue Phone icon to accept the call.

3. Tap to switch to the speakerphone, a Bluetooth headset (or your car's built-in Bluetooth), or your phone's earpiece.

4. Tap to mute the call. Tap again to turn off muting.

5. Tap to show the keypad if you need to type extra numbers after the call is connected.

6. Tap to put the call on hold.

7. Tap to create a conference call by adding a new caller. See more about conference calling later in the chapter in the "Make a Conference Call" task.

8. Tap to end the call.

>>>Go Further

EXTRA FUNCTIONS ON SAMSUNG PHONES

If you have a Samsung phone, while on a call you can tap the Menu icon to do a few additional things. You can put the call on hold; open your contacts; write an Action Memo using your S Pen (on the Galaxy Note series phones) and send it to the caller using MMS; send a regular text message to the caller; personalize the sound of the call; and boost the volume of the caller's voice.

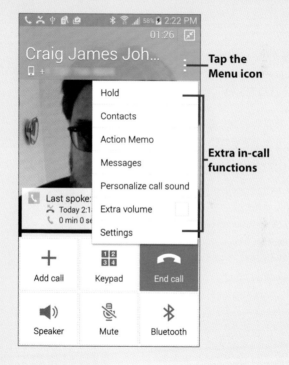

Tap the Menu icon

Extra in-call functions

Reject a Call

If you do not want to accept the call, you can reject it so that it goes to your voicemail.

1. When the phone rings, look at the contact name (if it is available) or the phone number (if it is not) and decide whether to take the call.

2. Drag the gray Phone icon to the red Phone icon to reject the call. The call goes to voicemail, and your Android phone displays the screen you were using before the call came in.

Reject a Call and Send a Quick Response

Instead of simply declining a call and sending it to your voicemail, you can send a Quick Response to the caller. Your Android phone provides a selection of canned Quick Response messages for general needs. You can also create your own messages or type custom messages for particular calls.

1. When the phone rings, look at the contact name (if it is available) or the phone number (if it is not) and decide whether to take the call.

2. Drag the gray Phone icon to the text message icon to reject the call and send a Quick Response message to the caller.

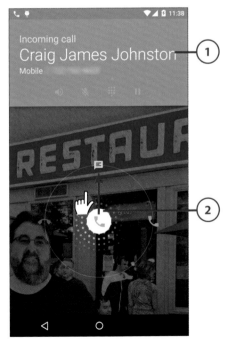

3. Tap one of the canned message suggestions to send that message.

Editing the Quick Responses

To edit your Quick Responses, open the Phone app and tap the Menu icon. On the menu, tap Settings. On the Settings screen, tap General Settings and then tap Quick Responses. Tap one of the Quick Responses to edit it.

Tap to create and send
a custom message

Handle a Missed Call

If you miss a phone call, you can quickly locate it in the Phone app's logs so that you can return it, but you can also take actions on missed calls from the Lock screen or any other screen.

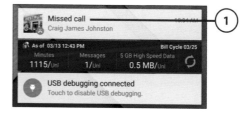

1. Tap twice on the missed call notification on the Lock screen. If you use a Lock screen password or other method of locking your phone, you are required to use that method to unlock your phone before you can continue.

2. Tap the missed call in the call History screen.

3. Tap Call Back to return the call.

See only missed calls   See only voicemail   Clear call history

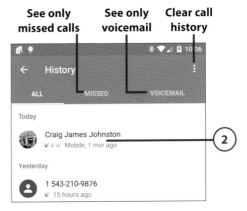

See full call details

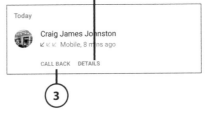

Make a Conference Call

You can quickly turn your current call into a conference call by adding more participants.

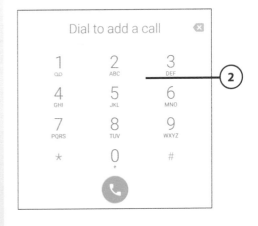

1. Tap the Add Call icon while you have a call in progress.

2. Dial the call in the most convenient way.

3. Tap to swap between the original call and the one you just added, if you need to.

4. Tap the Merge icon to merge the calls and complete the conference call setup.

5. Repeat steps 1–4 to add additional callers. The exact number of callers you can have on a conference call is governed by your wireless carrier.

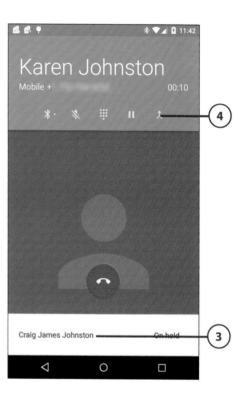

Managing the Conference Call

While on a conference call that you initiated, tap Manage Conference Call to see some options. Tap the Unmerge icon next to one of the callers to remove that person from the conference call while still keeping him connected and on hold. Tap the Hang Up icon next to one of the callers to hang up on her.

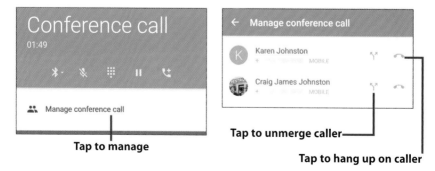

Tap to manage

Tap to unmerge caller

Tap to hang up on caller

Configure the Phone App

To make the Phone app work your way, you can configure its settings.

1. Tap the Menu icon and tap Settings.

2. Tap General Settings.

3. Tap to change the sort order when displaying the Contacts tab. You can sort by first name or last name.

4. Tap to change how names in the Contacts tab are formatted. You can format them with the first name first, or the last name first.

5. Tap to change the ringtone that plays when you receive an incoming call.

6. Check the box to hear the dialpad tones. Uncheck to silence them.

7. Check the box to also vibrate your phone when you have an incoming call.

8. Tap to manage your Quick Responses.

9. Tap to save your changes and return to the previous screen.

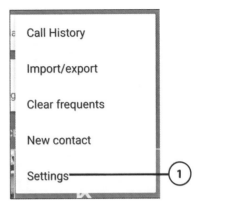

Call History

Import/export

Clear frequents

New contact

Settings ────── ① 1

─────────────

← Settings

General settings ───── ② 2
Contact display, sounds, and quick responses

Call settings
Voicemail, call waiting, and others

Advanced settings
Caller ID by Google, nearby places

─────────────

🔆 📵 ☎   ✻ ▼ 12:02

← General settings ───── ⑨ 9

Contact display options

Sort by ────────── ③ 3
First name

Name format ─────── ④ 4
First name first

Sounds and vibrate

Phone ringtone ────── ⑤ 5
Titania

Dialpad tones   ☑ ── ⑥ 6

Also vibrate for calls   ☐ ── ⑦ 7

Other

Quick responses ────── ⑧ 8

10. Tap Call Settings.

11. Tap to manage any Voice over IP (VoIP) accounts you want to use for calls, instead of the regular cellular voice network.

12. Tap to choose which voicemail service to use (if you have more than one option). If you use Google Voice, it is common to use the Google Voice voicemail system as opposed to the one provided by your wireless carrier.

13. Tap to manage Fixed Dialing Numbers (FDN).

14. Tap to manage which TTY mode you want to use or to turn TTY off. TTY stands for Teletype and it allows hearing-impaired people to connect a Teletype machine to the phone to type instead of speaking.

15. Check the box to make your phone compatible with hearing aids.

16. Tap to manage your call forwarding settings. You can choose to forward all calls to a specific number or to forward calls to specific numbers based on the situation. This screen is mostly used to change what voicemail system unanswered calls are forwarded to.

17. Tap to manage your Caller ID settings and whether you want to use Call Waiting.

18. Tap to save your settings and return to the previous screen.

19. Tap Advanced Settings.

← Settings

General settings
Contact display, sounds, and quick responses

Call settings ————————————— 10
Voicemail, call waiting, and others

Advanced settings
Caller ID by Google, nearby places

← Call settings

Phone account settings—————— 11

Voicemail ————————————— 12

Fixed Dialing Numbers ————— 13

TTY mode ————————————— 14
TTY Off

Hearing aids   ☐ — 15
Turn on hearing aid compatibility

Call forwarding ———————————— 16

Additional settings ———————— 17

← Settings

General settings
Contact display, sounds, and quick responses

Call settings
Voicemail, call waiting, and others

Advanced settings ————————— 19
Caller ID by Google, nearby places

20. Tap to enable a feature that allows Google to show names for people and businesses who call you, but whose contact information is not stored in your phone.

21. Tap to enable a feature that allows Google to show nearby places in the Phone app when you search.

22. Tap to save your settings and return to the previous screen.

Call Setting Differences with Verizon Phones

If you use a Verizon Android phone (or an Android phone on another CDMA provider), you may see slightly different settings on the Call Settings screen. If you see a setting called DTMF Tones, this setting allows you to change the length of the DTMF tone played. DTMF (Dual Tone Multi Frequency) Tones are played on a phone call when you tap the phone dialpad keys. You can choose to use short tones or long tones, which means that when your phone plays the DTMF tone, it either plays it the regular length, or it plays it for longer. If you see Assisted Dialing, tapping this allows you to set your home country so that when you travel, your phone will make sure it is dialing the numbers correctly, even when you travel internationally. If you see Voice Privacy, tap to choose whether you want your calls encrypted or not.

What Is VoLTE?

Some Android phones support VoLTE. First, LTE (or Long-Term Evolution) is the fourth generation of cellular data technology (not to be confused with the slightly faster version of 3G technology that has been incorrectly called 4G for years). VoLTE stands for Voice over LTE. Effectively, your voice call is sent as regular data over the LTE data channel as opposed to over the cellular voice channel. Voice quality is much better due to the higher rate at which the data is transmitted and received, and if the person you are calling also uses VoLTE, you can speak at the same time. Most wireless carriers treat VoLTE as regular voice minutes and don't count it against your data plan. However, you should verify the situation with your local wireless carrier; otherwise, your data plan might take an unexpected hit.

What Is FDN?

Fixed Dialing Number (FDN) is a feature that allows you to set up a fixed list of phone numbers that can be dialed from your phone. To use FDN, you first create a numeric PIN, then choose the numbers that can be dialed. This feature can be useful if you are lending your phone to someone and want to limit the dialing privileges, or you can use it on one of your children's phones to limit their dialing abilities.

What Is Wi-Fi Calling?

Some phones support Wi-Fi calling. The technical name for Wi-Fi calling is Universal Media Access (UMA). This technology is provided by some carriers around the world and enables your Android phone to roam between the cellular network and Wi-Fi networks. Typically when you are connected to a Wi-Fi network, any calls you make are free and of higher audio quality because of the faster speeds. As you move out of Wi-Fi coverage, your phone hands the call off to the cellular network—and vice versa—allowing your call to continue without interruption. If you want to read more about UMA or Wi-Fi calling, read this online article: http://crackberry.com/saving-call-charges-recession-your-black-berry. The article is on a BlackBerry blog, but the descriptions of the technology still apply.

Using SMS and MMS

Short Message Service (SMS), also known as text messaging, has been around for a long time. Multimedia Message Service (MMS) is a newer form of text messaging that can contain pictures, audio, and video as well as text. Your Android phone can send and receive both SMS and MMS messages.

Get to Know the Messenger App

The Messenger app is what you use to send and receive text messages. This app has all the features you need to compose, send, receive, and manage messages.

1. Tap the Messenger icon.

2. Tap to compose a new text message.

3. Tap the picture of someone who has sent you a message to show the contact information that allows you to contact the person using email, phone, and other methods.

4. Tap a message thread to open it. A message thread may have one or more messages in it.

5. Tap the Menu icon to see more options.

6. Tap to view archived messages. These are messages that you have previously deleted.

7. Tap to open the Settings screen. See the next section for more on Settings.

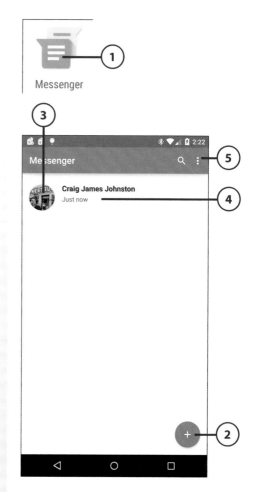

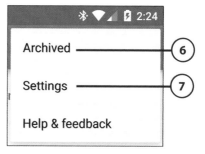

Manage Settings for the Messenger App

You use the settings of the Messenger app to manage how the app handles your SMS and MMS messages. Before you actually start working with SMS and MMS, let's take a look at the settings.

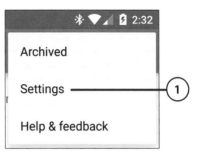

1. Tap the Menu icon and tap Settings.

2. Tap to change the default messaging app from Messenger to Google Hangouts. If you use Google Hangouts a lot for text and video chatting, you may decide to also use it for text and multimedia messages. Read more about using Google Hangouts in the "Using Google Hangouts for SMS and MMS" sidebar at the end of this chapter.

3. Choose to play a sound when you send messages.

4. Choose whether you want to be notified of incoming SMS and MMS messages.

5. Tap to choose the ringtone that plays when you are notified of a new message.

6. Choose whether your phone must vibrate when you receive a new message.

7. Tap to see Advanced settings.

8. Tap to choose how your phone handles group text messages when you choose to send a message to a group of people. You can either have your phone send the same text message to each person individually, or send one MMS message to all people.

9. Tap to edit your phone's phone number.

10. Choose whether you want your phone to automatically retrieve MMS messages.

11. Choose whether you want your phone to automatically retrieve MMS messages while you are roaming outside your carrier's home area.

12. Choose whether you want a delivery report when sending SMS messages.

13. Tap to manage which emergency alerts you want to receive. These alerts are sent out by your government or law enforcement (for example, AMBER alerts).

14. Tap to save your changes and return to the previous screen.

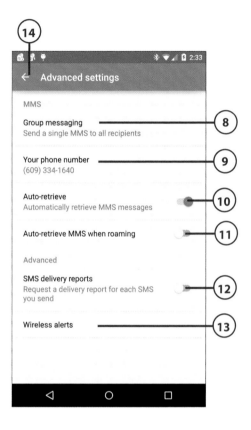

It's Not All Good

What Setting Should I Choose for Samsung Service Loading?

Samsung's Service Loading feature has been used for attacks that remotely wipe smartphones without the owner's consent. Because of this danger, never choose Always as the Service Loading setting. Choose Prompt if you want your Samsung phone to let you decide about service-loading requests. Choose Never if you prefer to suppress service-loading requests.

Don't Auto-Retrieve MMS While Roaming

Disable the automatic retrieval of multimedia messages when you travel to other countries because automatically retrieving these messages when you're roaming can result in a big bill from your provider. International carriers love to charge large amounts of money for people traveling to their countries and using their networks. The only time it is a good idea to leave this enabled is if your carrier offers an international SMS or MMS bundle, where you pay a flat rate up front before leaving. When you have the auto-retrieve feature disabled, you see a Download icon next to a multimedia message. You have to tap it to manually download the message.

What's the Difference Between a Delivery Report and a Read Report?

A delivery report indicates that the message has reached the destination device. Some Android phones allow you to also request a read report. A read report indicates that the message has been opened for viewing.

Compose a Message

When you compose a new message, you do not need to make a conscious decision whether it is an SMS message or an MMS message. As soon as you add a subject line or attach a file to your message, your Android phone automatically treats the message as an MMS message.

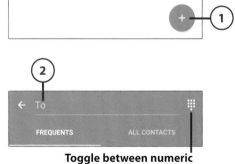

1. Tap the Compose icon to compose a new message.

2. Type the recipient's phone number, or if the person is in your contacts, type the name. If a match is found, tap the mobile number.

Toggle between numeric keypad and full keyboard

3. Tap and start typing your message.

4. Tap to send your message.

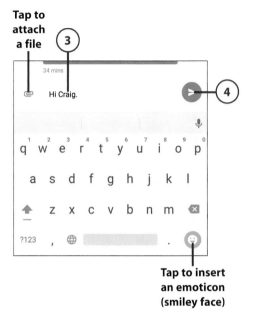

Tap to attach a file

Tap to insert an emoticon (smiley face)

It's Not All Good

Inserting Smiley Icons

By tapping the smiling face icon, you can insert emoticons (also known as smiley faces). Just be aware that the very first emoticon you insert into a new text message counts as 92 characters. Each additional emoticon counts as only one character each. Each text message is limited to 160 characters, so after inserting your first emoticon, you'll have only 68 characters left.

Schedule a Message To Be Sent at a Later Time

On some Android phones, you can decide that you want a text message to be sent automatically at a later time. To do this, before sending the message, tap the Menu icon and choose Schedule Message. Choose the date and time you want your message to be sent and tap Done. Then tap the Send button, and your message is sent at the time you scheduled.

>>>Go Further

MESSAGE LIMITS AND MESSAGES

Text messages can only be 160 characters long. To get around this limit, most modern phones simply break up text messages you type into 160-character chunks. Your Android phone displays a readout showing the number of characters remaining and the number of messages it will send: The readout starts at 160/1 when you begin a new message and runs down to 1/1; then it starts at 145/2 (fewer characters because there is some overhead in linking the messages). The phone receiving the message simply combines them into one message. This is important to know if your wireless plan has a text message limit. When you create one text message, your Android phone might actually break the message into two or more.

into multiple text messages so as not to go over the SMS character limits and to show how this will also cost more.

122 / 2 —— **Message count indicator**

Attach a File to a Message

If you want to send a picture, audio file, or video with your text message, all you need to do is attach the file. Be aware that attaching a file turns your SMS text message into an MMS multimedia message and may be subject to additional charges.

1. Tap the Paperclip icon to attach a file.

1

34 mins

Hi Craig.

2. Tap to attach a picture or video already stored in your Gallery or Photos app.

3. Tap to record and attach a voice note.

4. Tap to take a picture or record a short (50-second) video using your phone's camera.

5. Tap to send your MMS.

Toggle between picture and video   **Accept picture or video**

See full Camera app view

It's Not All Good

Is It Worth Attaching Files?

Attaching files to text messages is not as useful as you might desire. Most carriers limit the attachment size to around 300KB. This means that you can only really attach about 50 seconds of very low-quality video; pictures with low resolution, high compression, or both; and very short audio files. The Messenger app automatically compresses larger picture files to make them small enough to send, but you will often find that it simply refuses to send video files because they are too large. Choosing the option of capturing pictures, capturing video, or recording audio when you choose to attach is the only way you can guarantee that the files are small enough. This is because when you do this, the Camera and Audio Recorder apps are set to a mode that makes them record low-quality audio and take low-quality pictures.

Receive a Message

When you receive a new SMS or MMS message, you can read it, view its attachments, and even save those attachments to your Android phone.

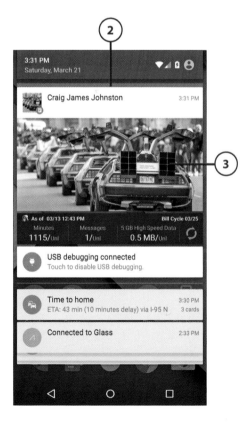

1. When a new SMS or MMS message arrives, your Android phone plays a ringtone and displays a notification in the status bar.

2. Pull down the Notification panel to see newly arrived messages.

3. Tap a message alert to display the message and reply to it.

4. Tap an attachment to open it for viewing.

5. Touch and hold a message to display the Message Options dialog.

6. Tap to delete the message. This deletes just the message and not the entire thread.

7. Tap to copy the message text so you can paste it elsewhere.

8. Tap to forward the message and attachment to someone else.

9. Tap to save the attachment to your Android phone.

10. Tap to share the message via social media or other methods.

11. Tap to view the message details, such as its size and the date and time it was sent.

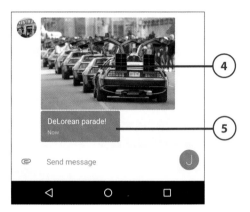

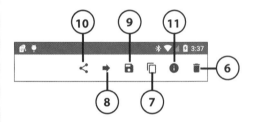

Usable Content

If a text message contains links to websites, phone numbers, or email addresses, tapping those links makes the Android phone take the appropriate action. For example, when you tap a phone number, your Android phone calls the number; when you tap a web link, the Android phone opens the page in Chrome or your other default browser.

>>>Go Further

USING GOOGLE HANGOUTS FOR SMS AND MMS

You may decide that because you already use Google Hangouts to instant message your friends and family, as well as to video chat with them, it makes sense to set the Google Hangouts app to handle text messages (SMS) and multimedia messages (MMS) so that all communications with your friends and family are in one place. To set this, from the Messenger app, tap the Menu icon and tap Settings. Tap Change Your Default SMS app and then choose Hangouts. The way in which you interact with SMS and MMS while using the Hangouts app is very similar to the way it works in the Messenger app, so the steps in this chapter should help you. Even the settings for handling SMS and MMS are similar. When one of your contacts has signed up for a Google account and has started using Google Hangouts, you can switch from sending and receiving SMS and MMS messages with them and start using Hangouts messages instead. Doing this saves you from costly SMS and MMS charges and just uses your data plan.

Choose type of message to send

Show only favorite contacts

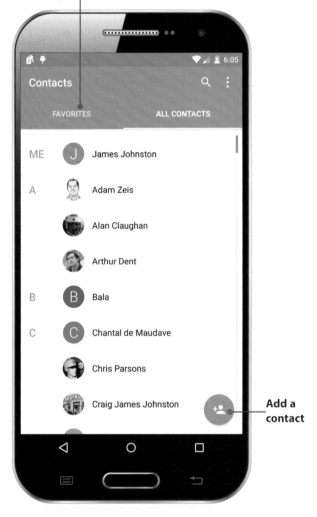

Add a
contact

In this chapter, you discover the app that's your Android phone's hub of all communication, Contacts. You learn how to add contacts, synchronize contacts, join duplicate contacts together, and even how to add a contact to your Home screen. Topics include the following:

2

→ Adding accounts
→ Adding and managing contacts
→ Synchronizing contacts
→ Creating favorite contacts
→ mporting contacts

Contacts

On the Android phone, you can synchronize your contacts from many online sites such as Facebook and Gmail so that as your friends change their Facebook profile pictures, their pictures on your Android phone change, too.

Contacts and People
On some Android phones, the Contacts app is called the People app. Please be aware of this as you read through this chapter.

Adding Accounts

Before you look around the Contacts app, try adding some accounts to synchronize contacts from. You already added your Google account when you set up your Android phone in the Prologue earlier in this book.

Adding Facebook, Twitter, LinkedIn, and Other Accounts

To add accounts for your online services, such as Facebook, Twitter, LinkedIn, and so on, install the apps for those services from Google Play Store. See Chapter 9, "Working with Android Applications," for information about how to install apps. After you have installed the apps and you have logged in to them, visit the Accounts section in Settings and add a new account as shown in the following sections to see new accounts for each online service.

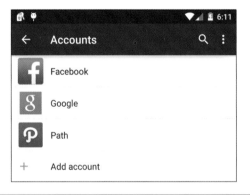

Mobile Device Management (MDM) and Containers

More and more companies are starting to use Mobile Device Management (MDM) systems to manage mobile devices. The steps in the following task describe a situation in which your company does not use an MDM system and you are manually adding your work account to your Android phone. If your company does use an MDM system, the setup of your work account will be handled automatically. With Android, many companies also deploy a Container or Dual Persona app. This Dual Persona app provides a secure area in which your email, contacts, and calendar reside. When a Container or Dual Persona is used, you use the Dual Persona app for email, contacts, and calendar instead of the built-in Android apps. Some examples of these Container or Dual Persona apps are Good Technology, Divide, and AirWatch Inbox. Samsung also provides one called KNOX on some models of its tablets and smartphones.

Add a Work Email Account

Your Android phone can synchronize your contacts from your work email account as long as your company uses Microsoft Exchange or an email gateway that supports Exchange ActiveSync (such as IBM Notes Traveler for Lotus Domino/Notes email systems). It might be useful to keep your work and personal contacts on one mobile device instead of carrying two devices.

1. From the Home screen, pull down the Quick Settings Bar.

2. Tap the Settings icon.

3. Tap Accounts in the Personal section. On Samsung phones, look for Accounts in the User and Backup section; on HTC phones, look for Accounts & Sync.

4. Tap Add Account.

5. Tap Exchange. Sometimes this account type is called Corporate, Microsoft Exchange ActiveSync, or Exchange ActiveSync.

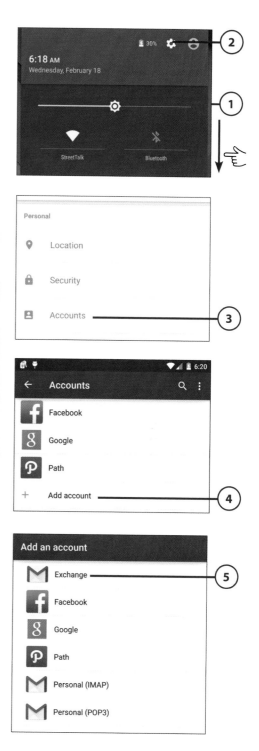

6. Enter your full corporate email address and tap Next.

7. Enter your corporate network password.

8. Tap Next.

What Is a Client Certificate?

Your company might require that you use a certificate as a method of authenticating to the email system, instead of using your username and password. There are advantages to doing this; for example, when your password changes, it doesn't stop your Android phone from receiving email.

Error Adding Account? Guess the Server

Your Android phone tries to work out some information about your company's ActiveSync setup. If it can't, you are prompted to enter the ActiveSync server name manually (as described in step 9). If you don't know what it is, you can try guessing it. If, for example, your email address is dsimons@allhitradio.com, the ActiveSync server is most likely webmail.all-hitradio.com or autodiscover@all-hitradio.com. If this doesn't work, ask your email administrator.

9. Enter your company's mail server name, and then tap Next at the bottom of the screen.

10. Tap OK to agree that your mail administrator might impose security restrictions on your Android phone if you proceed.

Remote Security Administration

Remote Security Administration is another way of saying that when you activate your Android phone against your work email servers, your email administrator can add restrictions to your phone. The restrictions can include forcing a Lock screen password, imposing the need for a strong password, and requiring how many letters and numbers the password must be. Your email administrator also has the power to remotely wipe your Android phone so that it is put back to factory defaults, which is what the administrator might do if you lose your phone or if it is stolen.

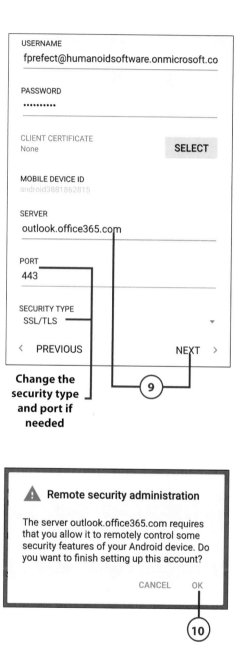

USERNAME
fprefect@humanoidsoftware.onmicrosoft.co

PASSWORD
··········

CLIENT CERTIFICATE
None   SELECT

MOBILE DEVICE ID
android3881862815

SERVER
outlook.office365.com

PORT
443

SECURITY TYPE
SSL/TLS   ▼

< PREVIOUS   NEXT >

Change the security type and port if needed

⑨

⚠ Remote security administration

The server outlook.office365.com requires that you allow it to remotely control some security features of your Android device. Do you want to finish setting up this account?

CANCEL   OK

⑩

11. Tap to choose how often your corporate email is delivered to your Android phone. Automatic means that as it arrives in your Inbox at work, it is delivered to your phone. You can set it to Manual, which means that your work email is delivered only when you open the Email app on your phone. You can also set the delivery frequency from every five minutes to every hour.

12. Tap to choose how many days in the past email is synchronized to your Android phone or set it to All to synchronize all email in your Inbox.

13. Tap to enable or disable being notified when new email arrives from your corporate Inbox.

14. Tap to enable or disable synchronizing your corporate contacts to your Android phone.

15. Tap to enable or disable synchronizing your corporate calendar to your Android phone.

16. Tap to enable or disable synchronizing your corporate email to your Android phone.

17. Tap to enable or disable automatically downloading email attachments when your Android phone is connected to a Wi-Fi network.

18. Tap Next.

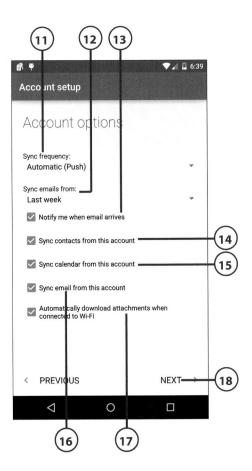

What to Synchronize

You might decide that you don't want to synchronize all your work information to your Android phone. You might decide to just synchronize email but not the calendar, or maybe just the calendar but not the contacts and email. Unchecking these boxes enables you to choose the information you don't want to synchronize. You can go back into the account settings and change it later if you change your mind.

19. Tap Activate to agree to the restrictions that are about to be imposed by your administrator on your phone.

20. Enter a name for this email account. Use something meaningful that describes the purpose of the account such as **Work Email**.

21. Tap Next to complete your work email setup.

Removing an Account

To remove an account, under the Accounts section in Settings, tap the account to be removed. For account types that can have multiple accounts (such as Corporate and Google), tap the account again on the next screen to show its sync settings. Tap the Menu icon on the top right of the screen and tap Remove Account.

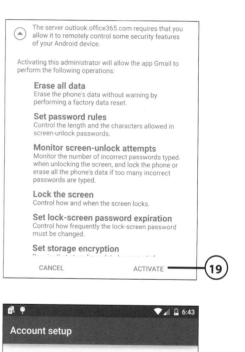

Navigating Contacts

The Contacts app actually has three screens. The middle one you see shows your list of contacts, but there are two others that have specific functions.

Navigate Contacts

1. Tap the Contacts icon.

2. Tap to add a new contact.

3. Tap to search for a contact.

4. Tap the Menu icon to change the settings for the Contacts app, manage accounts, import or export contacts, and choose which contacts to display.

5. Tap to see only favorite contacts and contacts you frequently contact.

Marking a Contact as a Favorite

To mark a contact as a favorite, while you have the contact's information open, tap the Star icon to the left of the Edit icon.

6. Tap a contact to view or edit it.

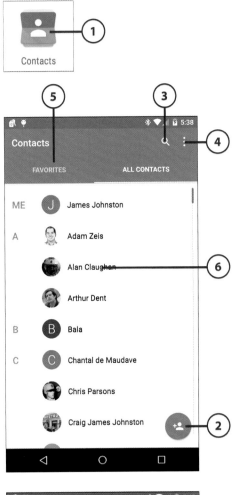

Tap to mark as a favorite

Contacts App Differences

The Contacts app may look a bit different on some Android phones, and even have a different name. On HTC phones, for example, the Contacts app is called People. The Contacts app and the Phone app are actually one app. The app has four tabs: Phone, Favorites, People, and Groups. To edit a contact in the HTC Contacts app, touch and hold a contact; when the pop-up screen appears, tap Edit. On Samsung phones, like the HTC phones, the Contacts app and the Phone app are actually one app. It has four tabs: Keypad, Logs, Favorites, and Contacts.

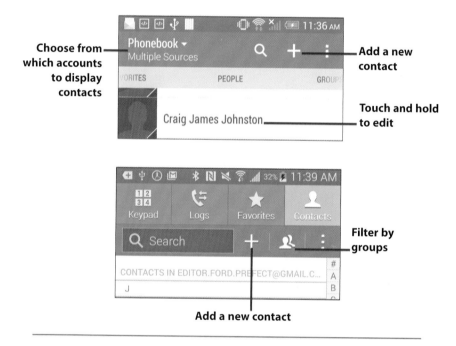

Choose from which accounts to display contacts

Add a new contact

Touch and hold to edit

Filter by groups

Add a new contact

Adding and Managing Contacts

As you add contacts to your work email accounts or Google accounts, those contacts are synchronized to your Android phone automatically. When you reply to or forward emails on your phone to an email address that is not in your Contacts, those email addresses are automatically added to the contact list or merged into an existing contact with the same name. You can also add contacts to your Android phone directly.

Add Contacts from an Email

To manually add a contact from an email, first open the email client (either email or Gmail) and then open an email message. See Chapter 5, "Email," for more on how to work with email.

1. Tap the blank contact picture to the left of the sender's name after you open the email.

2. Tap OK to add the sender's email address to your contacts.

3. Choose an existing contact that you want to add the email address to if you already have the contact in your list and want to add an additional email address to it. If you do this, skip the rest of the steps.

4. Tap Create New Contact to create a new contact and add this email address to it.

5. Tap to choose which email account you want to add this contact to (if you have more than one account).

6. Enter additional information about your new contact.

7. Tap the check mark to save the new contact.

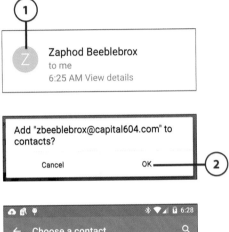

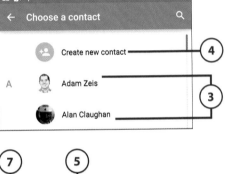

Add a Contact Manually

1. Tap the Contacts icon.

2. Tap to add a new contact.

3. Tap to select which email account the new contact is being added to. For example, you might want to add the new contact to your work email account instead of your personal account.

4. Enter the person's full name.

5. Tap to choose a contact picture.

6. Tap to enter a middle name, name prefix and suffix, and phonetic names.

7. Enter information including phone numbers, email address, and events.

8. Tap the check mark to save the new contact.

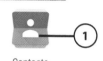

Contacts

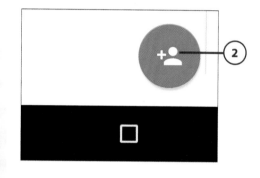

Add a Contact from a vCard

vCards are files that can be attached to emails. These vCards contain a virtual business card that you can import into the Contacts app as a new contact. Use the following steps to add a new contact from a vCard.

1. Tap the attachment that has the .vcf extension.

2. Tap to select which account you want to add the new contact to. For example, you might want to add the new contact to your work email account instead of your personal account.

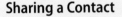

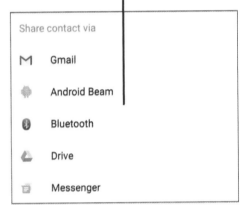

Sharing a Contact

To share a contact, tap the Menu icon and tap Share. The exact list of methods to share a contact is determined by the apps you have installed on your phone, but in general you should be able to share a contact via Android Beam (or S Beam if you are using a Samsung phone and sharing the contact with another Samsung user) or Bluetooth, save it to your Google Drive, or send it via the Email or Gmail app.

Sharing options

Share contact via

M   Gmail

        Android Beam

        Bluetooth

        Drive

        Messenger

>>>*Go Further*

WHAT IS NEAR FIELD COMMUNICATION (NFC)?

Your Android phone most likely has an NFC radio and antenna built in. When you hold either another device with built-in NFC or an NFC tag close to the phone's back cover, the NFC antenna and radio reads the data. You can learn more about NFC at http://en.wikipedia.org/wiki/Near_field_communication.

>>>*Go Further*

BEAMING BETWEEN PHONES

If you want to send a contact via NFC, you can use the Beaming feature, which is built in to your Android phone. To beam a contact, make sure the contact is selected, and bring the other person's NFC-enabled smartphone or phone back-to-back with your phone. After you hear a tone, you see the screen zoom out. Touch the screen to send the contact card to the other device.

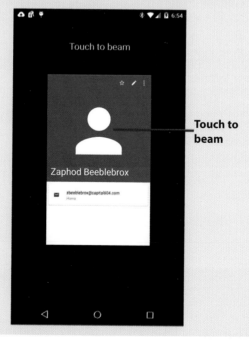

Touch to beam

Note that Samsung smartphones and phones support Android Beam, but they also use a Samsung-specific version of it called S Beam. If you are using an Android phone and are trying to beam a contact to a non-Samsung smartphone or phone, it may not work unless you go into Settings and disable S Beam. After S Beam is disabled, your Samsung phone reverts to using the standard Android Beam functionality. The same goes for someone using a Samsung smartphone and attempting to beam a contact to you.

Edit a Contact

Sometimes you need to make changes to a contact or add additional information to it.

1. Tap the contact to open the contact record.

2. Tap the Edit icon.

3. Tap the down-arrow icon to enter a middle name, name prefix, and name suffix.

4. Tap the X next to a field to delete it.

5. Tap to change the field subcategory. In this example, tapping Work enables you to change the phone subcategory from Work to Home to indicate that this is the contact's Home phone number.

6. Tap Add New to add a new field in a specific category. In this example, tapping Add New enables you to add a new email address.

7. Tap to put the contact in one or more contact groups. You can use a default contact group of family, friends, coworkers, or you can create a group.

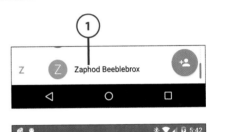

Indicates what account the contact originates from

8. Tap to add a new field to the contact's contact card. New fields could be phone numbers, IM (Instant Messaging) address, notes, nickname, website, a special date (such as a birthday or anniversary), your relationship to the contact, and even an Internet phone number (or SIP number).

9. Tap the check mark to save your changes.

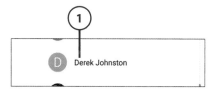

Add a Contact Photo

The contact photo is normally added automatically when a social network account is linked to a contact. However, you might want to manually add a picture or change the current picture.

1. Tap the contact.

2. Tap the Edit icon.

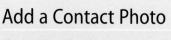

3. Tap the contact photo placeholder or, if there is already a photo, tap the photo.

4. Tap to add a photo already saved on your Android phone.

Taking a Photo

If you don't already have a photo you want to use, you can take a new photo with your phone's camera by tapping the Take Photo option.

5. Tap the photo you want to use.

6. Drag the cropping box to select the area of the photo you want to use as the contact photo.

7. Drag the outside of the cropping box to expand or contract it.

8. Tap Done to save the cropped photo as the contact photo.

Take a photo with the camera

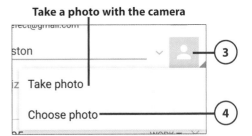

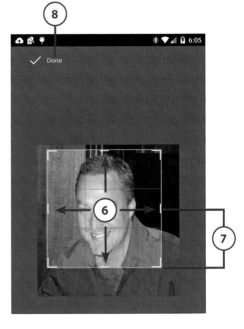

Customize Contacts Settings

There are a couple settings that you might want to customize for the Contacts app, such as choosing the contact list display order and whether to display contacts using their first names first or last names first.

1. Tap the Menu icon.

2. Tap Settings.

3. Tap to choose the sort order of the list of contacts in the Contacts app. You can sort the list by first name or last name.

4. Tap to choose how each contact is displayed. You can display contacts by first name first or last name first.

5. Tap the arrow to save the settings.

Manage Contact Groups

You can create contact groups—such as Friends, Family, Inner Circle—and then divide your contacts among them. This can be useful if you don't want to search through all your contacts to find a family member. Instead you can just tap the Family group and see only family members. The following steps describe how to manage which group(s) a particular contact belongs to.

1. Tap a contact.

2. Tap the Edit icon.

3. Tap Group Name to manage which groups this contact belongs to.

4. Select one or more groups to add the contact to.

5. Tap outside of the group selection area once you have made your changes.

6. Tap the check mark to save the changes to the contact.

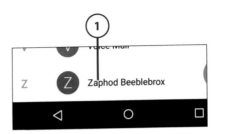

Tap to create a new group

GROUPS

Group name

Edit contact

Friends

Family

Coworkers

Project Purple ✓

The Vogons ✓

Bowling team

Create new group

Project Purple, The Vogons

ADD ANOTHER FIELD

It's Not All Good

You Can't Use Groups

Even though you can add contacts to groups, using the standard Android apps like Gmail, Contacts, and so on, you cannot actually use the groups for anything. For example, you might want to send an email to a group, and you'd think that you might be able to select a group so that all members of that group would receive the email. It's a great idea, but it's not possible. Even within the Contacts app, you cannot search a group name. The only thing that you can use groups for is for refining the Contacts display, as described in the "Choose Contacts to Display" section. Hopefully this will change in the future.

Choose Contacts to Display

You can choose to hide certain contact groups from the main contacts
display; for example, you can choose
to show only contacts from your
corporate account or only certain
groups of contacts from your Google
account.

1. Tap the Menu icon.
2. Tap Contacts to Display.

3. Tap to show all contacts from all accounts.

4. Tap an account to show only contacts from that account.

5. Tap to customize which groups in each account are displayed.

6. Tap to expand an account to see subgroups of contacts.

7. Tap to select or deselect a subgroup of contacts. In this example, we have chosen to only show contacts who are in the My Contacts and Starred in Android groups.

8. Tap OK to save the settings.

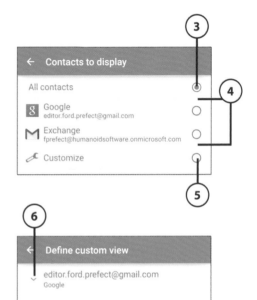

Join and Separate Contacts

As you add contacts to your Android phone, they are automatically merged if the new contact name matches a name that's already stored. Sometimes, you need to manually join contacts together or separate them if your Android phone has joined them in error.

Join Contacts Manually

1. Tap the contact that you want to join a contact to.

2. Tap the Edit icon.

3. Tap the Menu icon.

4. Tap Join.

5. Tap the contact you want to join with. The Contacts app suggests contacts but you can also search for them yourself.

6. Tap the check mark to complete the join process.

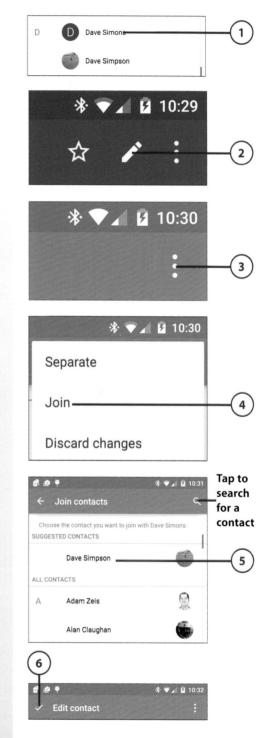

Tap to search for a contact

Separate Contacts Manually

When you follow these steps to separate contacts that have either been automatically or manually joined, all previous joins for this contact will be separated, including automatic ones that the Contacts app does when it sees duplicate contacts.

1. Tap the contact that you want to separate.

2. Tap the Edit icon.

3. Tap the Menu icon.

4. Tap Separate.

5. Tap OK to separate the contacts.

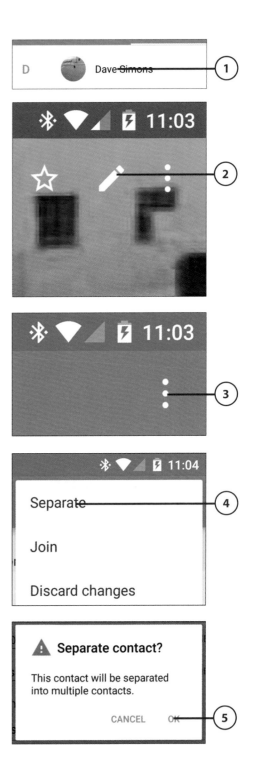

Adding a Contact to Your Home Screen

If you communicate with some contacts so much that you are constantly opening and closing the Contacts app, a quicker solution might be to add a shortcut to the contacts on the Home screen.

1. Tap the contact you want to add to your Home screen.

2. Tap the Menu icon.

3. Tap Place on Home Screen. A shortcut to the contact is placed on an available spot on the Home screen.

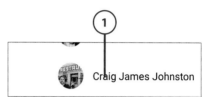

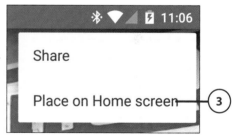

Repositioning or Removing the Shortcut

After you have a contact shortcut on your Home screen, you can reposition it by touching and holding it, and while you are still holding it, drag it around the screen, or off the sides of the screen to move it between the Home screen panes. Release the shortcut to complete the reposition. To remove the contact shortcut, touch and hold it, then drag it up to where you see the word Remove and release it.

Drag to remove the shortcut

Drag it around to reposition it

>>>Go Further
IMPORTING AND EXPORTING CONTACTS

You can import any vCards that you have saved to your Android phone's internal storage. You can also export your entire contact list to your Android phone's internal storage or share that entire contact list via Bluetooth, email, Gmail, or—if you have any NFC tag writer software installed—write it to an NFC tag. If you recently upgraded from an older phone on which you had saved your contacts on the SIM card, you can also import those contacts to your Android phone's Contacts app. To access the import/export functions, tap the Menu icon and tap Import/Export. When you export contacts to storage, you can find them in /mnt/sdcard when browsing your Android phone from your Mac or PC.

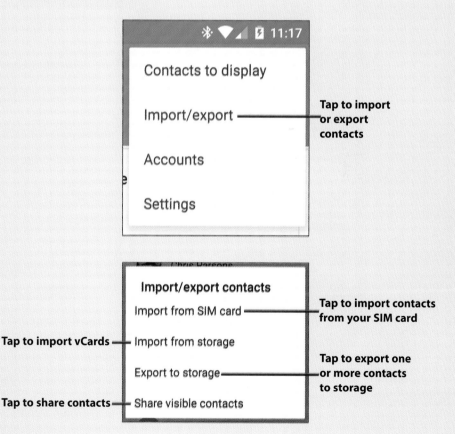

Tap to import or export contacts

Tap to import contacts from your SIM card

Tap to import vCards

Tap to export one or more contacts to storage

Tap to share contacts

Tap to find movies

Tap to find TV shows

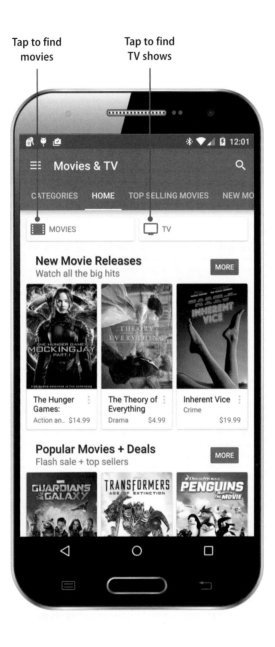

In this chapter, you discover your Android phone's audio and video capabilities, including how your Android phone plays video and music and how you can synchronize audio and video from your desktop computer or Google Play Music. Topics include the following:

→ Using Google Play Music for music
→ Using the Photos app for pictures and video
→ Renting movies with Google Play Movies
→ Working with YouTube

Audio, Video, and Movies

Your Android phone has strong multimedia capabilities. The large screen enables you to turn your Android phone sideways to enjoy a video in its original 16:9 ratio. You can also use your Android phone to search YouTube, watch videos, and even upload videos to YouTube right from your phone. Android fully embraces the cloud, which enables you to store your music collection on Google's servers so that you can access it anywhere.

Using Google Play Music

Your Android phone ships with a Google Play Music app, which enables you to listen to music stored on your phone as well as from your collection in the Google Play Music cloud. Using Google Play, you can also find and buy more music.

Find Music

The best place to discover and find music is in the Google Play Store.

Play Store

1. Tap the Play Store icon on the Home screen.

2. Tap to see only what's offered in the Music category.

3. Tap to sort music by genre.

4. Tap to see top-selling albums.

5. Tap to see new releases.

6. Scroll right to see top-selling songs.

7. Tap to search for music.

8. Scroll down to see more music.

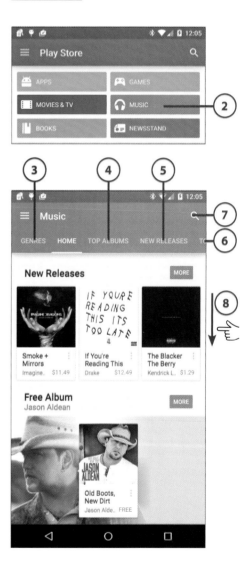

Purchase Music

After you find a song or album you're interested in, follow these steps to purchase it. Remember that when you purchase music, it does not download to your phone; instead, it's automatically added to your Google Cloud.

Free Music

Sometimes songs are offered for free. If a song is offered for free, you see the word FREE instead of a price for the song. Even though the song is free, you still need to follow the steps outlined in this section; however, the price is reflected as 0.

Adding a Payment Method

Before you purchase music, you need to make sure that you have a way to pay for it. To do that, you need to add a payment method to your Google Wallet account. Using your desktop computer, browse to http://wallet.google.com and log in. Click Payment Methods, and if you do not already have a valid payment method, click Add a Payment Method. Enter valid debit or credit card information.

1. Tap the price to the right of the song title. If you want to purchase the entire album, tap the price for the album (not shown).

2. Tap Buy.

Tap the song title to play a preview of it

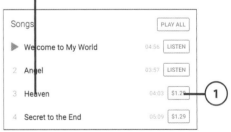

Tap to change payment methods

3. Tap Listen to hear your song after the purchase is complete. The song opens in the Play Music app and streams from your Google Cloud account over the air.

▶	Welcome to My World	04:56	LISTEN
2	Angel	03:57	LISTEN
3	Heaven	04:03	$1.29

3

It's Not All Good

Cloud and Data Usage

Although the idea of cloud storage (where your music is stored on Google computers as opposed to your Android phone) is beneficial, it does mean that anytime you listen to your music collection it is streamed over the Wi-Fi or cellular data network. If you are not connected to Wi-Fi or cellular data, you cannot access and listen to your music. You can plan for a no-coverage situation by keeping some music on your phone. See the section titled "Listen to Music with No Wireless Coverage" later in this chapter.

Add Your Existing Music to Google Play Music

You can upload as many as 50,000 songs from Apple iTunes, Microsoft Windows Media Player, or music stored in folders on your computer for free to your Google Play Music Cloud account by using the Google Music Manager app on your desktop computer. If you haven't already installed Google Music Manager, follow the steps in the "Install Google Music Manager" section in the Prologue of this book.

1

1. Click (right-click for Windows) the Google Music Manager icon. (This icon is in the Mac menu bar at the top of the screen or in the Windows taskbar at the bottom of the screen.)

2. Choose Preferences. (Use the Options command for Windows.)

3. Click to upload new songs you've added since you last used Google Music Manager to upload music.

4. Click to upload the remainder of songs that have not yet uploaded to Google Play Music.

5. Click to upload songs in certain playlists. This works only for iTunes or for Windows Media Player.

6. Choose the playlists to upload.

7. Click Upload after you have made your selections.

8. Click to allow Google Music Manager to automatically upload newly added songs.

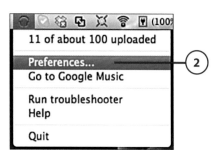

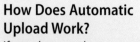

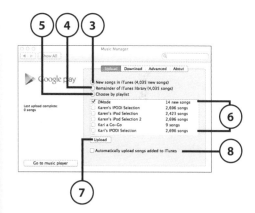

How Does Automatic Upload Work?

If you choose to have your music uploaded automatically in step 8, Google Music Manager continually monitors Apple iTunes, Microsoft Windows Media Player, or your Music folders to see when you add music. If it finds new music, Google Music Manager automatically uploads it. (After you install Google Music Manager, the software is always running on your computer.)

What if I Don't Have iTunes or Windows Media Player?

If you don't have or don't use Apple iTunes or Microsoft Windows Media Player to store and play your music, Google Music Manager can upload music from folders on your computer. Click the Advanced tab, click Change, and select either Music Folder (to use the folder on your computer called Music) or Other Folders (so you can choose folders where you store your music). Click Add Folder to add a new folder to the list.

Select to choose other folders

Can I Download Music to My Computer?

You can download your entire music collection from Google Play Music to your computer, or just download music you have purchased on your Android phone by clicking the Download tab in Google Music Manager Preferences.

Click to download your music

Use the Google Play Music App

Now that you have purchased some music and/or synchronized it from your computer, it's time to take a look at the Google Play Music app on your Android phone.

1. Tap the Play Music icon on the Home screen.

2. Scroll down to explore the Listen Now screen.

3. Tap to search for music. This includes music loaded on your phone, stored in the Google Cloud, available in All Access (if you subscribe to it), and playing on online radio stations.

4. Swipe in from the left side of the screen to see a menu.

What Is Listen Now?

Listen Now is the first screen you are presented with when you launch the Google Play Music app. This view is dynamically created based on what music you have uploaded, purchased, and listened to. It contains your music, music accessible via All Access, and radio stations. All Access is a subscription service that enables you to access a vast collection of music. As you scroll around the Listen Now screens, you are not visually cued as to what music is on All Access, and what music you have uploaded or purchased; everything is just seamlessly put together. For a free 30-day trial of All Access, use your computer to visit http://play.google.com/about/music/allaccess/#/.

5. Tap to return to the Listen Now screen.

6. Tap to see only music in your music library. This is the music you have purchased and uploaded.

7. Tap to see playlists that you have created and playlists that have been automatically created for you.

8. Tap to browse and create Instant Mixes (previously called Radio Stations) that will play your music. Read more about Instant Mixes later in this chapter.

Instant Mix Naming Confusion

Google seems unsure of what it should call Instant Mixes. In previous versions of Android this was called "Radio Stations." Then it was renamed to "Instant Mixes." On some Android phones, instead of Instant Mixes, this is now called "Radio."

9. Tap to explore music that is available to play and purchase.

10. Tap to switch between showing only music that is already downloaded to your phone or showing music no matter where it resides, including in your Google Cloud account.

11. Tap to change the Google Play Music app settings.

Work with My Library

My Library shows all music you have uploaded from your computer or purchased in the Google Play Store. After tapping My Library, as shown in step 6 of the "Use the Music App" task, continue with the following steps.

Swiping Between Views

As you follow the steps in this task, instead of tapping the view titles, such as Albums and Artists, you can swipe left and right to move between these views.

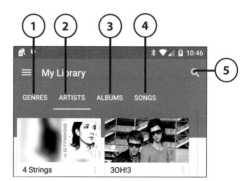

1. Tap Genres to filter the view by genre. Tap an album name to reveal songs on that album, and then tap a song to play it.

2. Tap Artists to filter the view by artist. Tap an artist's name to reveal songs by that artist, and then tap a song to play it.

3. Tap Albums to filter the view by album title. Tap an album name to reveal songs on that album, and then tap a song to play it.

4. Tap Songs to filter the view by song title. This shows all songs by all artists. Tap a song to play it.

5. Tap to search for music in your collection.

What's Playing?

If you are currently playing music, the bottom of the Google Play Music app shows the information about the song and allows you to pause the song. Tap the song to see more actions, including jumping backward and forward through a playlist.

Work with Playlists

Playlists can be created automatically for you, such as playlists of songs you have given a thumbs up to or music you last added to your library, but you can also manually create playlists. After tapping Playlists as shown in step 7 of the "Use the Music App" task, continue with the following steps.

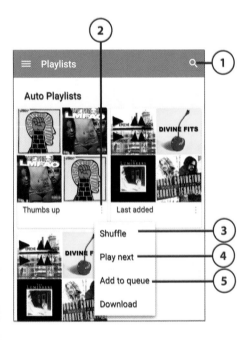

1. Tap to search for music by song or artist. This does not let you search for a playlist.

2. Tap the Menu icon at the bottom of a playlist to see a list of actions.

3. Tap to shuffle the songs in the playlist.

4. Tap to play the next song in the playlist.

5. Tap to add the playlist and all its songs to the queue of music currently playing.

6. Tap to download the playlist (and all the songs in the playlist) to your phone rather than storing it only in the Google Cloud. This enables you to play the songs even when your phone cannot connect to a Wi-Fi or cellular network.

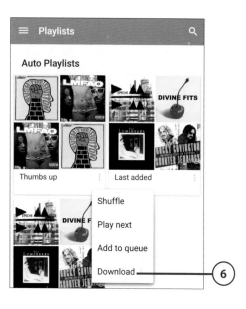

Creating or Adding to a Playlist

You can create a playlist from any song or add a song to any playlist. Tap the Menu icon to the right of the song and then tap Add to Playlist. When the list of playlists appears, either tap an existing playlist or tap New Playlist and provide a playlist name.

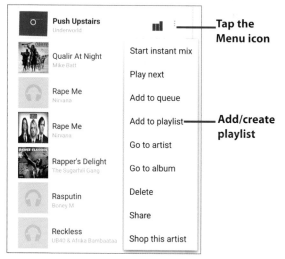

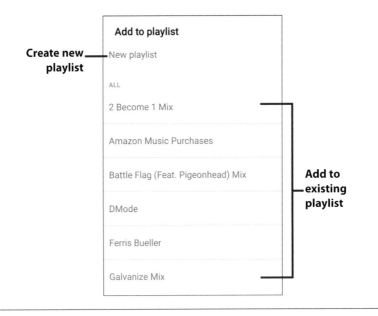

Create new playlist

Add to existing playlist

Edit or Delete Playlists

1. Tap the playlist you want to edit or delete.

2. Swipe a song left or right off the screen to remove it from the playlist.

3. Reposition a song in the playlist by dragging it up and down using the song anchor.

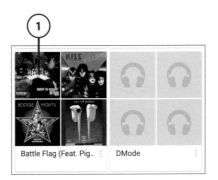

Song anchor

4. Tap the Menu icon to see more actions.

5. Tap to delete the playlist.

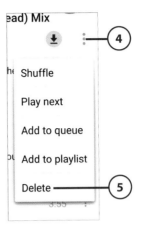

Work with Instant Mixes

Instant Mixes (previously called Radio Stations) are like channels that play music based on artist, genre, or some other shared criterion.

1. Swipe in from the left of the screen and tap Instant Mixes.

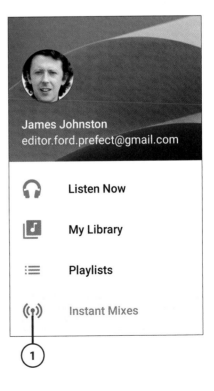

2. Tap a mix's thumbnail to start playing that Instant Mix.

3. Tap to see mixes that you have created.

4. Tap to see a list of mixes that are generated based on music you have purchased and listened to in the past.

5. Tap to add your own new Instant Mix.

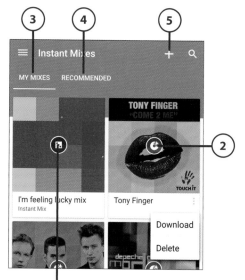

Special mix

Create Your Own Instant Mixes

You can create your own Instant Mixes based on an artist, song title, or genre. After you create a mix, it plays music from the artist or song you selected, but it also plays other similar songs. Use the following steps after tapping the plus symbol, as described in step 5 in the previous section.

1. Type the name of a song, artist, album, or music genre.

2. Tap a mix that matches your search. This example uses the sound track for the movie *Ferris Bueller's Day Off*. The mix should start playing immediately.

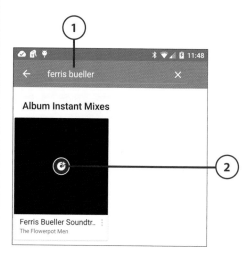

3. Tap the Music Queue icon to view and edit the list of songs queued up to play.

4. Swipe a song left or right off the screen to remove it from the mix.

5. Reposition a song in the queue by dragging it up or down by the song anchor.

Song anchor

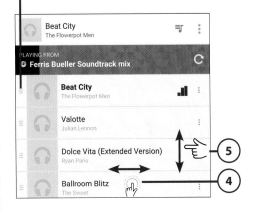

Control Playback

While your music is playing, you have some control over how a song plays and the selection of music that is queued to be played.

1. Tap to jump to the previous song in the album, playlist, or mix.

2. Tap to jump to the next song in the album, playlist, or mix.

3. Tap to pause the song. The button turns into the Play button when a song is paused. Tap again to resume playing a paused song.

4. Tap to indicate that you like the song. The Google Play Music app adds the song to the Thumbs Up playlist.

5. Tap to indicate that you do not like the song.

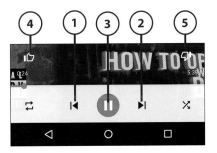

6. Tap to enable or disable song shuffling. When Shuffle is enabled, songs in the current playlist or album are randomly played. The Shuffle icon is not available when you are playing an Instant Mix.

7. Tap to enable repeating. Tap once to repeat all songs; tap again to repeat the current song only; tap again to disable repeating. The Repeating icon is not available when you play an Instant Mix.

8. Drag right and left to skip forward and backward through the song.

9. Tap to see and manage the list of songs in the album, playlist, or Instant Mix.

10. Tap the Menu icon to see more options.

11. Tap to make a new Instant Mix based on the song.

12. Tap to create a playlist and add the current song to it or add the song to an existing playlist.

13. Tap to show all songs by the artist.

14. Tap to show the album this song is on, and all songs you have purchased from the album.

15. Tap to share the link to the song on Google+.

16. Tap to clear the queue of songs you made earlier and stop playing the current song. If you didn't make a queue, the current song stops playing.

17. Tap to save the Now Playing queue if you made any changes.

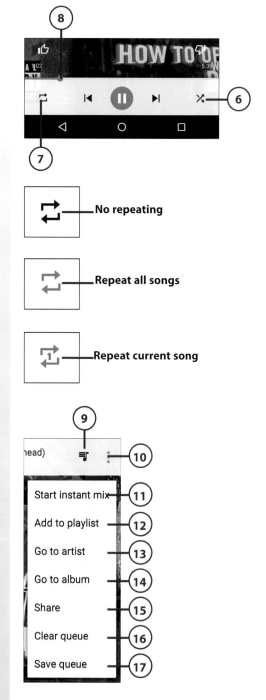

What Does Start Instant Mix Do?

If you are playing a song and choose the Start Instant Mix option, the Google Play Music app creates a new Instant Mix and adds songs to it that are similar to the one that's currently playing. The name of the mix becomes the name of the current song.

What Is the Queue?

The queue is mentioned in step 16, but what is the queue? Essentially, the queue is the Now Playing queue, a dynamic playlist that you can add songs to so that they are queued up to play one after the other. To add music to the queue, tap the Menu icon to the right of a song, playlist, or album and choose Add to Queue. This puts the song at the bottom of the current Now Playing queue. To have that song play as the next song in the queue, choose Play Next.

Work and Listen to Music

You don't have to keep the Google Play Music app open while you play music; you can switch back to the Home screen and run any other app while you still have the ability to control the music. The following steps work from the Home screen, while any app is running, or from the Lock screen.

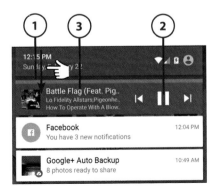

1. While on any screen, pull down the Notification panel. If you are on the Lock screen, you can skip this step because notifications are always visible in the middle of the screen.

2. Tap to pause the song.

3. Tap the song title to open the Google Play Music app for more control.

4. Tap to jump to the next song in the list, album, or playlist.

5. Tap to jump to the previous song in the list, album, or playlist.

6. Use two fingers and swipe down on the music control to expand it.

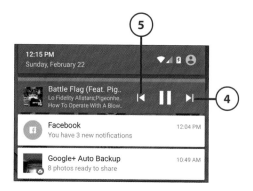

Listen to Music with No Wireless Coverage

As established earlier in the chapter, if you utilize Google Play Music to store your music in the Google Cloud, when you play that music on your Android phone, it is actually streaming over the Wi-Fi or cellular data network. If you know that you are going to be in an area without coverage but still want to listen to your music, follow these steps.

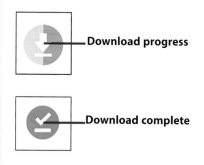

1. Tap the Download icon while viewing an album, song, or playlist.

2. The Download icon indicates the progress of the download. The amount of orange on the icon shows the progress of the download. The down arrow changes to a check mark when the download has completed.

Download progress

Download complete

Change Google Play Music Settings

1. Swipe in from the left of the screen to show the menu.

2. Tap Settings.

3. Tap to change the Google account being used for Google Play Music. You can also add a new Google account to be used with the Play Music app.

4. Tap to manually refresh the list of music shown on your Android phone.

5. Tap to subscribe to Google's All Access plan that gives you access to Google's 30-million-song collection. Tap to cancel your monthly All Access subscription, if you have one.

6. Tap to manage the devices you use to access your music. Google allows up to ten devices.

7. Tap to manage the audio equalizer settings.

8. Tap to enable or disable blocking explicit songs when listening to Instant Mixes.

9. Scroll down for more settings.

Trial All Access?

On some Android phones, step 5 may offer you a trial of Google's All Access plan. After the trial period, you can choose to cancel or continue using the plan.

James Johnston
editor.ford.prefect@gmail.com

🎧 Listen Now

🎵 My Library

≡ Playlists

((ŧ)) Instant Mixes

▶ Shop

Downloaded only

Settings

Music settings

GENERAL

Google account
Connect to Google Play using
editor.ford.prefect@gmail.com

Refresh
Refresh music from Google Play

Subscribe to All Access
Get access to millions of songs and unlimited radio

My devices
Access your music from up to 10 devices

Equalizer
Fine tune your audio settings

Block explicit songs in mixes

DOWNLOADING

Cache during playback
Temporarily store music while streaming

10. Tap to enable or disable caching of streamed music. When this is enabled, music you listen to is temporarily stored on your Android phone, so if you play one of the songs again, it plays it straight from memory.

11. Tap to enable or disable automatically caching music when you have your phone charging and connected to a Wi-Fi network. This setting refers to music you have chosen to store locally on your phone.

12. Tap to clear the local music cache. This removes all music you have previously chosen to be stored locally.

13. Check the box to only download music while connected to Wi-Fi, and not while connected to the cellular data network.

14. Tap to see the download queue. When you choose to make music available offline, that music is queued for download. You can see the download progress here.

15. Check the box to download music to your Android Wear smartwatch. See more about using Android Wear and playing music from your watch in Chapter 15, "Using Your Android Phone with an Android Wear Smartwatch."

16. Scroll down for more settings.

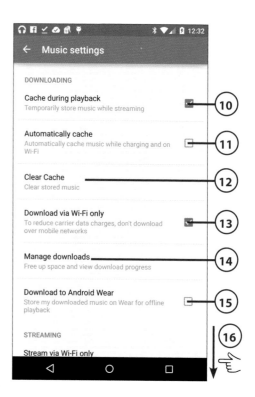

17. Check the box to only stream music while connected to Wi-Fi, and not while connected to the cellular data network.

18. Tap to change the audio quality when streaming music over cellular data networks. Your choices are Low, Normal, and High. The higher the audio quality, the more data needs to stream.

19. Tap to save your changes and return to the Play Music app's main screen.

Adjust the Equalizer

The Google Play Music app has a graphic equalizer that enables you to select preset audio configurations or set your own. As is shown in step 7 in the previous task, tap Equalizer in the Settings screen and use the following steps to use or adjust the equalizer.

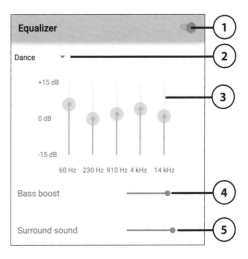

1. Tap to turn the Equalizer on/off.

2. Tap to select from a list of preset equalizer settings such as Dance, Hip Hop, and many more.

3. Drag the frequency response sliders to enhance or de-emphasize certain frequencies.

4. Drag the slider to adjust the Bass Boost. The Bass Boost setting is only available when you are using headphones.

5. Drag the slider to adjust the Surround Sound effect, which helps the music sound like it's surrounding the listener.

>>>Go Further

SYNCHRONIZING MUSIC AND OTHER MEDIA USING A CABLE

If for some reason you don't want to make use of Google Play Music or you can't because you live in a country where Google Play Music is not supported, you can synchronize music and other media using a cable (and sometimes over Wi-Fi). A great way to do this is to download an app called doubleTwist. doubleTwist has been providing media synchronization for many phones for a while now, and the product is very mature. Head to http://www.doubleTwist.com to download the Windows or Mac version, and then visit the Google Play Store to download the Android app companion.

>>>Go Further

BEAMING MUSIC BETWEEN ANDROID DEVICES

If you know someone with an Android smartphone or phone that has an NFC chip, you should be able to beam music to them. In theory, you should be able to send music to the other NFC-enabled device but as of the writing of this book, there seems to be a glitch preventing this from working correctly.

If this feature is fixed in the future, you need to find the song you want to send and then hold your Android phone back-to-back with the other Android device. You hear a sound and the screen also zooms out. Touch the screen to send the file. You can also send a link to a song in Google Play. To do that, find the song or album in the Google Play Store. Touch your Android phone back-to-back with the other device. The screen zooms out and you hear a sound. Touch the screen to send the link. The other person's device automatically opens Google Play and shows the song or album.

Recording Videos with the Camera Application

The Camera application enables you to take pictures and record video. This chapter covers the video-recording feature of the Camera app. Chapter 14, "Taking and Managing Pictures," covers information on using the Camera app to take pictures (including Panorama and Photo Spheres).

Record Video

1. Tap to launch the Camera app.

2. Swipe in from the left of the screen to see the Camera options.

3. Tap the Video icon to select the video camera mode.

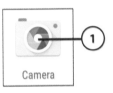

Camera

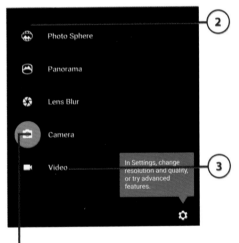

Photo Sphere

Panorama

Lens Blur

Camera

Video

In Settings, change resolution and quality, or try advanced features.

Tap for still camera

4. Tap to start recording video. Tap the icon again to stop recording.

Indicates you must rotate your phone into Landscape view

4

>>>Go Further
TAKING PICTURES WHILE RECORDING VIDEO

While you are recording video, you can still take pictures. To take a picture while recording video, tap the screen. Each time you tap the screen, that frame of video is stored as a picture.

Change Video Settings

Before you record a video, you can change some settings that can alter how the video is recorded or config-ure it to record Time Lapse video.

1. Tap the Menu icon.

2. Tap to turn the grid pattern on or off. The grid pattern is seen only in the view finder view to help you line objects up in the shot; it does not appear on your final video.

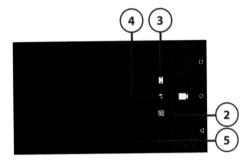

3. Tap to switch between the front-facing and rear-facing cameras (if your phone has both cameras).

4. Tap to use the rear LED flash as a light while recording video.

5. Tap anywhere on the screen to close the settings.

6. Swipe in from the left of the screen.

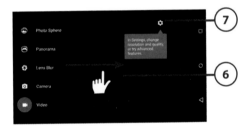

7. Tap the Settings icon.

8. Tap to enable or disable storing your current geographic location with the video that you record.

9. Tap Advanced to enable or disable manual exposure. This feature only works when using the still camera mode, not video recording.

10. Tap to change the format of video recorded by the rear-facing or front-facing cameras.

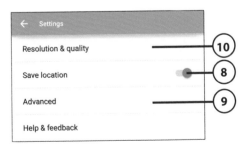

11. Tap to select the format of the video for the rear-facing camera. You can choose Ultra High Definition (UHD, also known as 4K), 1080p High Definition, 720p High Definition, or 480p Standard Definition. The exact choices available are dependent upon the rear camera's capabilities on your phone.

12. Tap to select the format of the video for the front-facing camera. You can choose 1080p High Definition, 720p High Definition, 480p Standard Definition, or a low-quality CIF format, which is 325×288 pixels. The exact choices available are dependent upon the front camera's capabilities on your phone.

13. Tap to return to the main camera Settings screen.

(13)

← **Settings**

Camera

Back camera photo
(4:3) 13.0 megapixels

Front camera photo
(16:9) 2.1 megapixels

Video

Back camera video
HD 1080p   **(11)**

Front camera video
HD 1080p   **(12)**

Play Videos

If you have personal videos you have recorded or people have sent you, use the following steps to find them and play them.

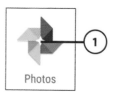

Photos

1. Tap the Photos icon to launch the Photos app.

2. Swipe in from the left of the screen to see the list of photos and videos in different locations.

3. Tap Videos to filter the Photos app view to only show videos.

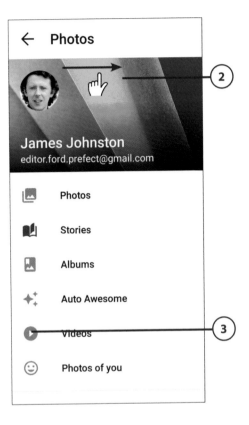

>>>Go Further
WHERE ARE ALL MY PHOTOS AND VIDEOS STORED?

In addition to allowing you to view photos and videos on your device, the Photos app shows you a lot of other options; so what are they? If you tap Photos, you see all photos and videos on your device and also ones that have previously been copied to your Google Cloud account from this and all other devices you own. If you tap Stories, you access a feature of Google+ that creates stories from photos and videos that have previously been copied to your Google Cloud account. Tapping Albums shows you all albums on your device and in the Google Cloud. Tapping Auto Awesome shows you any photos and videos that have been automatically backed up to your Google Cloud account and turned into little movies. You can also manually create them. Tapping Videos shows you only videos on your device and in your Google Cloud account.

4. Tap a video to open it.

5. Tap to edit the video. This feature did not work at the time this book was written.

6. Tap to delete the video.

7. Tap to share the video on YouTube; on social media including Facebook, Instagram, or Google+; via Beam; via Bluetooth; or via email.

8. Tap to start playing the video.

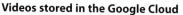

Videos stored on your phone

Videos stored in the Google Cloud

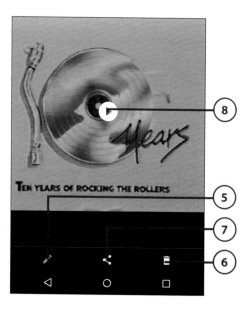

9. Tap the screen while the video is playing to reveal the video controls.

10. Tap to pause or unpause the video.

11. Drag the slider to quickly skip forward and backward.

12. Tap to skip back five seconds.

13. Tap to skip forward five seconds.

14. Rotate your Android phone sideways to allow the video to fill the screen.

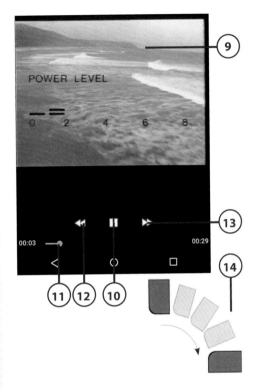

Share Videos

You can share videos with people from the Photos app. The list of methods of sharing is dependent on the applications you have installed on your Android phone. Many sharing methods require that you already have an account on the service you want to share on, including YouTube, Google+, Instagram, Facebook, and Path.

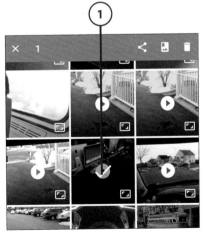

1. Touch and hold the video you want to share. You see a check mark on the video indicating that it is selected. Tap additional videos you want to share if you want to share more than one.

2. Tap the Share icon to see all the ways you can share the video(s). The list of choices is dependent on the apps you have installed.

3. Tap to send the video via Bluetooth. This allows you to send the video to another device (of any kind) using Bluetooth.

4. Tap to share the video on YouTube. This allows you to upload the video to your YouTube account.

5. Tap to share the video on Google+ to certain people, your circles, or share it publicly so everyone can see it.

6. Tap to share the video with specific people you know on Google+.

7. Tap to share the video with specific Google+ Circles.

8. Tap to share the video publicly on Google+.

9. Tap to email this video using Gmail.

10. Tap to upload the video to your Google Drive account.

11. Tap to share the video on the Path social network.

12. Tap to share with another person using Android Beam.

13. Tap to share the video on the Facebook social network.

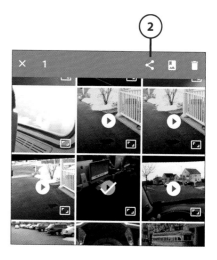

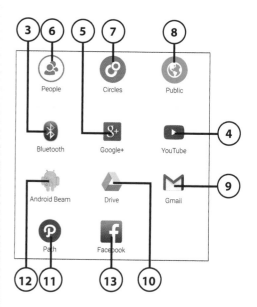

Bluetooth Sharing Might Fail

Many phones do not accept incoming Bluetooth files, but devices like computers do. Even on computers, the recipient must configure her Bluetooth configuration to accept incoming files.

Uploading or Sharing Multiple Videos

You can share or upload multiple videos at the same time, instead of one by one. After you touch and hold a video, tap more videos to add them to your list. When you select more than one video to share, however, the option to share on Facebook is disabled because you can only upload videos to Facebook one at a time. After you reduce your list of videos to share to only one video, the Facebook sharing option returns.

Delete Videos

1. Touch and hold the video you want to delete. Tap additional videos or photos if you'd like to delete more than one file at a time.

2. Tap the Trash icon to delete the video(s).

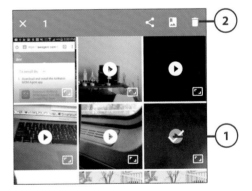

Undeleting a Video

After you delete a video, you have six seconds to change your mind and undo the delete. Within six seconds, tap the Undo button to restore your deleted video(s).

Tap to undo
your last delete

Change Photos App Settings

1. Tap the Menu icon in the Photos app.

2. Tap Settings.

3. Tap to change your Google account Auto Backup settings. Auto Backup automatically makes backup copies of your photos and videos to your Google+ account. They remain private and cannot be seen by others.

4. Tap to turn Auto Backup on or off.

5. Tap to change the Google account used for Auto Backup, if you have more than one account.

6. Tap to change the size of the photos that are uploaded. You can choose Standard or Full. Full size is the untouched full resolution photo, whereas Standard is a greatly reduced quality photo meant for quick sharing.

7. Tap to purchase more storage if your free storage is starting to fill up.

8. Scroll down for more settings.

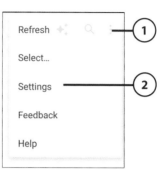

Refresh — **1**

Select...

Settings — **2**

Feedback

Help

← Settings   ⋮

General Settings

Auto Backup — **3**
Automatically back up new photos and videos to
Google Photos.

4

← Auto Backup   ⋮

Active Account

James Johnston — **5**
editor.ford.prefect@gmail.com
14.6 GB available

Backup Storage

Photo size — **6**
Full size

Get more storage — **7**
Purchase additional storage for full-size photos

8

9. Tap to select whether to back up photos only when on a Wi-Fi network, or over cellular data and Wi-Fi networks.

10. Tap to select whether to back up videos only when on a Wi-Fi network, or over cellular data and Wi-Fi networks. If you change the setting in step 9 to Wi-Fi only, this setting is grayed out.

11. Tap to indicate whether it's okay to back up photos and videos while you are roaming on cellular data outside your home area.

12. Tap to select whether you want to back up your photos and videos only when your phone is charging.

13. Tap to back up all photos and videos immediately.

14. Tap to save your changes and return to the main Photos settings screen.

15. Tap to change your Google account settings for Photos.

(14)

← **Auto Backup**   ⋮

Backup Settings

Back up photos ———————————————— (9)
When there is a Wi-Fi or mobile data connection available

Back up videos ———————————————— (10)
Only when there is a Wi-Fi connection available

Roaming ————————————————————— (11)
Back up photos & videos when roaming on a data network

While charging only ———————————— (12)
Back up photos & videos only when a charger is connected

Back up all —————————————————— (13)
Back up all photos & videos now (if connection settings allow)

Account Settings ————————————————— (15)

James Johnston
editor.ford.prefect@gmail.com

16. Tap to choose whether the Photos app should show any photos and videos that you have stored in your Google Drive.

17. Tap to choose whether you want the Photos app to show the geographic location of where newly uploaded photos and videos were taken. The accuracy of that geographic location is set in the next step.

18. Tap to change how accurately your geographic location is reported when you take photos or videos.

19. Tap to choose whether you want your photos and videos automatically enhanced when they are backed up to Google. If enabled, Google automatically modifies your photos to make them look better.

20. Tap to choose whether Google can automatically create Auto Awesome images, movies, and stories using your photos and videos that are backed up. The Auto Awesome images, movies, and stories are only viewable by you unless you choose to share them with others.

21. Tap to choose whether you want to use this phone to create Auto Awesome images, movies, and stories, instead of relying on the Google servers.

22. Tap to choose whether you want Google to prompt your friends to tag you in photos it can see that you are in.

23. Tap to save your changes and return to the main Photos settings screen.

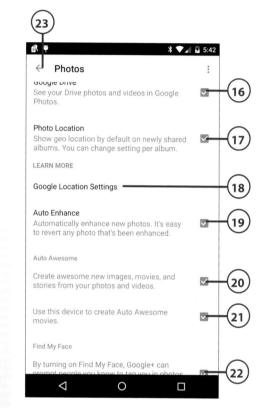

Changing How Your Phone Determines Your Location

When you tap Google Location Settings, you can choose High Accuracy, which uses GPS, mobile networks, and nearby Wi-Fi networks to determine your location; Battery Saving, which uses only nearby Wi-Fi networks and mobile networks to determine your location; or Device Only, which uses only the GPS chip in your phone to determine your location.

My Phone Has the Gallery App

Android phones used to ship with the Gallery app. This app handled all photos and video on the phone, but has been replaced by the Photos app. Although Google has moved away from the Gallery app (in fact, you cannot find it in the Google Play Store anymore), some phone vendors who heavily modify Android (such as Samsung) still ship their phones with a modified version of the Gallery app. They do this because they have integrated certain vendor-specific features into the Gallery app. The Gallery app has many of the same functions as the Photos app, so the steps you see for the Photos app work for the Gallery app as well.

Managing Movies and TV Shows

Google Play enables you to rent and purchase movies. (Most movies are available only as rentals.) You can also buy TV shows—even whole season passes of TV shows.

Buy and Rent Movies

As with music, when you buy or rent movies, they remain in the Google Cloud and stream to your phone when you want to watch them.

Play Store

1. Tap to launch Google Play.

2. Tap Movies & TV.

3. Scroll through the movie options, or use the Search icon to look for a specific title. Tap a movie title when you find one you want to watch.

4. Tap to watch a trailer of the movie.

5. Scroll down to see information about the movie, including other viewers' reviews and ratings. You can also add your review and rating. If you see a red tomato icon, this means that the Rotten Tomatoes score is included in the reviews.

6. Tap to add the movie to your Wishlist.

7. Tap to buy the movie in either Standard Definition (SD) or High Definition (HD).

8. Tap to rent the movie in either Standard Definition (SD) or High Definition (HD).

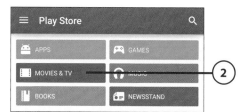

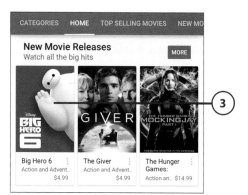

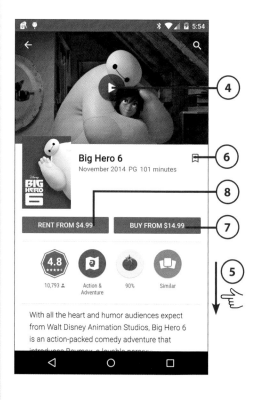

9. Choose whether you want to buy or rent the High Definition (HD) or Standard Definition (SD) version of the movie. In this example, we are buying the movie.

10. Tap to accept and buy or rent the movie. This example is about buying the movie.

Tap to change the payment method

Adding a Payment Method

Before you purchase or rent movies, you need to make sure that you have a way to pay for it. To do that, you need to add a payment method to your Google Wallet account. Using your desktop computer, browse to http://wallet.google.com and log in. Click Payment Methods, and if you do not already have a valid payment method, click Add a Payment Method. Enter valid debit or credit card information. Some cellular providers allow you to add your Google purchases to your bill.

11. Tap to first download the movie to your phone so that you can watch it when you are not in Wi-Fi or cellular data coverage. If you purchased an HD version of the movie, you are asked whether you want to download the SD or HD version. (The HD version is a larger file.)

12. Tap to start watching the movie. This streams the movie to your phone from the Google Cloud.

Movie Download Progress

If you choose to download the movie you rented or purchased because you know you want to watch it when you will be out of Wi-Fi or cellular data coverage (on a plane, for example), you can see the progress of the movie download right on the screen. Wait until it shows Downloaded before you move out of Wi-Fi or cellular data coverage. You can also pull down the Notification panel to see the progress of your download. To cancel the movie download, tap the Push Pin icon.

Download progress

Buy TV Shows

As with music and movies, when you buy TV shows, they remain in the Google Cloud and stream to your phone when you want to watch them.

1. Tap to launch Google Play.

2. Tap Movies & TV.

3. After browsing the available TV shows or searching for a specific show, tap a show title.

4. Tap to expand the synopsis.

5. Tap a star to rate the TV show yourself.

6. Tap to change the season if the TV show has multiple seasons.

7. Tap to buy the entire season. When you buy a season that is not yet complete, as new episodes air on TV you automatically have access to them on your phone.

8. Tap to buy just one episode. The rest of the example is for a single-episode purchase.

9. Tap to buy the Standard Definition (SD) version of the TV show season or episode. SD is lower quality.

10. Tap to buy the High Definition (HD) version of the TV show season or episode. HD is the best quality.

11. Tap Buy to complete your purchase.

Adding a Payment Method

Before you purchase TV shows, you need to make sure that you have a way to pay for it. To do that, you need to add a payment method to your Google Wallet account—if you haven't already done so. Using your desktop computer, browse to http://wallet.google.com and log in. Click Payment Methods, and if you do not already have a valid payment method, click Add a Payment Method. Enter valid debit or credit card information.

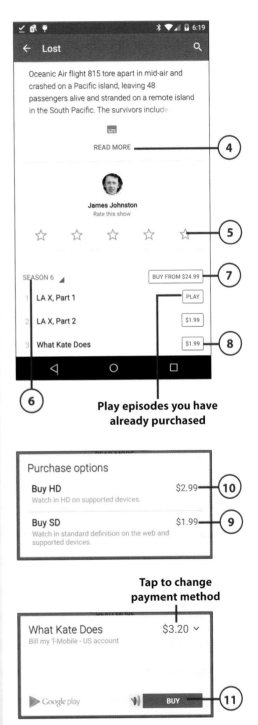

Play episodes you have already purchased

Tap to change payment method

Use the Play Movies & TV App

When you watch movies and TV shows, they are actually playing inside an app called Play Movies & TV. You can launch this app when you want to watch movies and TV shows you have previously purchased or rented.

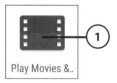

Play Movies &..

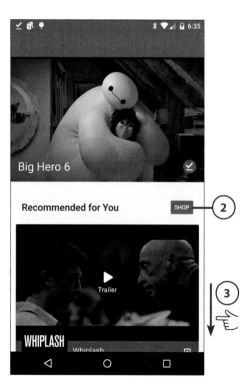

1. Tap to launch Play Movies & TV. You should see the Watch Now screen.

2. Tap to find more movies or TV shows in the Google Play Store.

3. Scroll down to see movies and TV shows Google recommends for you based on what you have previously searched for, rented, or purchased.

4. Swipe in from the left of the screen to reveal the menu.

5. Tap My Library to see only movies you have purchased or rented no matter whether they are physically located on your phone or still in the cloud.

6. Tap to see movies and TV shows that you have added to your Wishlist.

7. Tap to shop for more movies or TV shows in the Google Play Store.

8. Tap to change the settings for the Play Movies & TV app. See the next section for an explanation of the settings.

James Johnston
editor.ford.prefect@gmail.com

Watch Now

My Library — 5

My Wishlist — 6

Shop — 7

Downloaded only

Settings

Help & feedback

8

Show only movies and TV shows that have been downloaded to your phone

Change Play Movies & TV Settings

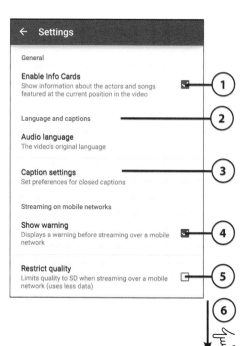

1. Check the box to choose whether you want to see information about actors and songs featured at the current position in the movie or TV show you have paused.

2. Tap to choose to play back the original language from the movie or TV show, or try to force the playback of English audio when it's available.

3. Tap to enable or change the way Captions (Closed Captioning) looks systemwide (in this app and all other apps).

4. Check the box to show a warning when you are about to stream content over the cellular data network.

5. Check the box to restrict the quality of the media you are streaming to lower-quality Standard Definition (SD) when streaming over a cellular data network.

6. Scroll down for more settings.

7. Tap to manage downloaded movies and TV shows. You can delete them to free up space and view any downloads already in progress.

8. Tap to choose whether to download media over only Wi-Fi or over both Wi-Fi and cellular networks.

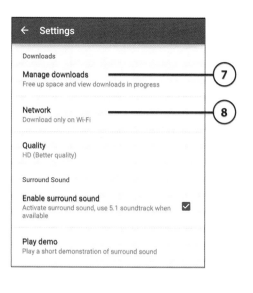

9. Tap Quality to choose whether to default to downloading High Definition (HD) content or Standard Definition (SD) content.

10. Tap to choose whether you want to hear 5.1 Surround Sound if the content you are playing supports it.

11. Tap to play a short demo of how 5.1 Surround Sound works.

12. Tap to save your changes and return to the Movies & TV main screen.

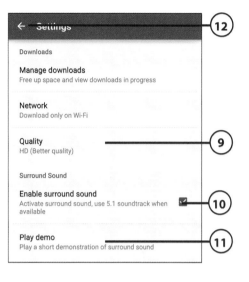

Copy Videos from Your Computer

You can copy videos from your computer to your Android phone via the USB cable. You start by creating a folder on your phone to store the videos and then you drag them from your computer to the new folder.

Copy from a Windows Computer

1. Connect your phone to your PC using the supplied USB cable. Your phone shows up as an option in Windows Explorer.

2. Click the phone. This example uses a Google Nexus 7.

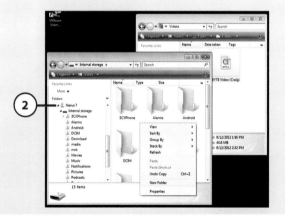

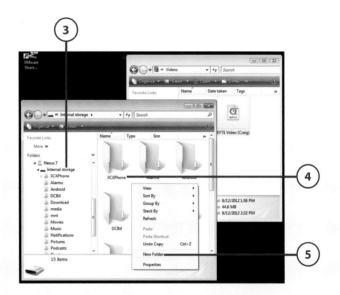

3. Click Internal Storage to expand the list of folders on your phone.

4. Right-click in the right pane.

5. Select New Folder.

6. Type a name for your new folder. The sample folder is My Videos.

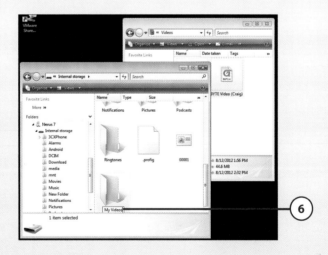

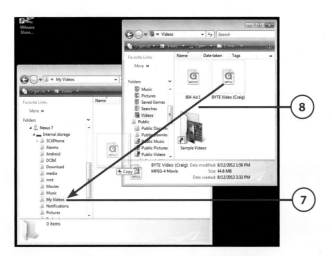

7. Click the newly created folder in the left pane.

8. Drag a movie from another folder on your PC to the new folder.

Copy from an Apple Mac OS X Computer

To copy files from your Mac to your phone, you must install Android File Transfer. You should have done this already, but if not, please follow the instructions in the Prologue earlier in this book.

1. Connect your phone to your Mac using the supplied USB cable. Android File Transfer automatically launches.

2. Click File.

3. Select New Folder.

4. Type a name for your new folder The sample folder is My Videos.

5. Drag a movie from another folder on your Mac to the new folder.

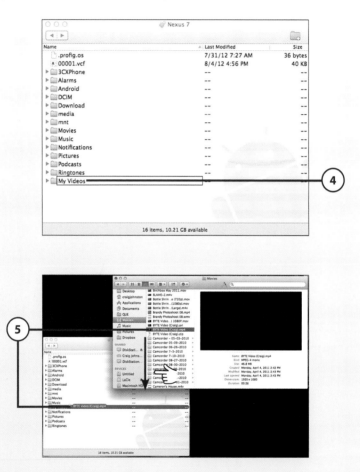

Watching Videos with YouTube

Your Android phone comes with a YouTube app that enables you to find and watch videos, rate them, add them to your favorites, and share links to YouTube videos. The YouTube application even enables you to upload new videos.

Navigate the YouTube Main Screen

1. Tap the YouTube icon to launch the YouTube application.

2. Tap a video to open it.

3. Tap to search for a video on YouTube.

4. Tap to change the YouTube app settings.

5. Scroll down to see all videos in your What to Watch feed.

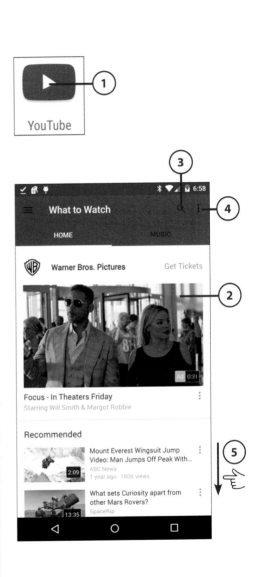

Navigate the YouTube App

1. Swipe in from the left of the screen to reveal a menu.

2. Tap My Subscriptions to see a mixture of videos from YouTube channels you subscribe to.

3. Tap to see videos you have uploaded to YouTube.

4. Tap to see your YouTube history, including videos you have previously watched.

5. Tap to see a list of videos you have chosen to watch later. You find out how to set videos to be watched later in the next section.

6. Tap to see movies and TV shows you have previously purchased in the Google Play Store. You can play that content in YouTube.

7. Tap one of your YouTube playlists to see videos that have been added to it.

8. Scroll down for more options.

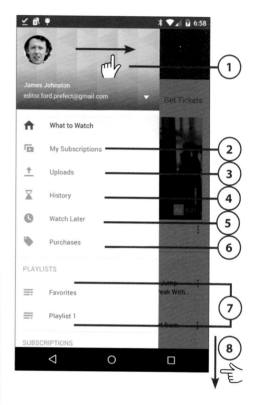

9. Tap one of the channels you subscribe to in order to see videos in it.

10. Tap to browse YouTube channels.

11. Tap one of the Best of YouTube categories to see videos in that category.

Play a Video

While playing a YouTube video, you can rate the video, read video comments, and share the video with someone.

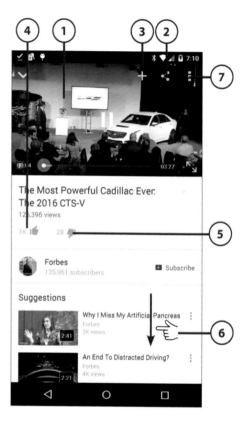

1. Tap on the playing video to see options.

2. Tap to share a link to this video. You can share it on Facebook, Twitter, Google+, or by more traditional ways, such as email and text message.

3. Tap to add this video to your favorites, save the video to an existing or new YouTube playlist, or add the video to your Watch Later queue.

4. Tap to give this video a thumbs up. Thumbs up tells the video's creator that you liked the video.

5. Tap to give this video a thumbs down. Thumbs down tells the video's creator that you disliked the video.

6. Scroll down to read and post comments for this video. You can also see suggested videos. YouTube suggests videos that are related to the one you are watching based on content and keywords.

7. Tap to choose whether you want to show the Closed Captions (CC), play the Standard Definition (SD) or High Definition (HD) version of the video, or flag the video as inappropriate.

8. Tap to pause the video.

9. Tap to subscribe to the YouTube Channel where this video is found.

Viewing Videos Full Screen

To view a video at a larger size, simply rotate your Android phone, and the video will be played in Landscape mode.

Swiping Videos Away

While playing a video in a window (not full screen), if you swipe it down, it moves to the bottom right of the screen as a thumbnail. Swipe the thumbnail of the video up to make it large, or swipe it left to dismiss it.

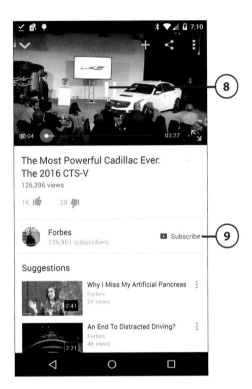

Upload a Video

You can upload one of your personal videos to YouTube. When uploaded, you can share the video with others.

1. Swipe in from the left of the screen to reveal the menu.

2. Tap Uploads. You see videos that you have previously uploaded to YouTube.

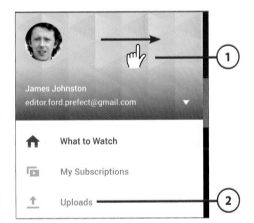

3. Tap the Upload icon.

4. Select a video to upload from videos you have stored in the Photos app.

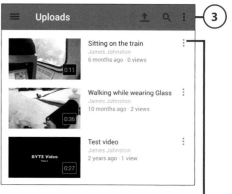

Previously——
uploaded videos

Tap to see
other videos

Modifying Properties of Uploaded Videos

You can edit the YouTube properties of videos that you have previously uploaded. While in the Uploads screen, tap the Menu icon to the right of a video, then tap Edit.

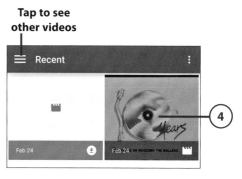

Edit properties

5. Tap to enter a title for your video.

6. Tap to enter a description for your video.

7. Tap to choose whether the video is private, public, or unlisted.

8. Tap to add any tags or keywords so that your video shows up in the results when people search using the tags you enter.

9. Tap to upload your video.

You Can Trim Some Videos Before Uploading

If you have recorded the video you are planning to upload to YouTube, you can trim the video. Blue trim handles on a video indicate that it is editable. Drag the trim sliders left and right to trim your video. To trim with more precision, touch and hold the sliders and then drag them.

Drag the sliders to trim your video

Change YouTube Settings

You can clear your YouTube search history, set the video caption font size, or choose the SafeSearch Filter using the YouTube application's Settings screen.

1. Tap the Menu icon.

2. Tap Settings.

3. Tap General to choose whether to prioritize videos from a specific country, specify whether you want videos with restricted content to be hidden when you search, whether to send Google anonymous data about your YouTube usage, and whether you want to receive notifications about YouTube content.

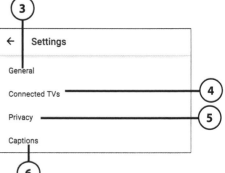

4. Tap to manage connected TVs.

5. Tap to clear your YouTube search and watch history, or to temporarily pause your device from keeping track of your search history.

6. Tap to choose how Captions (Closed Captioning) look in the YouTube app.

>>>Go Further

WHAT ARE CONNECTED TVS?

Smart TVs and game consoles that include the YouTube app can be used by your Android phone's YouTube app as a second screen. After you pair a Smart TV or game console with your Android phone, you can "send" a YouTube video to the TV or game console to be played. This enables you to let others watch the video with you.

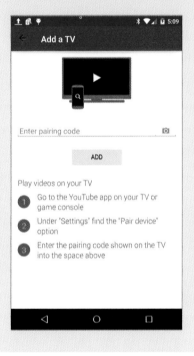

>>>Go Further
PLAY YOUR AUDIO AND VIDEO ON YOUR TV

If you have purchased one or more Chromecast devices from Google, you can use them to play your music, movies, and TV shows via a Chromecast, on your TV. If your Android phone detects one or more available Chromecast devices on the local network while you are playing music, or watching a TV show or movie, you will see the Chromecast icon on the screen. Tap the Chromecast icon, and choose which Chromecast you want to use. After your Android phone successfully connects to the Chromecast, your music will play out of the TV speakers, and any TV shows and movies will play right on the TV. You will still be able to control playback on your Android phone. When you want to stop using the Chromecast, tap the Chromecast icon again, and choose Disconnect. Read more about Chromecast here: https://www.google.com/chrome/devices/chromecast/

Tap to start Chromecasting

Capital 604 Documentary Trailer

Choose a Chromecast device

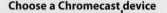

Tap to stop Chromecasting

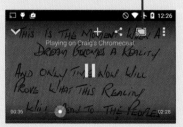

Adjust the volume of the audio

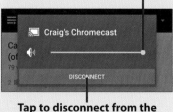

Tap to disconnect from the Chromecast

Quickly control your
Wi-Fi and Bluetooth

This chapter covers your Android phone's connectivity capabilities, including Bluetooth, Wi-Fi, Wi-Fi Direct, VPN, and NFC. Topics include the following:

→ Pairing with Bluetooth devices
→ Connecting to Wi-Fi networks
→ Connecting to virtual private networks (VPNs)
→ Using Wi-Fi Direct between two Android devices
→ Using Near Field Communications (NFC)

Connecting to Bluetooth, Wi-Fi, and VPNs

Your Android phone can connect to Bluetooth devices—such as headsets, computers, and car in-dash systems—as well as to Wi-Fi networks. Your Android phone can also connect to virtual private networks (VPN) for access to secure networks and can send information between your phone and another Android device using Wi-Fi Direct.

Connecting to Bluetooth Devices

Bluetooth is a great personal area network (PAN) technology that enables short-distance wireless access to all sorts of devices, such as headsets, phones, and computers. The following tasks walk you through how to pair your Android phone to your device and how to configure options.

Pair with a New Bluetooth Device

Before you can take advantage of Bluetooth, you need to connect your Android phone with that device, which is called *pairing*. After you pair your Android phone with a Bluetooth device, they can connect to each other automatically in the future.

Putting the Bluetooth Device into Pairing Mode

Before pairing a Bluetooth device to your Android phone, you must first put the device into Pairing mode. If you pair with a Bluetooth headset, for example, the process normally involves holding the button on the headset for a certain period of time. Consult your Bluetooth device's manual to find out how to put that device into Pairing mode. If you are pairing your phone with your car, use the car's menu system to put it in Pairing mode.

1. Pull down the Quick Settings Bar.

2. Tap the word Bluetooth to open the Bluetooth settings.

3. Tap the On switch to enable Bluetooth, if it is not already in the On position.

4. Tap the Bluetooth device you want to connect to. This example uses a vehicle's built-in Bluetooth, in this case called Your Vehicle.

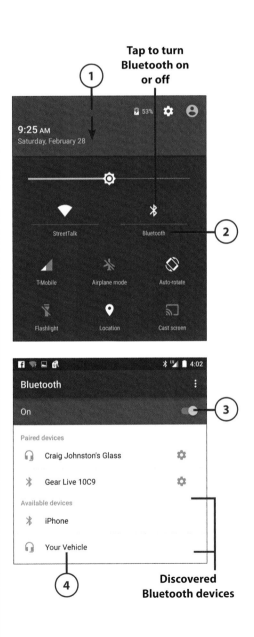

Tap to turn Bluetooth on or off

Discovered Bluetooth devices

5. If all goes well, your Android phone should now be paired with the new Bluetooth device.

>>>Go Further
USING BLUETOOTH PAIRING CODES

If you pair with a device that requires a pairing code, such as a computer or another smartphone, the screen shows a pairing code. Make sure the pairing code is the same on your Android phone and on the device you are pairing with. Tap Pair on your Android phone, and confirm the pairing code on the device you are pairing with.

Bluetooth pairing request

Device
Craig's iMac (2)

Pairing code
339713

Pairing grants access to your contacts and call history when connected.

CANCEL   PAIR

Tap to confirm the pairing code

In some cases, such as older Bluetooth headsets or your vehicle's built-in Bluetooth, you are asked to type a PIN on your Android phone to complete the pairing. If you pair with an older Bluetooth headset, you might be prompted to enter a PIN. Try using four zeros or 1234 as the pairing code. It normally works. If not, refer to the headset's manual. If you pair with your vehicle's built-in Bluetooth, you are asked to type the PIN you see on your vehicle's dashboard screen.

Bluetooth pairing request

Device
Your Vehicle

Usually 0000 or 1234

☐ PIN contains letters or symbols

You may also need to type this PIN on the other device.

Pairing grants access to your contacts and call history when connected.

CANCEL   OK

Enter the PIN you see

Tap OK

Reverse Pairing

The steps in this section describe how to pair your Android phone with a Bluetooth device that is in Pairing mode and listening for an incoming pairing command. You can pair Bluetooth another way by asking others to search for and pair with your phone. Anytime you have the Bluetooth screen open, your phone is in Pairing mode and listening for incoming pairing requests.

Manage Extra Bluetooth Options

You can change the name your Android phone uses when pairing over Bluetooth to make it easier to find, see any files people have sent you via Bluetooth, and rescan for devices.

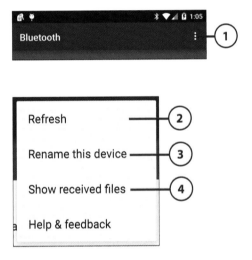

1. Tap the Menu icon.

2. Tap to refresh the list of discovered Bluetooth devices by rescanning.

3. Tap to rename your Android phone so that it has a friendlier name when seen over Bluetooth, Wi-Fi, and NFC.

4. Tap to see any files people have sent you via Bluetooth.

Change Bluetooth Device Options

After a Bluetooth device is paired, you can change a few of its options. The number of options depends on the Bluetooth device you connect to. Some have more features than others.

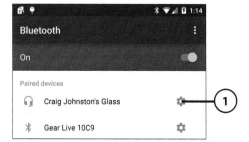

1. Tap the Settings icon to the right of the Bluetooth device.

2. Tap to rename the Bluetooth device.

3. Tap to disconnect and unpair from the Bluetooth device. If you do this, you can't use the device until you redo the pairing as described in the earlier task.

4. Tap to enable and disable what you want to use the Bluetooth device for. These features are called profiles, and sometimes Bluetooth devices have more than one profile (as in this example).

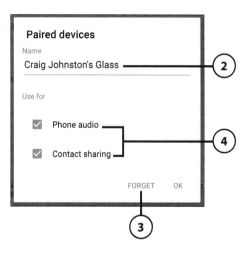

What Are Bluetooth Profiles?

Each Bluetooth device can have one or more Bluetooth profiles. Each Bluetooth profile describes certain features of the device. This tells your Android phone what it can do when connected to it. A Bluetooth headset normally has only one profile, such as Phone Audio. This tells your Android phone that it can use only the device for phone call audio. Some devices might have this profile but provide other features, such as a Contact Sharing profile, which would enable it to synchronize your Android phone's Contacts app, or Media Audio, which is for playing stereo music via Bluetooth. Read more about Bluetooth profiles at http://en.wikipedia.org/wiki/List_of_Bluetooth_profiles.

Quickly Disconnect from a Bluetooth Device

To quickly disconnect from a Bluetooth device, tap the device on the Bluetooth Settings screen, and then tap OK.

Working with Wi-Fi

Wi-Fi (Wireless Fidelity) networks are wireless networks that run within free radio bands around the world. Your local coffee shop probably has free Wi-Fi, and so do many other public areas, such as airports, train stations, and malls. Your Android phone can connect to any Wi-Fi network to provide you access to the Internet.

Connect to Wi-Fi

The following steps explain how to find and connect to Wi-Fi networks. After you connect your Android phone to a Wi-Fi network, you are automatically connected to it the next time you are in range of that network.

1. Pull down the Quick Settings Bar.

2. Tap the word Wi-Fi to go to the Wi-Fi settings.

3. Tap to turn Wi-Fi on if the slider is in the Off position.

4. Tap the name of the Wi-Fi network you want to connect to. If the network does not use any security, you can skip to step 7.

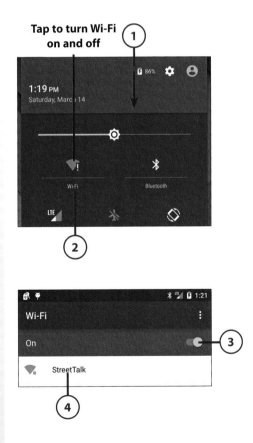

Tap to turn Wi-Fi on and off

5. Enter the Wi-Fi network password.

6. Tap to show advanced options if you need to specify a proxy or change the way that your IP address is assigned.

7. Tap to connect to the Wi-Fi network.

StreetTalk

Password

....

☐ Show password

☐ Advanced options

CANCEL   CONNECT

5

6

7

Adding a Hidden Network

If the network you want to connect to is not listed on the screen, it might be purposely hidden. If it is hidden, it does not broadcast its name, which is also known as its Service Set Identifier (SSID). Tap the Menu icon, and tap Add Network. Type in the SSID, and choose the type of security that the network uses. You need to get this information from the network administrator before you try connecting.

Add network

Network name

Enter the SSID

Security

WEP

Password

☐ Show password

☑ Advanced options

Proxy

None

IP settings

DHCP

CANCEL   SAVE

Type network name (SSID)

Choose type of security used (if any)

Type network password (if needed)

8. If all goes well, you see the Wi-Fi network in the list with the word Connected under it.

Indicates Wi-Fi signal strength

Can't Connect to Wi-Fi?

If all does not go well, you might be typing the password or encryption key incorrectly. Verify both with the person who owns the Wi-Fi network. It might be easier to make use of Wi-Fi Protected Setup (WPS) if it is available. WPS still allows for a secure connection, but it removes the need to type long network passwords.

Connecting to Wi-Fi Protected Setup (WPS) Networks

Many new Wi-Fi routers include a method of connecting called Wi-Fi Protected Setup (WPS). The idea is that on the Wi-Fi router, you press a button to start the WPS connection. On your phone, you touch the WPS icon, and the two devices automatically connect to each other in a secure way. Sometimes, a WPS-enabled router uses a method in which you swap PINs. Your phone supports both methods of connecting via WPS. Tap the Menu icon, then tap Advanced, and choose the method of WPS you want to use.

Tap to use the WPS push-button method

Tap to use the WPS PIN method

Adjust Wi-Fi Network Options

1. Tap a Wi-Fi network to reveal a pop-up that shows information about your connection to that network.

2. Tap Forget to tell your Android phone to not connect to this network in the future.

3. Touch and hold on a Wi-Fi network to reveal three actions.

4. Tap to forget the Wi-Fi network and no longer connect to it.

5. Tap to change the Wi-Fi network password that your Android phone uses to connect to the network, or modify other settings for this network.

6. Tap to write the information about this Wi-Fi network onto an NFC tag, allowing others to simply scan the tag to connect. You need to have the NFC radio turned on and an NFC tag in range.

On

StreetTalk
Connected (1)

(3)

StreetTalk

Status
Connected

Signal strength
Excellent

Link speed
144Mbps

Frequency
2.4GHz

Security
WPA/WPA2 PSK

FORGET   DONE

(2)

StreetTalk

Forget network (4)

Modify network (5)

Write to NFC tag (6)

Set Advanced Wi-Fi Options

You can configure a few advanced Wi-Fi settings that can help preserve the battery life of your Android phone.

1. Tap the Menu icon.

2. Tap Advanced.

3. Tap to enable or disable the capability for your Android phone to automatically notify you when it detects a new Wi-Fi network.

4. Tap to enable or disable the capability for Google's location service and other apps to scan for Wi-Fi networks, even if you have turned Wi-Fi off.

5. Tap to change the Wi-Fi sleep policy. This enables you to choose whether your Android phone should keep its connection to Wi-Fi when the phone goes to sleep.

6. Tap to manually set the frequency bands that your phone uses when communicating over Wi-Fi. You can choose 2.4GHz or 5GHz. It is better to leave this set to Automatic to allow your phone to automatically select the best option.

7. Tap to install certificates used to secure Wi-Fi communications. Your company's IT administrator may email you a certificate to install before you connect to your company's Wi-Fi network.

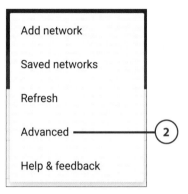

8. Tap to manage Wi-Fi Direct connections.

9. Tap to connect using WPS Push Button or WPS Pin Entry.

10. Use this Wi-Fi MAC address if you need to provide a network administrator with your MAC address to use a Wi-Fi network.

11. This shows the IP address that has been assigned to your Android phone when it connected to the Wi-Fi network.

12. Tap to save your changes and return to the previous screen.

(12)

← Advanced Wi-Fi   🔍

Network notification
Notify whenever a public network is available

Scanning always available
Let Google's location service and other apps scan for networks, even when Wi-Fi is off

Keep Wi-Fi on during sleep
Always

Wi-Fi frequency band
Automatic

Install certificates

Wi-Fi Direct ────────── (8)

WPS Push Button ──────────

WPS Pin Entry ────────── (9)

MAC address
ec:88:92:7a:5f:5d ────────── (10)

IP address
fe80::ee88:92ff:fe7a:5f5d ────────── (11)

Should You Keep Wi-Fi on During Sleep?

In step 5, you can choose how your Android phone handles its connection to Wi-Fi when it goes to sleep. If your phone has no cellular data, Wi-Fi is the only way that it can connect to the Internet. You should keep this option set to Always; otherwise, any real-time updates cannot be delivered to you, and your phone cannot update things such as email. However, battery usage can be affected by always maintaining a Wi-Fi connection, and you might want to set this to Only When Plugged In, which means that if your Android phone is not charging, and it goes to sleep, it turns Wi-Fi off. When the phone is charging and it goes to sleep, it stays connected to Wi-Fi. If you set this setting to Never, it means that when your Android phone goes to sleep, it turns Wi-Fi off.

>>>*Go Further*

WHAT ARE IP AND MAC ADDRESSES?

A MAC address is a number burned into your Android phone that identifies its Wi-Fi adapter. This is called the *physical layer* because it is a physical adapter. An IP address is a secondary way to identify your Android phone. Unlike a MAC address, the IP address can be changed at any time. Modern networks use the IP address when they need to deliver some data to you. Typically, when you connect to a network, a device on the network assigns you a new IP address. On home networks, this device is typically your Wi-Fi router.

Some network administrators use a security feature to limit who can connect to their Wi-Fi networks. They set up their networks to allow connections from only Wi-Fi devices with specific MAC addresses. If you try to connect to such a network, you have to give the network administrator your MAC address so that he can add it to the allowed list.

What Is Passpoint?

Some phone vendors, like Samsung, include the ability to use Passpoint. Passpoint is a technology that is being used increasingly by operators of Wi-Fi hotspots, and its purpose is to allow your phone to automatically roam onto the hotspots with no need for you to search for them or log in to them using the typical hotspot login web page. Simply based on the SIM card in your phone, you are automatically authenticated onto these hotspots and provided a secure encrypted connection.

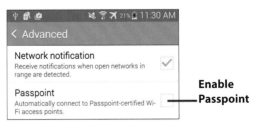

Enable Passpoint

Managing Virtual Private Networks (VPNs)

Your Android phone can connect to virtual private networks (VPNs), which are normally used by companies to provide a secure connection to their inside networks or intranets.

Add a VPN

Before you add a VPN, you must first
have all the information needed to
set it up on your Android phone.
Speak to your network administrator
and get this information ahead of
time to save frustration. This information includes the type of VPN
protocol used, the type of encryption
used, and the name of the host to
which you are connecting.

1. Pull down the Notification panel
    and tap the Settings icon.

2. Tap More under the Wireless &
    Networks section.

3. Tap VPN.

4. Tap OK to set up a Lock screen
    PIN. If you already have a Lock
    screen lock or password, you
    won't be prompted at this point,
    and you can proceed to step 7.

Why Do You Need to Set a PIN?

If you don't already have a Lock
screen PIN, password, or pattern
set up before you create your first
VPN network connection, you are
prompted to create one. This is
a security measure that ensures
your Android phone must first
be unlocked before anyone can
access a stored VPN connection.
Because VPN connections are usually used to access company data,
this is a good idea.

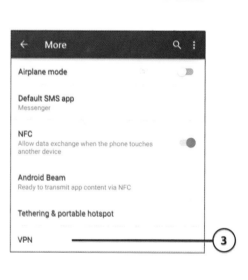

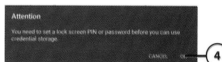

5. Choose either Pattern, PIN, or Password to unlock your Android phone.

6. Enter your Lock screen PIN, pattern, or password (not shown). After you make your entry, you are taken back to the main VPN screen.

7. Tap the plus icon to add a VPN profile.

8. Enter a name for your VPN network. You can call it something like **Work VPN** or the name of the provider, such as **Public VPN**.

9. Tap to choose the type of security the VPN network uses. Based on what you choose here, the additional information that you need to enter in step 10 will vary.

10. Enter the remaining parameters that your network administrator has provided.

11. Tap Save.

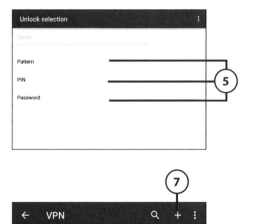

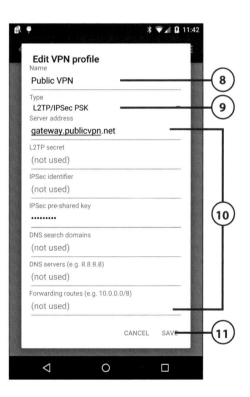

Connect to a VPN

After you create one or more VPN connections, you can connect to them when you want to.

1. Pull down the Notification panel, and tap the Settings icon.

2. Tap More under the Wireless & Networks section.

3. Tap VPN.

4. Tap a preconfigured VPN connection.

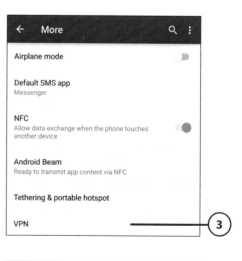

5. Enter the VPN username.

6. Enter the VPN password.

7. Tap Connect. After you connect to the VPN, you can use your Android phone's web browser and other applications normally, but you now have access to resources at the other end of the VPN tunnel, such as company web servers or even your company email.

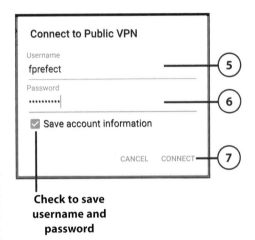

Check to save
username and
password

How Can You Tell If You Are Connected?

After your Android phone successfully connects to a VPN network, you see a key icon in the Notification panel. This indicates that you are connected. If you pull down the Notification panel, you can tap the icon to see information about the connection and to disconnect from the VPN.

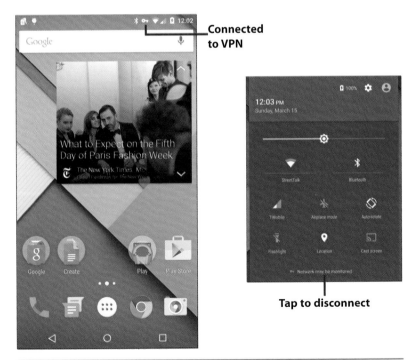

Connected
to VPN

Tap to disconnect

Editing or Deleting a VPN

You can edit an existing VPN or delete it by tapping and holding on the name of the VPN. A window pops up with a list of options.

>>>Go Further
ACCESSING YOUR VPN QUICKLY

As you can see from the preceding task, it takes three steps to get to the VPN Settings screen. If you use a VPN connection often and want to minimize the steps, you can create a shortcut on your Home screen that takes you straight to the VPN Settings screen. To do this, you need to find the Settings Shortcut widget. Touch and hold on the Home screen and tap Widgets. Find the Settings Shortcut widget, touch and hold it, and then drag it to the Home screen where you want it to stay. When you release the widget, you see a list of settings screens. Scroll down to VPN and tap it. Learn more about Home screen widgets in Chapter 10, "Customizing Your Android Phone." This trick does not work on all Android phones due to the manufacturer customizations.

Tap Widgets

Touch and hold

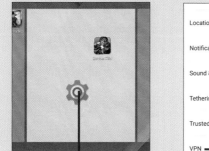

**Drag into position
and release it**

Location

Notification log

Sound & notification

Tethering & portable hotspot

Trusted credentials

VPN ⎯⎯⎯⎯⎯⎯⎯⎯⎯⎯ **Tap VPN**

>>>*Go Further*

SETTING UP AN ALWAYS-ON VPN

Some companies require you to use an always-on VPN. Your Android phone supports these kinds of VPNs, and to use an always-on VPN, first set up the VPN connection as detailed in this section. From the VPN screen, tap the Menu icon, and tap Always-On VPN. Finally, choose which previously configured VPN connection you want to be always on.

Managing Near Field Communications (NFCs)

Your Android phone has the capability to swap data via its Near Field Communications (NFC) radio with other devices that use NFC or read data that is stored on NFC tags. You can also use NFC to pay for items you have purchased using Google Wallet. Here is how to start using NFC.

>>>*Go Further*

WHAT IS NFC?

NFC stands for Near Field Communications, a standard that enables devices such as smartphones and tablets to swap information or simply read information. Think of NFC as a much lower-power version of Radio Frequency Identification (RFID), which has been used for decades in applications such as electronic toll (e-toll) payments (when you drive through toll plazas and have the money automatically deducted from your account). The only difference is that with NFC you must bring the two devices within about an inch from each other before they can communicate.

Your Android phone has an NFC radio, which you can use to read NFC tags, swap information between two NFC-enabled devices (such as two NFC-enabled phones or tablets), pay for items at a store, and send information to another phone or device. As more phones start shipping with NFC built in, this technology will become more useful.

Enable NFC and Android Beam

To get the full benefit from NFC, you need to enable the NFC radio. You should also enable Android Beam and S Beam (Samsung only).

1. Pull down the Quick Settings Bar and tap the Settings icon.

2. Tap More.

3. Move the NFC switch to the On position.

4. Tap to enable Android Beam. (See the next section for more about Android Beam.)

5. Tap to save your changes.

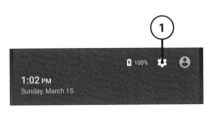

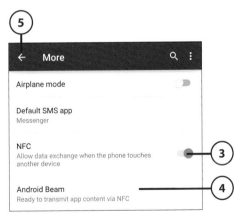

Enabling Samsung S Beam

Samsung phones include an additional beaming function called S Beam. It is not compatible with Android Beam and only works between Samsung devices. To enable NFC, Android Beam, and S Beam, from the Settings screen, tap NFC under the Connect and Share section. Tap the switch at the top right of the screen to turn on the NFC radio, then enable Android Beam and S Beam from the same screen.

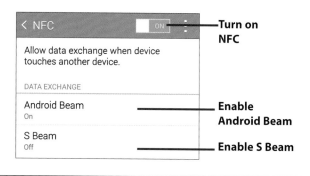

What Is Android Beam?

All Android devices running version 4.0 (Ice Cream Sandwich) or later have a feature called Android Beam. This feature sends small bits of data via NFC (such as links to YouTube videos or links to apps in Google Play) to enable you to effectively share content, but it also automates sending actual files (such as pictures and videos) between devices via Bluetooth.

Use Android Beam to Send Links to Content

You can use Android Beam to send links to content—such as apps, music, and video in the Google Play Store or website links—to another device. Android Beam only works between devices that are both running Android 4.0 (Ice Cream Sandwich) or later.

1. Open a website that you'd like to share the link to. Put the back of your phone about 1" from the back of another NFC-enabled phone. You know that the two devices have successfully connected when the web page zooms out, as shown in the figure.

2. Tap the web page after it zooms out.

3. The browser on the other device opens and immediately loads the link you shared.

Beaming Google Play Content and YouTube Videos

If you like a song, movie, book, or app that is in the Google Play Store, you can beam it to someone. Simply open the song, movie, book, or app in Google Play, touch your devices together, and touch to beam. To beam a YouTube video, open the video in the YouTube app, touch the devices together, and touch to beam. The other device opens YouTube and jumps directly to the video.

Use Android Beam to Send Real Files

You can also use Android Beam to send real content such as pictures, music, and video that's stored on your phone. Sending real files using Android Beam only works between devices that are running Android 4.1 (Jelly Bean) or later. This task describes how to beam a picture.

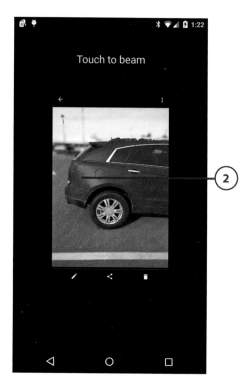

1. Open the picture you want to beam. (Note that the picture must reside on your phone and not in the Google Cloud.) Then put the back of your phone about 1" from the back of another NFC-enabled Android phone or tablet. You know that the two devices have successfully connected when the picture zooms out, as shown in the figure.

2. Tap the picture after it zooms out.

3. Your phone sends the picture to the other device. The file is sent using Bluetooth in the background.

It's Not All Good

Beaming to Samsung Devices

Android Beam is designed to work between any Android devices running version 4.1 (Jelly Bean) or later; however, Samsung includes a feature called S Beam that works in a slightly different way to Android Beam. If you want to beam files from your phone to a Samsung Android device, the owner of the Samsung phone may need to disable S Beam first if the beaming fails.

Managing Cellular Network Settings

Your Android phone can connect to many different cellular networks around the world. The exact networks that it can connect to are determined by the variant of phone you have because not all carriers use the same technology. To complicate things even more, many countries use different frequencies from one another.

Change Mobile Settings

Your phone has a few options when it comes to connecting to cellular (or mobile) networks.

1. Pull down the Notification panel and tap the Settings icon.

2. Tap More in the Wireless & Networks section.

3. Tap Cellular Networks.

What Is Wi-Fi Calling?

Some phones support Wi-Fi calling. Wi-Fi calling, also known as Universal Mobile Access (UMA), is provided by some cellular carriers to both augment their coverage and to provide free calls over Wi-Fi. This is not Voice over IP (VoIP) calling but a regular GSM voice call, routed via a Wi-Fi hotspot, over the Internet, to your carrier. Because the call is not using the cellular network infrastructure, the calls are free, and because of the speeds at which Wi-Fi networks operate, the call quality is much higher because much less compression is needed. To read more about UMA, try this online article: http://crackberry.com/saving-call-charges-recession-your-blackberry.

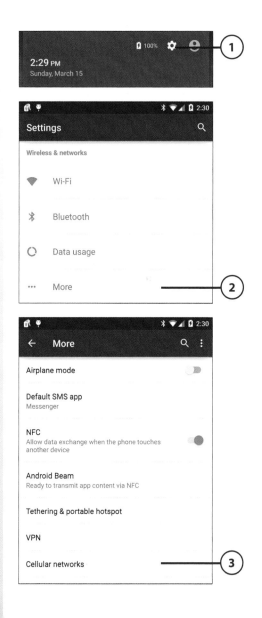

4. Tap to enable or disable cellular data roaming. If this is turned off, your phone does not attempt to use data while you roam away from your home cellular network.

5. Tap to change the network type. This setting enables you to choose to force your phone to connect to a slower 2G network to save battery or always to a faster 3G or 4G (LTE) network for the best speed, or to leave it set to Global and let your phone choose for you.

6. Tap to view, edit, and add Access Point Names (APNs). It is unlikely that you need to make any APN changes.

7. Tap to view and choose network operators to use manually.

8. Tap to save your changes and return to the previous screen.

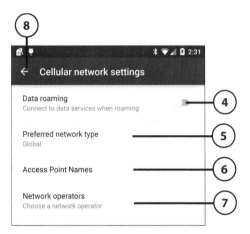

What Is an Access Point Name?

Access Point Name can be shortened to APN. You normally don't have to make changes to APNs, but sometimes you need to enter them manually to access certain features. For example, if you need to use tethering, which is where you connect your laptop to your phone and your phone provides Internet connectivity for your laptop, you might be asked by your carrier to use a specific APN. Think of an APN as a gateway to a service.

Can I Disable Mobile Data?

If you disable mobile data, you can save on battery life; however, you effectively kill the functionality of any app that needs to be connected all the time, such as Instant Messaging apps (Yahoo! or Google Talk) or apps like Skype. You also stop receiving email in real time. When this feature is disabled, about five minutes after your phone goes to sleep, it disconnects from the mobile data network; however, it remains connected to the mobile voice network.

>>>*Go Further*

WHY SELECT NETWORK OPERATORS MANUALLY?

When you are roaming in your home country, your phone automatically selects your home cellular provider. When you are roaming outside your home country, your phone registers on a cellular provider based on its name and how it scores alphabetically. The lowest score always wins. For example, a carrier whose name starts with a number is always chosen over carriers whose names start with letters. A carrier whose name starts with the letter *A* is chosen over a carrier whose name starts with the letter *B*, and so on. As you roam, your home carrier might not have a good roaming relationship with a carrier that your phone has chosen based on its name, so it's better for you to choose the carrier manually to ensure the best roaming rates and, many times, basic connectivity. You will notice that sometimes carriers are represented not by their names but by their operator codes (or Public Land Mobile Network [PLMN] number). For example, 53024 is actually 2Degrees in New Zealand, and 53005 is Telecom in New Zealand.

Using Your Mobile Wi-Fi Hotspot

Your phone has the ability to share its cellular data connection with up to eight devices over Wi-Fi. Before you use this feature, you need to sign up for a tethering or hotspot plan with your cellular provider, which is normally an extra monthly cost.

Set Up and Start Your Mobile Wi-Fi Hotspot

1. Pull down the Notification panel and tap the Settings icon.

2. Tap More in the Wireless & Networks section.

3. Tap Tethering & Portable Hotspot.

4. Tap Set Up Wi-Fi Hotspot to configure the settings.

What Is USB and Bluetooth Tethering?

USB and Bluetooth tethering are features that enable you to share your phone's Internet connection with a computer via the USB port or via Bluetooth. To use this, connect your phone to the computer using the supplied USB cable and enable USB tethering, or pair your phone with your computer using Bluetooth and enable Bluetooth tethering. On the computer, there will be some extra setup to do, which includes choosing your phone as an Internet access point. (And on older Windows computers, you might need to install a device driver. Please consult the computer's manual for instructions.)

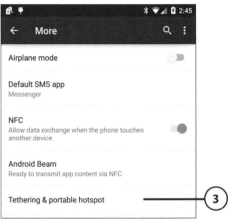

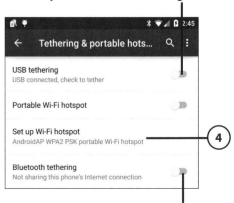

Tap to enable USB tethering

Tap to enable Bluetooth tethering

5. Choose a network name (also known as the SSID) for your mobile hotspot. You can leave it set to the auto-generated name or change it to something more friendly.

6. Tap to choose the type of security to use for your mobile hotspot or choose None to use no security. Depending on the manufacturer of your Android phone, you may have more or fewer security choices in this step.

7. Enter a password for your hotspot if you chose to use security in step 6.

8. Tap to save your settings.

9. Tap to enable your portable hotspot.

10. Provide the network connection information to anyone you want to have connecting to your hotspot.

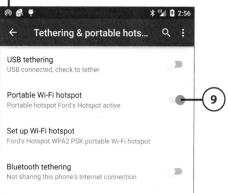

Set up Wi-Fi hotspot

Network name
Ford's Hotspot — ⑤

Security
WPA2 PSK — ⑥

Password
dontpanic — ⑦

The password must have at least 8 characters.

☑ Show password

CANCEL   SAVE — ⑧

— **Indicates your hotspot is active**

⊛ ☐ ⚘   ∗ LTE ◢ 🔋 2:56

←   Tethering & portable hots...   ⚲   ⋮

USB tethering
USB connected, check to tether

Portable Wi-Fi hotspot — ⑨
Portable hotspot Ford's Hotspot active

Set up Wi-Fi hotspot
Ford's Hotspot WPA2 PSK portable Wi-Fi hotspot

Bluetooth tethering
Not sharing this phone's Internet connection

Gaining More Control over Your Hotspot

Some Android phone manufacturers have modified the hotspot features to allow more control. For example, some Android phones allow you to control how many people can connect to your hotspot, and even restrict exactly which devices can connect based on their MAC addresses.

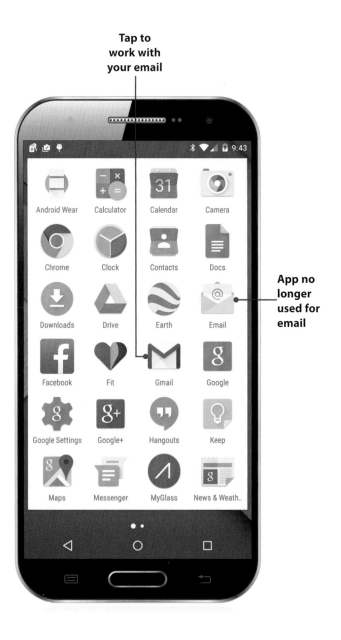

Tap to work with your email

App no longer used for email

In this chapter, you find out about your Android phone's email application—Gmail—and how to use it for your Gmail account but also for other personal accounts using POP3 or IMAP. You can even use it for your work email using Exchange. Topics include the following:

→ Sending and receiving email
→ Working with attachments
→ Working with Gmail labels
→ Changing settings

5

Email

Your Android phone comes with an email app called Gmail. This app works with Google's free email service called Gmail, but it also supports other email services provided by other companies that support the POP3 and IMAP post office protocols, and even corporate email systems such as Microsoft Exchange and Lotus Notes (with an IBM Notes Traveler Gateway).

What About the Email App?

In previous versions of Android, you would use the Email app for Exchange, POP3, and IMAP, and use the Gmail app only for Gmail. Now the Gmail app does it all, and if you tap the Email app, you just see a message telling you to use Gmail. Some Android phones may still use the Email app because they have heavily customized it to support certain special device features. In these situations, there will be an overlap of functionality between the Gmail app and the Email app.

Adding Accounts to Gmail

When you first set up your Android phone, you used your existing Gmail account. The Gmail application enables you to have multiple Gmail accounts, which is useful if you have a business account and a personal account. This section explains how to set up an additional Gmail account, a POP3/IMAP account, and an Exchange account for work emails.

Start Setting Up Accounts

1. Tap to open the Gmail app.

2. Swipe in from the left of the screen to reveal the Gmail folders and the menu.

3. Tap Settings near the bottom of the menu (swipe down past the folders to see the Settings menu item if needed).

4. Tap Add Account.

5. Follow the steps in the next few sections to add a Google account, personal account, and work account.

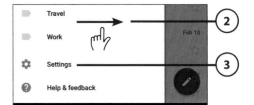

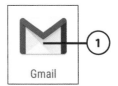

Add a Google Account

When you first set up your Android phone, you added your first Google (Gmail) account. The following steps describe how to add a second account.

1. Tap Google.

2. Tap OK.

3. Enter your existing Google account name. This is your Gmail address.

4. Tap Next.

What If I Don't Have a Second Google Account?

If you don't already have a second Google account but want to set one up, in step 3, tap Create a New Account. Your Android phone walks you through the steps of setting up a new Google account.

5. Enter your existing Google password.

6. Tap Next.

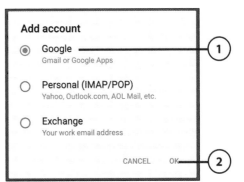

Add account

1 — ◉ Google
Gmail or Google Apps

○ Personal (IMAP/POP)
Yahoo, Outlook.com, AOL Mail, etc.

○ Exchange
Your work email address

CANCEL   OK — 2

Add your account   ⋮

Google

Sign in to get the most out of your device. ⓘ

Enter your email
zaphodbeeblebrox75@gmail.com — 3

OR CREATE A NEW ACCOUNT

NEXT > — 4

**Tap to get a new
Google account**

👤 zaphodbeeblebrox75@gmail....

Password
.... — 5

Forgot password? · Privacy & Terms

NEXT > — 6

7. Select the components from your Google account that you want to synchronize with your Android phone. Scroll up and down to see all components.

8. Tap Next.

Scroll down to see all options

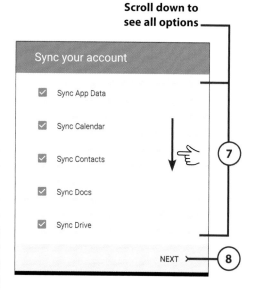

Why Would I Want Multiple Google Accounts?

You are probably wondering why you would want multiple Google accounts. Isn't one good enough? Actually it is not that uncommon to have multiple Google accounts. It can be a way to compartmentalize your life between work and play. You might run a small business using one account, but email only friends with another. Your Android phone supports multiple accounts but still enables you to interact with them in one place.

Add a New POP3 or IMAP Account

You can skip to the next section if you don't want to add a POP or IMAP email account. Email accounts from your Internet service provider or personal website probably use either POP3 or IMAP.

1. Tap Personal (IMAP/POP).

2. Tap OK.

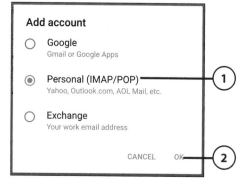

3. Enter the email address for this account.

4. Tap Next.

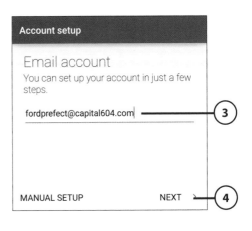

Why Would I Use Manual Setup?

Your Android phone tries to figure out the settings to set up your email account. This works most of the time when you use common email providers such as Yahoo! or Hotmail. It also works with large ISPs such as Comcast, Road Runner, Optimum Online, and so on. It might not work for smaller ISPs, in smaller countries, or when you create your own website and set up your own email. In these cases, you need to set up your email manually.

5. Tap either POP3 or IMAP as the type of account. If your email provider supports it, always choose IMAP. This example uses IMAP.

6. Enter the password for this email account and then tap Next.

7. Ensure that the information on this screen for the incoming mail server is accurate. Pay close attention to the Server and Security Type fields as they may not be correct. Change them if needed.

8. Tap Next.

Where Can I Find This Information?

Always check your ISP's or email service provider's website and look for instructions on how to set up your email on a computer or smartphone. This is normally under the support section of the website.

Entering Your Username and Password

On the Incoming Server and Outgoing Server screens, your username and password should already be filled out because you typed them in earlier. If not, enter them. Typically for POP3 and IMAP setups, the username is your full email address.

Carried over from previous screens

Incoming server settings

USERNAME
fordprefect@capital604.com

AUTHENTICATION
Password ••••••••••

SERVER
imap.capital604.com

PORT
143

SECURITY TYPE
STARTTLS

‹ PREVIOUS   NEXT ›

9. Ensure that the information on this screen for the outgoing mail server is accurate. Pay close attention to the SMTP Server and Security Type fields as they may not be correct. Change them if needed.

10. Tap Next.

11. Tap to change the frequency with which email from this account synchronizes to your Android phone, or set it to Never to only get new mail when you open the Gmail app.

12. Check the box if you want to be notified when new email arrives into this account.

13. Check the box if you want email to synchronize between this account and your Android phone.

14. Check the box if you want email to be automatically downloaded when you are connected to a Wi-Fi network. Tap the right arrow at the bottom of the screen when you're done with the options on this page.

Account setup

Outgoing server settings

SMTP SERVER
smtp.capital604.com

PORT
587

SECURITY TYPE
None

☑ Require signin

USERNAME
fordprefect@capital604.com

AUTHENTICATION
Password ·········· ✕

< PREVIOUS   NEXT >

Carried over from previous screens

Account setup

Account options

Sync frequency:
Every 15 minutes

☑ Notify me when email arrives

☑ Sync email from this account

☑ Automatically download attachments when connected to Wi-Fi

15. Enter a friendly name for this account, such as **Capital 604 Mail**.

16. Enter your full name or the name you want to display when people receive emails sent from this account.

17. Tap Next.

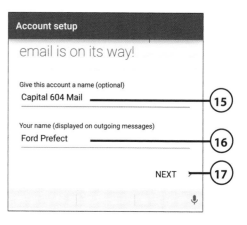

Be Secure if You Can

If your mail provider supports email security such as SSL or TLS, you should strongly consider using it. If you don't, emails you send and receive go over the Internet in plain, readable text. Using SSL or TLS encrypts the emails as they travel across the Internet so that nobody can read them. Set this under the Advanced settings for the Incoming and Outgoing Servers.

Add a Work Email Account

You can skip to the next section if you don't want to add a work email account. Work email systems must support Microsoft Exchange (or Lotus Notes using an IBM Notes Traveler Gateway) to work on your phone.

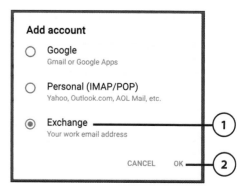

1. Tap Exchange.

2. Tap OK.

3. Enter your company email address.

4. Tap Next.

5. Type the password for your work email account.

6. Tap Next.

7. Check the username and change it if necessary. Many times, the username is not your email address but rather the username you use to log in to your company's network.

8. Enter the email server.

9. Tap Next.

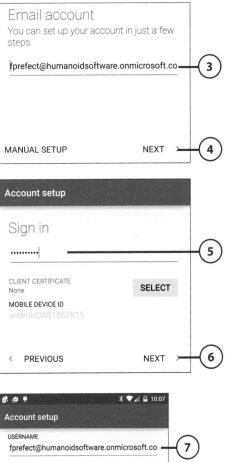

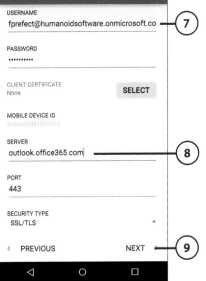

10. Tap OK to allow the company's email server to remotely control your phone. The extent to which the company controls it differs by company.

11. Tap to choose to either have your email pushed to your phone in real time as it arrives in your company Inbox or on a schedule.

12. Tap to choose how many days in the past email is synchronized to your Android phone or set it to All to synchronize all email in your Inbox.

13. Tap to enable or disable being notified when new email arrives from your corporate Inbox.

14. Tap to enable or disable synchronizing your corporate contacts to your Android phone.

15. Tap to enable or disable synchronizing your corporate calendar to your Android phone.

16. Tap to enable or disable synchronizing your corporate email to your Android phone.

17. Tap to enable or disable automatically downloading email attachments when your Android phone is connected to a Wi-Fi network.

18. Tap Next.

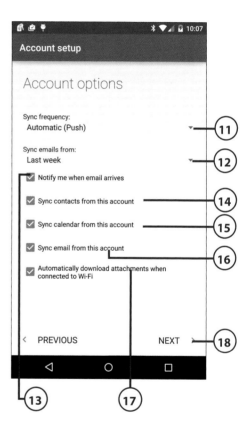

Choosing What to Synchronize

You might decide that you don't want to synchronize all your work information to your Android phone. You might decide to just synchronize email but not the calendar, or maybe just the calendar but not the contacts and email. Unchecking these boxes enables you to choose the information you don't want to synchronize. You can go back into the account settings and change it later if you change your mind.

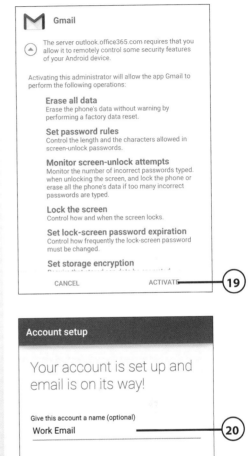

19. Tap Activate to allow your company's email server to add restrictions on your phone. The message displayed on the screen is a standard message indicating what your company can do, but is not representative of what they will do.

20. Enter a friendly name for your work email account, if you want to.

21. Tap Next to complete your company email setup.

Using the Gmail App

Now that you have added some email accounts that the Gmail app supports, you can start sending and reading emails with it.

Navigate the Gmail App

Let's take a quick look at the Gmail app and find out how to navigate the main screen.

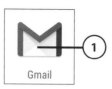

Gmail

1. Tap the Gmail icon to launch the app. Your initial view is of the Inbox of your primary Google (Gmail) account, which is the account you used when setting up your phone.

2. Tap to search the current folder for an email.

3. Tap to compose a new email.

4. Tap to see only new messages received from your social networking sites such as Facebook and Google+. When you have tapped it once, the Social option disappears until new social media emails arrive.

5. Tap to see any new emails that are promotions for products. When you have tapped it once, the Promotions option disappears until more promotional emails arrive.

6. Tap to see any new updates. Updates include messages about updating an app, but can also include update email relating to things you have purchased, bills you need to pay, and even updates to meeting invites. After you have tapped Updates once, the option disappears until there are more new updates.

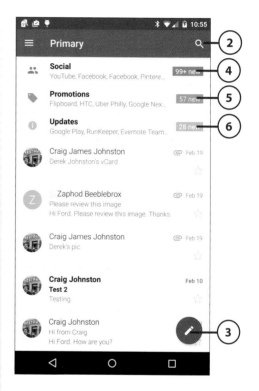

7. Swipe in from the left of the screen.

8. Tap to switch between your email accounts, if you have more than one.

9. Tap to add a new email account.

10. Tap to manage your existing email accounts.

11. Tap the current email account to see a list of folders (or as the Gmail app calls them, labels).

12. Tap to view Social, Promotions, Updates, and Forums. These are only visible when viewing Google (Gmail) accounts.

13. Tap to switch between your different folders, or as the Gmail app calls them, labels.

14. Scroll down to see all of your labels.

15. Swipe the vertical action bar to the left to minimize it.

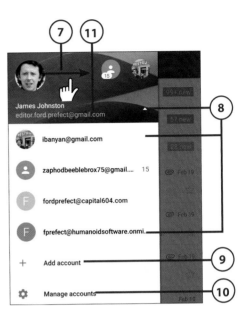

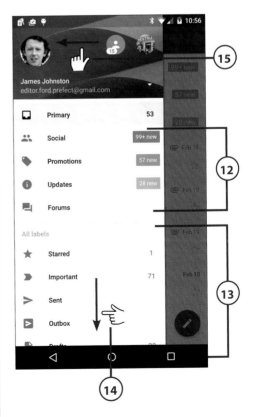

Using Stars and Labels

In the Gmail app, you use stars and labels to help organize your email. In most email clients, you can create folders in your mailbox to help you organize your emails. For example, you might create a folder called "emails from the boss" and move any emails you receive from your boss to that folder. The Gmail app doesn't use the term *folders*; it uses the term *labels* instead. You can create labels in Gmail and choose an email to label. When you label the email, it actually moves it to a folder with that label. Any email that you mark with a star is actually just getting a label called "starred." But when viewing your Gmail, you see the yellow star next to an email. People normally add a star to an email as a reminder of something important.

Compose an Email

1. Tap the Compose icon.

2. Tap to change the email account from which the message is being sent (if you have multiple accounts).

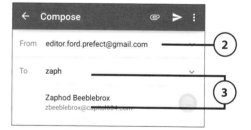

3. Type names in the To field. If the name matches someone in your Contacts, a list of choices is displayed and you can tap a name to select it. If you only know the email address, type it here.

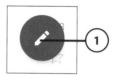

4. Tap to add Carbon Copy (CC) or Blind Carbon Copy (BCC) recipients.

5. Tap the Paperclip icon to add one or more attachments or insert links to one or more Google Drive files.

6. Type a subject for your email.

7. Type the body of the email.

8. Tap to save the email as a draft, or discard it.

9. Tap to send the email.

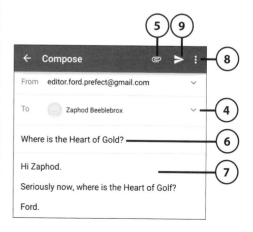

Add Attachments or Insert Drive Links

Before sending an email, you can add one or more attachments or insert links to files you have in your Google Drive account. The Gmail app can attach files from your phone and in your Google Drive account.

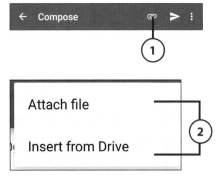

1. After filling in the fields as described in the "Compose an Email" task, tap the Paperclip icon.

2. Tap either Attach File or Insert from Drive. This example demonstrates attaching a file.

3. Choose where you want to search for the file. This can include your recent downloads, your Google Drive account, the Downloads folder, internal phone storage, or the Photos app.

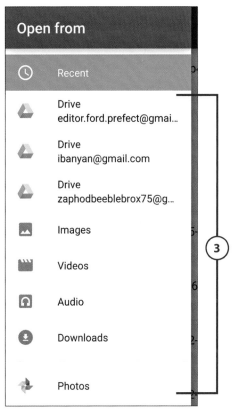

What Is the Difference Between Attaching and Inserting?

When you choose to attach a file to an email, you can choose a file located on your phone, in the Photos app, or in your Google Drive account. The file is then copied from that location and attached to the email. If you choose to insert a file from Google Drive, then the file you choose is not actually copied out of Google Drive and attached to the email; instead, a link to that file is placed in the body of the email. This allows the recipients to tap the link and open the document right in your Google Drive account.

4. Tap the file to attach it. In this example, the attachment is a document in my Google Drive account.

5. Tap the Paper Airplane icon to send the email.

My Drive ▾

W Craig James Johnston - Mobile - Short.docx
Nov 29, 2014 —————————— ④

Screenshot_2014-10-14-10-57-33.png
Nov 29, 2014

Links to Drive files ⑤

← Compose

From | editor.ford.prefect@gmail.com ∨

To | Zaphod Beeblebrox ∨

Where is the Heart of Gold?

Hi Zaphod.

Seriously now, where is the Heart of Golf?

Ford. 🖼 Screenshot_2014-10-14-10-57-33.png
▢ Untitled Presentation

📎 Craig James Johnston - Mobile - Short.docx ✕
30 KB

Attachment

Tap the X to remove an attachment

6. If you inserted files from Google Drive, then you need to choose what privileges recipients have. Tap to choose whether recipients can simply view the files, comment on them, or edit them.

7. Tap Send.

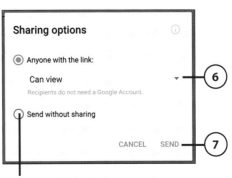

Force recipients to request access

Read an Email

1. Tap an email to open it. Unread emails are in bold, whereas emails that you have already read are not bold.

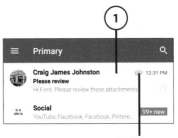

Indicates
attachments

What Is Rich Text Formatting?

Rich Text Formatting (RTF) is a message formatted with anything that is not plaintext. RTF includes bulleted lists; different fonts; font colors; font sizes; and styles such as bold, italic, and underline. Although you cannot type an email on your phone with the standard keyboard using RTF, if you are sent an RTF email, your phone preserves the formatting and displays it correctly.

---

2. Tap to mark the email as unread and return to the email list view.

3. Tap to reply to the sender of the email. This does not reply to anyone in the CC field.

4. Tap the Menu icon to reply to the sender of the email and any recipients in the To and CC fields (Reply All). You can also choose to print the email.

What Are Conversations?

Conversations are Gmail's version of email threads. When you look at the main view of the Gmail app, you are seeing a list of email conversations. The conversation might have only one email in it, but to Gmail that's a conversation. As you and others reply to that original email, Gmail groups those emails in a thread, or conversation.

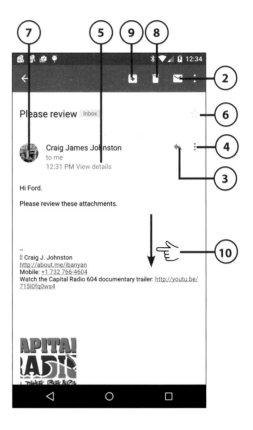

5. Tap to expand the email header to see all recipients and all other email header information.

6. Tap to "star" the message, or move it to the "starred" label.

7. Tap the sender's contact picture to see more contact information about him.

8. Tap to move the email to the Trash folder.

9. Tap to move the email to a different label.

10. Scroll down to see attachments and additional options.

11. Tap to reply to the sender, and any recipients in the CC field.

12. Tap to forward the email, including its attachments to new recipients.

13. Tap attachments to open them.

Using Gmail Messages' Extra Options

If you are receiving email in your Gmail Inbox, then you will have a few extra options while reading an email that are specific to Gmail. You will be able to archive an email as well as send it to Trash. You will also be able to mark an email as important, mute the email conversation, report an email as spam, or report an email as a phishing scam. When you mute a conversation, you will no longer see any emails in that conversation (or email thread). For more information on printing emails, and an explanation of what an important email is, see the "How Do I Print Emails?" and the "What Is Important" notes, respectively later in the chapter.

Move to

Change labels

Mark important

Mute

Print

Report spam

Report phishing

>>>Go Further

HOW DO I PRINT EMAILS?

When you choose to print an email, the Print dialog enables you to choose to print the email to a PDF (which turns the email into a Portable Document Format [PDF] file) or to print the email to any printers that you have previously connected to Google Cloud Print using your desktop Chrome web browser. To learn more about how to connect your printers to your Google Cloud Print account, look at the instructions at https://support.google.com/chrome/answer/1069693?hl=en.

Tap to choose a printer or save as a PDF

What Is Important?

Gmail tries to automatically figure out which of the emails you receive are important. As it learns, it might sometimes be wrong. If an email is marked as important but you don't consider it important, you can change the status to not important manually by tapping the Menu icon and tapping Mark As Not Important. Important emails have a yellow arrow, whereas emails that are not important have a clear arrow. All emails marked as Important are also given the Priority Inbox label.

What Happens to Your Spam or Phishing Emails?

When you mark a Gmail message as spam or as a phishing scam, two things happen. First, it gets a label called Spam. Second, a copy of that email is sent to Gmail's spam servers so that they are now aware of a possible new spam email that is circulating around the Internet. Based on what the servers see for all Gmail users, they block the emails that have been marked as spam and phishing emails from reaching other Gmail users. So the bottom line is that you should always mark spam emails because it helps all of us.

Customize Gmail App Settings

You can customize not only the way the Gmail app works, but also how each independent email account functions.

1. Swipe in from the left of the screen and tap on the current email account to reveal its folders.

2. Tap Settings.

3. Tap General Settings.

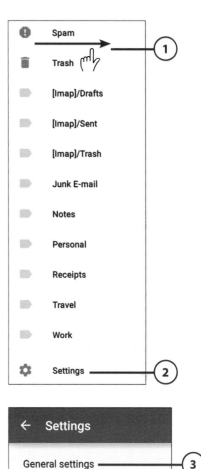

Using Additional Options in General Settings

While in the General Settings screen, if you tap the Menu icon, you can clear your email search history, or clear picture approvals. When you clear picture approvals, you are clearing your previous decisions on which emails you wanted to automatically load the images for.

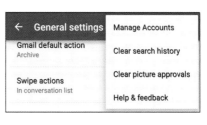

4. Tap to choose what must happen when you swipe across a message. The choices are to Archive the message or Delete the message.

5. Check the box to enable the ability to swipe an email left or right to archive or delete it. You can decide what action occurs in step 4 above.

6. Check the box to enable showing the email sender's contact image in the conversation list.

7. Check the box to enable making Reply All the default reply action.

8. Tap to enable automatically shrinking the emails to fit on the screen.

9. Tap to choose what happens when you archive or delete a message. Your choices are to show newer messages, older messages, or the conversation list.

10. Choose which actions you want to show a confirmation screen for.

11. Tap to save your changes and return to the main Settings screen.

12. Tap one of your accounts to change settings specific to that account, and use the steps in the following sections.

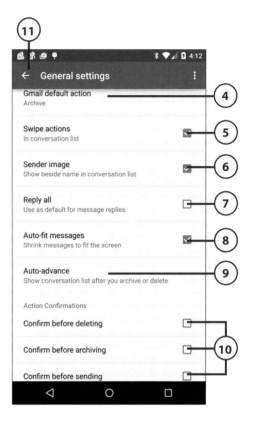

Customize Google Account Settings

1. Tap to choose whether you want to see your Priority Inbox instead of your regular Inbox when opening the Gmail app.

2. Tap to choose what Inbox categories will be shown. As shown earlier in the chapter, by default the Social and Promotions categories are displayed. You can also show Updates and Forums.

3. Tap to enable or disable notifications when new email arrives for this Gmail account.

4. Tap to select how to get notified when new email arrives for this account. You can choose a different notification for each label and also decide which labels in addition to the Primary label you will be notified for.

5. Tap to enter a signature to be included at the end of all emails composed using this account.

6. Tap to set your Vacation Responder. This is a message that is automatically sent to people when you are on vacation.

7. Scroll down for more settings.

← editor.ford.prefect@gmail.com

Inbox type
Default Inbox ①

Inbox categories
Primary, Social, Promotions, Updates, Forums ②

Notifications ③

Inbox sound & vibrate
Sound on, notify once ④

Signature
Not set ⑤

Vacation responder
Off ⑥

⑦

What Is the Priority Inbox?

Google introduced the Priority Inbox as a way to automatically figure out which emails are important to you and place them in a special folder. It does this by analyzing which emails you open and reply to. If the app makes a mistake, you can mark a message as less important or more important. Over time, Google's handle on which emails are important to you gets more accurate. Because the Priority Inbox probably has the most-important emails, you might want to open it first and then go to the regular Inbox later to handle less-important emails.

8. Tap to choose whether to synchronize Gmail to this phone. Turning this off stops Gmail from arriving on your phone.

9. Tap to choose how many days of email to synchronize to your phone.

10. Touch to manage labels. Labels are like folders. You can choose which labels synchronize to your phone, how much email synchronizes, and which ringtone to play when new email arrives in that label.

11. Check the box to automatically download attachments to recently received emails while connected to a Wi-Fi network.

12. Tap to choose how images embedded in emails are handled. They can be automatically downloaded, or you can be prompted before they are downloaded for each email.

13. Tap the left arrow at the top of the screen (not shown) to save your changes and return to the main Settings screen.

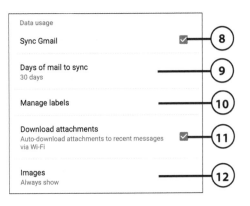

What Is an Email Signature?

An email signature is a bit of text that is automatically added to the bottom of any email you send from your Android phone. It is added when you compose a new email, reply to an email, or forward an email. A typical use for a signature is to automatically add your name and maybe some contact information at the end of your emails. Email signatures are sometimes referred to as email footers.

Customize POP/IMAP Account Settings

1. Tap to change the name of your account. This is the friendly name you may have typed when you originally set it up on your phone.

2. Tap to change the full name you want people to see when you reply to emails using this account.

3. Tap to enter a signature to be included at the end of all emails composed using this account.

4. Tap to change the frequency in which your phone checks for new email for this account. You can set it to Never, which means that your phone only checks for email when you open the Gmail app, or you can set it to automatically check on a specified schedule.

5. Check the box to automatically download attachments to recently received emails while connected to a Wi-Fi network.

6. Scroll down for more settings.

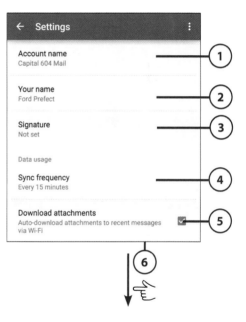

7. Tap to enable or disable notifications when new email arrives for this email account.

8. Tap to select the ringtone to play when you are notified of new email for this account.

9. Check the box if you want your phone to also vibrate when a new email arrives for this account.

10. Tap to change the incoming email server settings for this account.

11. Tap to change the outgoing email server settings for this account.

12. Tap the left arrow at the top of the screen (not shown) to save your changes and return to the main Settings screen.

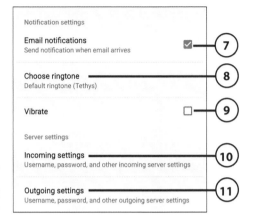

Customize Exchange Account Settings

1. Tap to change the name of your account. This is the friendly name you may have typed when you originally set it up on your phone.

2. Tap to change the full name you want people to see when you reply to emails using this account.

3. Tap to enter a signature to be included at the end of all emails composed using this account.

4. Tap to change the frequency in which your phone checks for new email for this account. You can set it to Automatic (Push) to have emails automatically pushed to your phone as soon as they arrive in your Inbox back at the office. You can also set it to Never, which means that your phone only checks for email when you open the Gmail app, or you can set it to automatically check on a specified schedule.

5. Tap to choose how much email to synchronize to your phone. You can choose All to have every email synchronize, or choose between the last day up to the last month.

6. Tap to choose which folders to synchronize to your phone. You are presented with a list of all mail folders, and you can choose whether to synchronize it or not, plus decide how much email should synchronize on a folder-by-folder basis.

7. Check the box to synchronize email from this account with your phone. If you uncheck this box, email stops synchronizing to your phone.

8. Check the box to synchronize contacts from this account with your phone. If you uncheck this box, contacts stop synchronizing to your phone.

9. Scroll down for notification settings.

10. Check the box to synchronize the calendar from this account with your phone. If you uncheck this box, the calendar stops synchronizing to your phone.

11. Check the box to automatically download attachments to recently received emails while connected to a Wi-Fi network.

12. Tap to enable or disable notifications when new email arrives for this email account.

13. Tap to select the ringtone to play when you are notified of new email for this account.

14. Check the box if you want your phone to vibrate when new email arrives for this account.

15. Tap to change the incoming email server settings for this account.

16. Tap to save your changes and return to the main Settings screen.

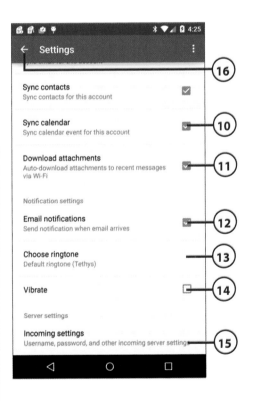

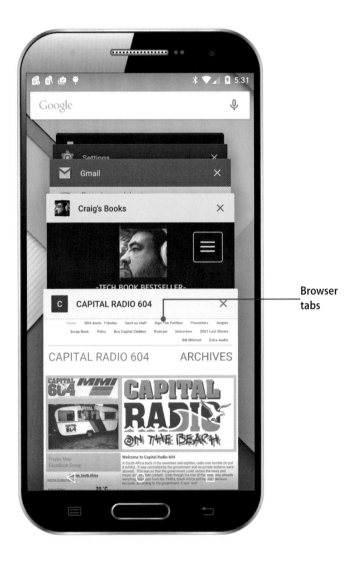

Browser tabs

In this chapter, you discover how to browse the World Wide Web using the browser capabilities of your Android phone. Topics include the following:

→ Bookmarking websites
→ Sharing websites with your friends
→ Keeping track of sites you have visited
→ Using GPS and browsing together
→ Browsing Incognito

Browsing the Web with Chrome

Your Android phone has a fully featured web browser called Chrome. In fact, the experience of using the Android phone's browser is similar to using a desktop browser, just with a smaller screen. You can bookmark sites, hold your Android phone sideways to fit more onto the screen, and even share your GPS location with websites.

Navigating with Chrome

Let's dive right in and cover how to run the Chrome web browser and use all its features. You can customize the Chrome browser, share your GPS location, bookmark sites, maintain your browsing history, and even access bookmarks stored on your computer.

Get Started with Chrome

1. Tap the Chrome icon.

2. Tap to type a website address or one or more search terms. Some websites move the web page up to hide the address field. When this happens, you can drag the web page down to reveal the address bar again.

3. Tap the Overview button to see open Chrome browser tabs.

4. Tap to go to the previous page on the current website, or to the previous website you were viewing.

5. Tap the Menu icon to see more options.

6. Tap to open a new browser tab from which you can go to a new website.

7. Tap to bookmark the website that you are currently looking at. If the site is already bookmarked, you can edit the bookmark.

8. Tap to manually refresh the website.

9. Tap the right arrow to go to the next page on the current website, or to go to the next website, if you had previously tapped the Back button.

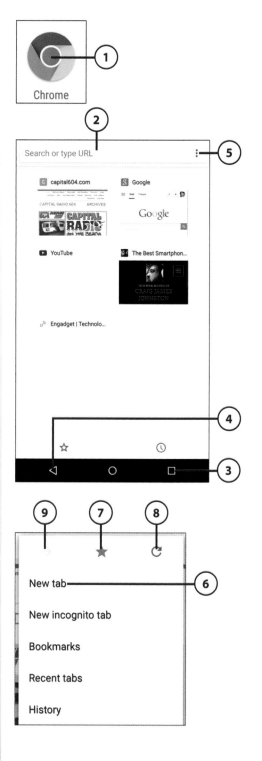

Using Chrome Browser Tabs

Chrome browser tabs work the same way that your desktop web browser tabs work. If you open a new tab, you can load a different website and then switch between the tabs, effectively switching between multiple open websites. In previous versions of Chrome, you could navigate between tabs using the Chrome interface. In the latest versions of Android and the Chrome browser, the management of Chrome tabs has moved to the Overview screen. When you open a new tab, the Chrome browser opens the new tab for you, and it looks like your previous tab disappears. To navigate between Chrome browser tabs, tap the Overview button. Among the open apps, you will see your browser tabs. You can then tap tabs to switch to them, and close them by swiping or tapping the X in the top right of each tab.

Old tab management

New tab management

Tap to see tabs

Use Web Page and Chrome Options

While a web page is open, you have a number of options, such as finding text on a web page and forcing Chrome to load the desktop version of a website.

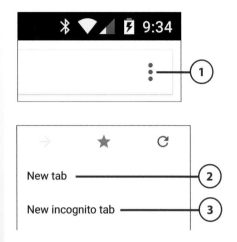

1. Tap the Menu icon.

2. Tap to open a new browser tab.

3. Tap to open a new Incognito browser tab.

Browsing in Secret (Going Incognito)

If you want to visit a website in secret, you can. Visiting a website in secret using an Incognito browser tab means that the site you visit does not appear in your browser history or search history and does not otherwise leave a trace of itself on your Android phone. To create a new Incognito browser tab, while in the browser tab screen, tap the Menu icon and then tap New Incognito Tab. One thing to remember is that although all traces of the website you are browsing to in an Incognito tab are not stored on your phone, there are certainly traces of your browsing stored other places, including your Internet service provider (ISP), the website you are visiting, and the routers that your data passes through. To close all open Incognito tabs, but leave regular tabs open, pull down the Notification panel and tap Close All Incognito Tabs.

Tap to close all Incognito tabs

4. Tap to open the Chrome bookmarks screen.

5. Tap Recent Tabs to see websites that were recently opened in Chrome browser tabs on your desktop computer and all other devices where you have the Chrome browser installed and running.

6. Tap to see the history of all websites you have visited on all devices where you run the Chrome web browser. History from Incognito tabs are not visible as they are not stored.

7. Tap to share the current web page's address using a number of methods, including Facebook, Twitter, Skype, Bluetooth, and Android Beam, or to copy the link to the Clipboard.

8. Tap to print the web page on a printer that is linked to your Google Chrome Cloud Print account, or print the web page to a Portable Document Format (PDF) file.

9. Tap to find a word on the current web page.

10. Tap to add a shortcut for the current web page on your phone's Home screen.

11. Tap to request the desktop version of the current website if you are seeing a mobile version. When you check the box, Chrome refreshes the page with the desktop version.

12. Tap to change the Chrome web browser settings.

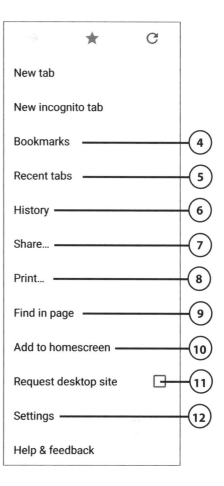

How Can I See My Desktop Computer's Browser Tabs?

To see your desktop computer's Chrome browser tabs, make sure you install Chrome on your desktop computer and use it as your default web browser. When setting up Chrome, use the same Google account as you use on your Android phone. Then not only are your bookmarks kept in sync between your phone and desktop (and all other devices where Chrome is installed), but also any browser tabs you have open in Chrome on your desktop computer (called browser windows on the desktop version of Chrome) can be seen as described in step 5. Even if you close Chrome and shut down your computer, you still see the last tabs that were open.

Master Chrome Browser Tricks

Your Android phone has some unique tricks to help you browse regular websites on a small screen.

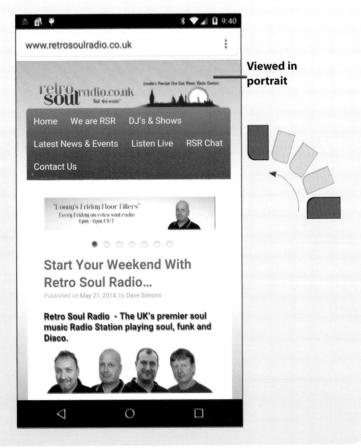

Viewed in portrait

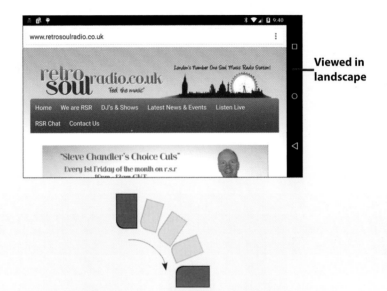

Viewed in landscape

1. Rotate your Android phone on its side to put the phone into *landscape orientation*. Your Android phone automatically switches the screen to Landscape mode.

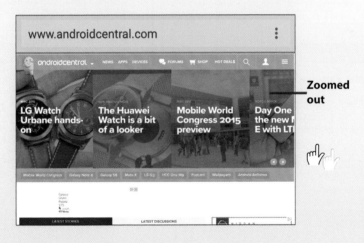

Zoomed out

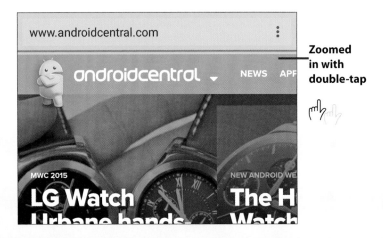

Zoomed
in with
double-tap

2. Double-tap the screen to zoom in and out.

Zooming with Pinch to Zoom

An alternative way to zoom, which enables you to actually zoom in much further, is to place your thumb and forefinger on the screen and spread them apart to zoom in and then move them back together to zoom out.

Zoomed in
with pinch to
zoom

3. If menu choices on a web page are too small, when you touch a menu item, the Chrome browser shows you a zoomed-in portion of the menu to enable you to more easily touch your menu item.

Zoomed in to menu choices

Managing Bookmarks and History

Your Android phone enables you to bookmark your favorite websites, but it also keeps track of where you have browsed and can show you your browsing history broken up by days, weeks, and months. The history also enables you to read web pages offline.

Manage Bookmarks

1. Tap the Menu icon (not shown).

2. Tap Bookmarks.

3. Tap to switch between your mobile bookmarks and bookmarks that you have on your desktop computer.

4. Tap a bookmark to open it.

Work with Bookmarks

1. Tap a bookmark to open it in the current tab.

2. Touch and hold a bookmark to see more options.

3. Tap to open the bookmark in a new browser tab.

4. Tap to open the bookmark in an Incognito tab (secretive browsing).

5. Tap to edit the bookmark.

6. Tap to delete the bookmark.

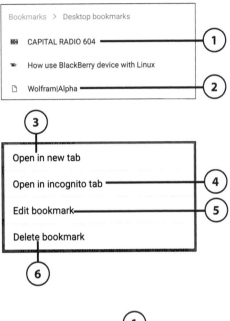

Add a Bookmark

While you are viewing a web page, you can add it to your list of bookmarks.

1. Tap the Menu icon and then tap the Star icon. The Add Bookmark screen displays.

2. Change the bookmark name if you want to. It defaults to the web page's title.

3. Edit the web page link if you want to or leave it as is (normally best).

4. Select where to save the bookmark. You can choose to save it in Mobile Bookmarks (only on your phone) or in one of the bookmark folders that you have synchronized from your desktop computer.

5. Tap to save the bookmark.

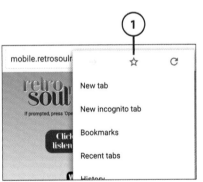

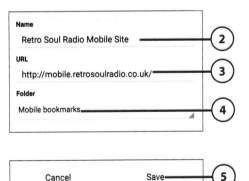

Where Should I Save Bookmarks?

When you save bookmarks, you can choose to save them locally or to one of your desktop bookmark folders. If you choose to save a bookmark locally, it is saved only to your Android phone. The bookmark is not synchronized to the Google Cloud or made available anywhere other than on your phone. If you choose to save the bookmark to one of your desktop bookmark folders, that bookmark is stored in the Google Cloud and is then available to you on any device where you use that same Google account. This includes when you log in to your Google account on your desktop version of the Chrome browser on your computer and any Android smartphone or phone that you purchase and use in the future.

Manage Browsing History

Your browsing history is a list of all websites that you have visited. Browsing your history can help find websites you have visited in the past but forgotten about.

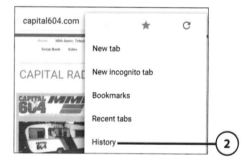

1. Tap the Menu icon (not shown).

2. Tap History.

3. Tap Clear Browsing Data at the bottom of the screen to clear all Chrome browser data, including browser history, cache, cookies, and saved passwords.

4. Tap the X icon to the right of a browser history item to remove it.

5. Touch and hold an item to see more options for that item.

6. Tap to open the website in a new browser tab.

7. Tap to open the website in a new Incognito browser tab.

8. Tap to copy the link for this website to the Clipboard.

9. Tap to copy the link's title text to the Clipboard.

10. Tap to save the contents of the web page to your phone. Only the text and layout is saved, not the images. You can find the downloaded web page by opening the Downloads app.

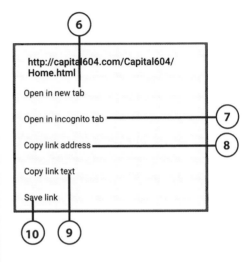

Customizing Browser Settings

Your Android phone's Chrome browser is customizable. This section describes the different settings you can adjust.

1. Tap the Menu icon (not shown).

2. Tap Settings.

3. Tap your Google account.

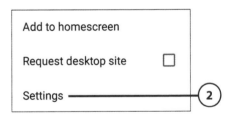

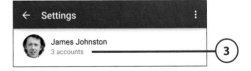

4. Tap the Google account you want to change on the next screen (if you have more than one account).

5. Tap to enable or disable synchronization, and choose what to synchronize.

6. Check the box to synchronize everything, or uncheck it to selectively choose what to synchronize.

7. Tap to choose whether you want to encrypt saved passwords using your Google credentials, or encrypt everything using a new passphrase.

8. Tap to save your changes and return to the account choice screen.

9. Tap to save your changes and return to the main Settings screen.

← James Johnston ⋮

ACCOUNTS

You're signed in to the following Google Accounts. Add or remove accounts in Android settings.

editor.ford.prefect@gmail.com
Sync is on — 4

ibanyan@gmail.com

zaphodbeeblebrox75@gmail.com

8   5

← Sync ⋮

Data types

Sync everything — 6

Autofill

Bookmarks

History — 6

Passwords

Open tabs

Encryption — 7

9

← James Johnston ⋮

10. Tap to choose the search engine to use. You can choose Google, Yahoo!, Bing, Ask, or AOL.

11. Tap to change the way that Chrome browser tabs are handled.

12. Tap to enable or disable the Autofill Forms feature and create profiles that contain your information and credit card information for Chrome to use in those forms.

13. Tap to enable or disable the capability for Chrome to save your website passwords. This setting also enables you to view and remove any passwords already stored.

14. Tap to see the Privacy settings. Read more about Chrome privacy settings and what information is sent for each setting, by going to https://support.google.com/chrome/ and searching for *privacy settings*.

Alternative Handling of Tabs

In step 11, you can turn off the default behavior. The default behavior is where browser tabs are merged with the running apps on the Overview screen; when you turn off the default behavior, the browser tabs are handled inside Chrome. When Chrome is handling its own tabs, a small number appears in a box to indicate the number of open tabs. Tap the number to switch between tabs.

capital604.com/Capital604/Send_us_ — **Tap to switch tabs**

15. Tap to enable or disable Chrome making suggestions of alternatives when you mistype a website address. If enabled, Chrome sends Google what you have typed in the address bar.

16. Tap to enable or disable Chrome making suggestions as you type in the address bar. If enabled, Chrome sends Google what you have typed in the address bar.

17. Tap to enable or disable the feature where Chrome preloads the IP address of every link on a web page to speed up browsing. If enabled, Chrome sends Google the name of the website you are visiting. You can choose to pre-fetch resources on Wi-Fi Only, always (Wi-Fi or cellular data), or never.

18. Tap to enable or disable sending usage and crash reports. If enabled, Chrome might send personal information to Google.

19. Tap to enable the Do Not Track feature. When enabled, Chrome sends a request that you not be tracked to websites you visit. What the website does with that request is unpredictable, so this feature might not be effective.

20. Tap to clear some or all of your browsing data. This includes your browsing history, browser cache, cookies and other site data, any saved passwords, and any autofill info.

21. Tap to save your changes and return to the main Settings screen.

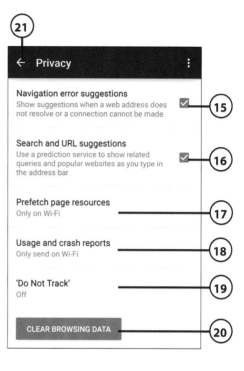

>>>*Go Further*

WHERE DOES MY PERSONAL INFORMATION GO?

In steps 15–20 of the "Customizing Browser Settings" section, you see options to allow Chrome to send your personal information to Google. In each case, the information is either used to make your web browsing experience quicker and easier or to help Google figure out why the Chrome browser is crashing. For example, in step 18, you can allow Chrome to send information about what you were busy doing when the Chrome web browser crashed (if it crashes in the future). Because debugging software means trying to figure out every possible combination of tasks, it is never possible to come up with every combination unless Google has visibility into how people like you are using the software in the real world. The information that is sent to Google is not shared with anyone and is kept private and confidential, so you will not suddenly start receiving spam emails after Google has received your information.

22. Tap to change the size of text displayed on web pages (text scaling) and to override a website's capability to prevent zooming.

| Accessibility | — (22) |
| Site settings | — (23) |

23. Tap to change website content settings such as accepting cookies, blocking pop-up ads, and sharing your location.

← **Site settings**

≡ All sites

✪ Cookies
   Allow sites to save and read cookie data   ☑ — (24)

24. Tap to enable or disable accepting cookies.

● Location
   Ask first — (25)

25. Tap to enable or disable allowing websites to access your location and specify how accurately your location is identified. This screen also allows you to manage each website that has asked for your location.

26. Tap to decide whether a website must ask you before it uses your camera and microphone, or if you want to block this access to all websites.

27. Tap to enable or disable the capability for Chrome to run JavaScript. This is normally left on because many websites use JavaScript to enhance their site and make it easier to use.

28. Tap to enable or disable blocking web pop-ups.

29. Tap to enable or disable content protection. Having this enabled allows websites to authenticate your phone so that they can let you watch premium protected videos.

30. Tap to enable or disable Google Translate. When this is enabled, you can translate web pages into other languages.

31. Tap to browse settings for all websites you have visited so that you can clear any data stored by those individual websites.

32. Tap to save your changes and return to the main Settings screen.

33. Tap Reduce Data Usage to allow Google servers to compress the data coming from websites so that it reduces how much data it takes to load each web page. On some phones this setting may be called Data Saver.

34. Tap to save your changes and return to the Chrome main screen.

(32)

← Site settings

☰   All sites

🍪   Cookies
    Allow sites to save and read cookie data   ☑

📍   Location
    Ask first

📹   Camera or microphone
    Ask first   — (26)

⇥   JavaScript
    Allow sites to run JavaScript   ☑ (27)

🔲   Pop-ups
    Blocked   — (28)

📥   Protected content
    Ask first   — (29)

🔤   Google Translate
    Ask first   — (30)

☰   Storage   — (31)

(34)

← Settings   ⋮

Reduce data usage
Off   — (33)

What Is Text Scaling?

When you use text scaling, you instruct your Android phone to always increase or decrease the font sizes used on a web page by a specific percentage. For example, you can automatically make all text 150 percent larger than was originally intended.

What Are Cookies?

Cookies are small files that are placed on your phone by websites. They contain information that might enhance your browsing experience if you return to the website from which they came. For example, they could contain information about what pages you visited before and your browsing history on the website. When you return to the website that placed the cookie, it can read the information in the cookie. Cookies can contain any kind of information, so it is possible for them to be used maliciously, although it's not likely.

How Does Pop-Up Blocking Work?

When you enable pop-up blocking, your Android phone automatically blocks any website request to pop up a window. This is good because almost every pop-up on a website is some kind of scam to get you to tap a link so that you go to a new site. Sometimes, though, pop-ups are legitimate, and a website that needs you to allow pop-ups will ask you to allow them. You can disable the pop-up blocker any time and then re-enable it when you stop using that website. Unlike desktop computers, you cannot temporarily stop blocking pop-ups, so you need to remember to manually disable and enable the pop-up blocker.

How Does Reduce Data Usage Work?

When you enable Reduce Data Usage, behind the scenes a setting is changed so that every web page you visit (with the exception of secure web pages and web pages opened in an Incognito tab) are rerouted via the Google servers before proceeding to your phone. This is called a *proxy*, and it means that the Google servers act like a proxy for your web data. Although this feature reduces the size of web pages being downloaded, bear in mind that the way it does this is by compressing images so that they look washed out and end up at a lower resolution.

Taking Actions on a Link

If you touch and hold a link on a website, you can choose to open it in a new tab, open it in an Incognito tab (secretive browsing), copy the link's address (to paste into another app, such as an email you are composing), copy the text of the link, and save the link (and its associated web page) as a file on your phone.

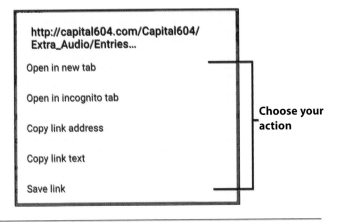

http://capital604.com/Capital604/
Extra_Audio/Entries...

Open in new tab

Open in incognito tab

Copy link address

Copy link text

Save link

Choose your action

>>>Go Further

MY PHONE DOESN'T HAVE CHROME

Some Android phones do not come preloaded with the Chrome web browser, but they do have a built-in web browser simply called Internet. Most of the steps in this chapter apply to the Internet web browser. Sometimes there are additional features in the Internet browser, such as a Reader View (on Samsung phones). Tapping the R to the left of the address bar shows a "book-like" text view of the website.

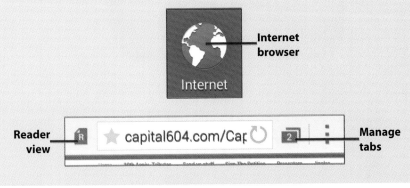

Internet browser

Reader view

Manage tabs

Search Google

See places nearby

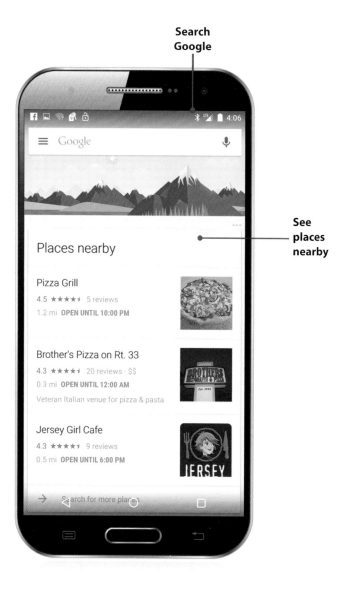

In this chapter, you find out how to use Google Maps, Navigation, and Google Now. Topics include the following:

→ Staying up to date with Google Now
→ Navigating with Google Maps
→ Taking map data offline

Google Now and Navigation

You can use your Android phone as a GPS navigation device while you walk or drive around. Your phone also includes an app called Google Now that provides all the information you need when you need it.

Using Google Now

You can access Google Now from the Lock screen or from any screen, which enables you to search the Internet. Google Now provides you with information such as how long it takes to drive to work and the scores from your favorite teams.

Accessing Google Now

You can access Google Now from any app or the Home screen pane by swiping from the bottom of the screen up onto the screen and toward the word Google. If you are on the Home screen, you can also swipe all the way to the left to see Google Now. It is the leftmost Home screen pane.

Swipe up from the bottom of the screen

Use Google Now

After you access Google Now, you can see current information, or search the Internet.

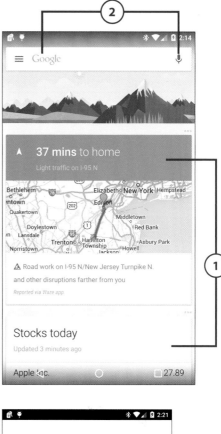

1. Cards automatically appear based on your settings. Examples of these cards are scores for the sports teams you follow, upcoming meetings, weather in the location where you work, and traffic on the way to work.

2. Tap the Microphone icon to speak a search term or to command Google Now to do something. You can also type your search terms.

3. Information relevant to your search appears.

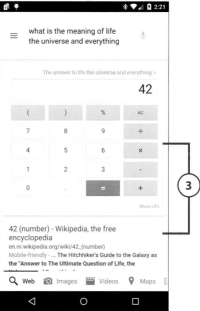

Commanding Google Now

In addition to searching the Internet using Google Now, you can command Google Now to do things for you. For example, you can tell Google Now to set an alarm for you, compose a text message, or even send an email. This is just a small list of the types of things you can have Google Now do for you. To see a comprehensive list of commands, visit http://trendblog.net/list-of-google-now-voice-commands-infographic/.

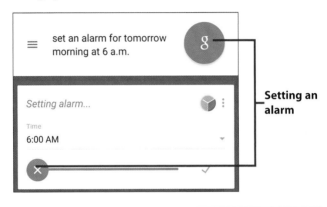

Setting an alarm

Set Up Google Now

For Google Now to work for you, you need to set it up correctly. This also means sharing your location information with Google.

1. Swipe in from the left side of the screen to reveal the menu.

2. Tap to add and manage reminders. After adding a reminder, Google Now notifies you of the activity when the reminder is due.

3. Tap Customize to customize what kinds of Google Now cards are displayed. This includes choosing sports teams, stocks, places, and TV and video.

4. Tap Settings.

5. Tap to manage what Google Now can search for. This can include apps you have installed, bookmarks and web history in the Chrome web browser, your contacts, Google Play Books, Movies & TV, and Music.

6. Tap Voice to manage how and when Google Now responds to your voice.

7. Tap to choose the languages that Google Now responds to.

8. Tap to choose when Google Now should be listening for you to say "OK Google," which is the key phrase that launches Google Now. You can choose to have Google Now listening only from the Google Now app, from any screen, or from the Lock screen.

9. Tap to choose whether Google Now works when your phone is locked, and how it should listen for your commands. You can choose to let Google Now use a paired Bluetooth device, a headset connected by a cable, or both.

10. Tap to choose when Google Now speaks back to you. Your choices are On (which means *always*), Off (which means *never*), or only when you are using a hands-free device (such as a Bluetooth headset or your car's built-in Bluetooth connection). Some phones may not include the "Off" choice here.

Beware of Others Speaking to Your Phone

Be careful about deciding when Google Now can listen for commands. If you allow Google Now to listen for "OK Google" on any screen (which means on any screen plus while running any app), the only drawback could be battery life suffering, but if you let Google Now listen for "OK Google" from the Lock screen, there is the potential for someone else to instruct your phone to do things. Even though when you enable this feature, you are asked to say "OK Google" three times so that Google Now can become familiar with your voice, it is possible for others to command your phone to send emails, read emails back to them, and so on.

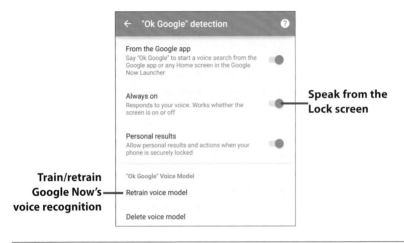

11. Tap to manage whether Google Now speech recognition can work even when there is no Internet connection. This is achieved by downloading one or more languages to your phone.

12. Tap to block offensive words being spoken when search results are returned by voice.

13. Tap to allow Google Now to record your voice using your Bluetooth headset or built-in car Bluetooth.

14. Tap to save your changes and return to the main Google Now Settings screen.

15. Tap Accounts & Privacy.

16. Tap to choose which of your Google accounts (if you have more than one) you want to use for Google Now.

17. Tap to manage whether apps can share your data with Google and clear any data that apps on your phone have shared with Google.

18. Tap to enable or disable the SafeSearch Filter that blocks offensive content.

19. Tap to choose whether you want to share your commute status, such as when you leave for home or leave for work. People need to be in your Google+ Circles to receive your Commute updates.

20. Tap to enable or disable high-contrast text if you have a vision disability.

21. Tap to enable or disable Google Now sending Google information on how you use Google Now.

22. Tap to save your changes and return to the main Google Now Settings screen.

23. Tap to manage how Google Now alerts you when new cards are ready, and choose the ringtone that plays when they are ready to view.

24. Tap to save your changes and return to Google Now.

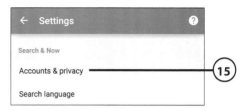

Telling Google Maps Where You Live and Work

Google Now can be even more effective if you configure your work and home addresses in Google Maps. Google Now uses that information to tell you things like how long your commute to work will be, whether there is heavy traffic on the route, and so on. See step 3 in the "Configure Google Maps Settings" task later in this chapter on how to do that.

Navigating with Google Maps

Google Maps enables you to see where you are on a map, find points of interest close to you, get driving or walking directions, and review extra layers of information, such as a Satellite view.

1. Tap to launch Google Maps.

2. Tap to type a search term, the name of a business, or an address.

3. Tap to speak a search term, the name of a business, or an address.

4. Tap to get walking or driving directions from one location to another. You can also choose to use public transit or biking paths to get to your destination.

5. Tap to switch between the top-down view that always points North, and the 3D view that follows the direction your phone is pointing.

6. Tap to explore what's around your current location.

7. Swipe in from the left of the screen to reveal the menu.

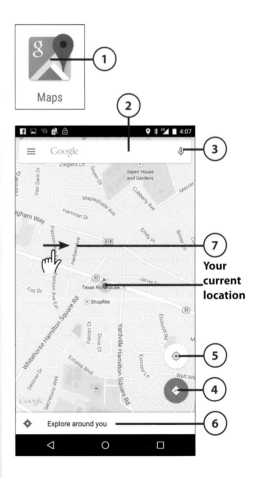

Maps

Your current location

How To Explore Around You

When you tap Explore Around You, you are presented with restaurants and businesses within a 20-minute drive and a time of day. The time of day should be the current time of day (for example, "Morning") and that determines the search criteria for restaurants. For example, if it's morning, the screen will show nearby restaurants that serve breakfast. Where possible, a star rating is provided for each restaurant so you can quickly see if it is rated highly. Tapping on a restaurant or business shows more information about it, including the address, hours of operation, the menu (if available), and the ability to quickly get directions. You can also tap the star icon to save the restaurant to your favorites, and in the future the restaurant will be displayed with a star on the map.

8. Tap to switch to a different Google account for use with Google Maps.

9. Tap to see your work and home address, plus addresses you have recently searched for, and any places you have saved to your favorites.

10. Tap to toggle between the Map view and the Satellite view.

11. Tap to show the current traffic conditions on the Map view or Satellite view.

12. Tap to show all public transport locations on the Map view or Satellite view.

13. Tap to show all bicycling routes on the Map view or Satellite view.

14. Tap to see the Terrain view.

15. Tap to launch the Google Earth app.

16. Tap to change the settings for Google Maps.

Changing Google Maps Settings

See the "Configure Google Maps Settings" task later in this chapter for more information about customizing Google Maps.

Get Directions

You can use Google Maps to get directions to where you want to go.

1. Tap the Directions icon.

2. Tap to set the starting point or leave it as Your Location (which is where you are now).

3. Tap to flip the start and end points.

4. Tap to use driving directions.

5. Tap to use public transportation.

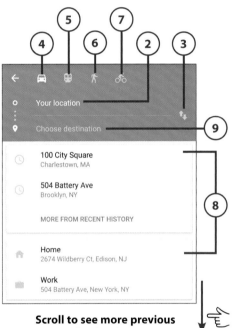

Scroll to see more previous destinations

Using Public Transportation

If you choose to use public transportation to get to your destination, you have two extra options to use. You can choose the type of public transportation to use, including bus, subway, train, or tram/light rail. You can also choose the best route (fewer transfers and less walking).

6. Tap to walk to your destination.

7. Tap to use bike paths (if available).

8. Tap to choose a previous destination. If you need to type the address of your destination, skip to step 9; if not, skip to step 10.

9. Type or speak the destination address.

10. Tap to make changes to your route, including choosing alternative routes to travel and modifying options (such as avoiding toll roads). If you are happy with the route as is, skip to step 14.

11. Tap to decide whether you want to avoid highways, tolls, or ferries.

12. Tap to choose an alternative route. If you choose an alternative route, the screen automatically returns to the Map view.

13. Tap to return to the Map view.

14. Tap to start the navigation.

15. Tap to see and select alternative routes as they appear on the map.

16. Tap the Menu icon to mute the voice guidance, show traffic conditions, choose the Satellite view, and show the entire route alternatives.

17. Tap to speak commands such as "Show alternative route," "How's traffic ahead?" or "What time will I get there?"

18. Tap to cancel the route.

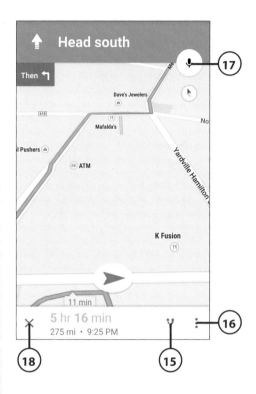

Configure Google Maps Settings

1. Swipe in from the left side of the screen.

2. Tap Settings.

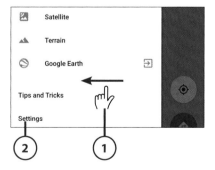

3. Tap to edit your work and home addresses. Telling Maps your home and work addresses is important for Google Now to work more efficiently, but it also helps you quickly plan new routes to work and home.

4. Tap to enable or disable the capability for your phone to report its location. You can also choose the accuracy of your location by changing the mode.

5. Tap to improve your location accuracy if you think that your phone is not reporting it correctly.

6. Tap to see addresses you have looked up and received directions to. You can also delete items in this list.

7. Tap to set the distance unit of measure. You can either set it to Automatic so that Google Maps adjusts it based on where you are on the planet, or you can manually set it.

8. Tap to change the volume level for the voice that speaks the turn-by-turn directions, and choose whether you want to always start navigation using the Tilt Map. The Tilt Map presents the view as if you are looking ahead from behind the navigation arrow.

9. Tap to save your changes and return to the main Google Maps screen.

9

← **Settings**

Edit home or work — **3**

Google location settings — **4**

Location accuracy tips — **5**

Maps history — **6**

Distance units — **7**
Automatic

Navigation settings — **8**

Shake to send feedback ☑

Use Offline Google Maps

Google Maps enables you to download small parts of the global map to your phone. This is useful if you are traveling and need an electronic map but cannot connect to a network to download it in real time.

1. Swipe in from the left of the screen.

2. Tap Your Places.

Tap to view previously saved maps

3. Scroll down to the bottom of the Your Places screen, and tap View All and Manage. If you have never saved an offline map, skip to step 4.

4. Tap Save a New Offline Map.

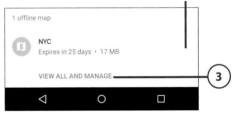

5. Pan around to find the area of the map you want to save offline.

6. Pinch to zoom out or unpinch to zoom in to the area of the map you want to save offline.

7. Tap Save when the area of the map fills the screen.

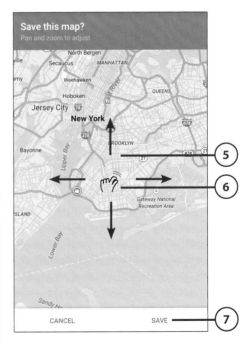

8. Type a name for the offline map and tap Save.

Name offline map

NYC

CANCEL   SAVE

⑧

How Much Map Can I Take Offline?

When selecting the area of the map to take offline, you are limited to approximately 100Mb of map data. You don't need to worry about the size of the data because if you have selected an area that is too large, Google Maps gives you a warning.

Your selection area is too large warning ———

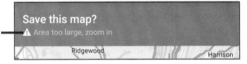

Save this map?
⚠ Area too large, zoom in
Ridgewood   Harrison

It's Not All Good

Offline Maps Have Limited Use

If you download some map data to your phone, you can use it to zoom in and out of the area you downloaded. You can also see where you are on the map in real time even though you have no network coverage. You cannot, however, get turn-by-turn directions within the downloaded map area. You also cannot search for things in the downloaded map area or see points of interest.

So how useful is having map data already downloaded to your phone? Because offline maps are already downloaded, they help when you have a network connection and are getting driving directions because Google Maps does not need to download the map data in real time, which could save you a lot of money in data roaming charges.

Tap to see Day, Week, or Schedule views

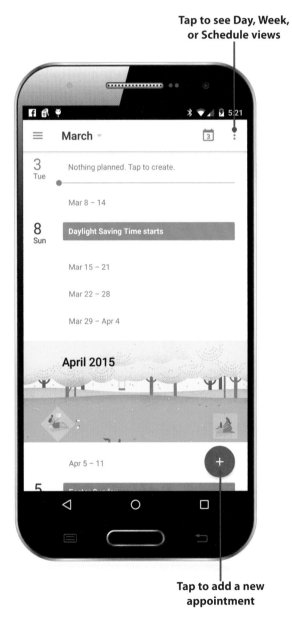

Tap to add a new appointment

In this chapter, you find out how to set the time, use the Clock app, and use the Calendar app. Topics include the following:

→ Synchronizing to the correct time
→ Working with the Clock app
→ Setting alarms
→ Working with the Calendar

Working with Date, Time, and Calendar

Your Android phone has a Clock app that you can use as a bedside alarm. The Calendar app synchronizes to your Google or corporate calendars and enables you to create meetings while on the road and to always know where your next meeting is.

Setting the Date and Time

Before you start working with the Clock and Calendar apps, you need to make sure that your Android phone has the correct date and time.

1. Pull down the Quick Settings Bar and tap Settings.

2. Tap Date & Time under the System section.

3. Check the box to have your phone's clock automatically updated by the cellular provider it is connected to. It is best to leave this enabled.

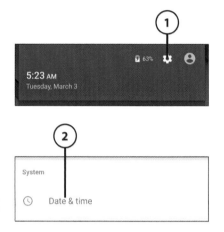

Does Network Time Sync Always Work?

Your phone updates its clock from the cellular service provider it is connected to. As you travel around the country or around the world, your time zone and clock are updated by the cellular providers you connect to. If you don't connect to cellular networks for a long time, don't worry; your clock remains accurate within a second or two.

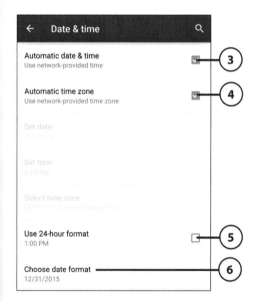

4. Check the box to have you phone's time zone automatically updated by the cellular provider it is connected to. It is best to leave this enabled.

5. Tap to enable or disable the use of 24-hour time format. This makes your Android phone represent time without a.m. or p.m. For example, 1:00 p.m. becomes 13:00.

6. Tap to change the way in which the date is represented. Leaving it set to Regional allows your phone to modify how the date is displayed based on the region you are in (using your GPS location), or you can manually set it.

Using the Clock App

The Clock app is preinstalled on your Android phone and provides the functionality of a bedside clock and alarm clock.

Navigate the Clock App

1. Tap the Clock icon.

2. Tap to manage alarms.

3. Rotate your Android phone onto its side to increase the size of the digits.

4. Tap the Menu icon to change the Clock app's settings and activate Night mode. When Night mode is active, the screen becomes dim until you touch it.

5. Tap to manage which extra cities you want to see time for.

6. Tap to use the Stopwatch function.

7. Tap to use the Timer function.

8. Tap to see the main Clock screen (the clock shown in the figure).

Manage Alarms

The Clock app enables you to set multiple alarms. These can be one-time alarms or recurring alarms. Even if you exit the Clock app, the alarms you set still trigger.

1. Tap to manage your alarms.

2. Tap the down arrow on an existing alarm to edit it.

3. Tap the On/Off switch to enable or disable an existing alarm.

4. Tap to add a new alarm.

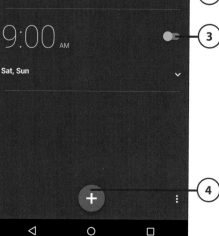

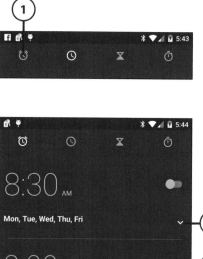

5. Drag the purple hour selector to the hour you want your alarm to trigger, or just tap the hour. After you select an hour, the screen automatically changes.

6. Tap the minutes past the hour you want your alarm to trigger. You can also drag the purple minute selector to choose a more precise time.

7. Tap AM or PM.

8. Tap OK to continue setting the alarm's extra settings.

Drag to be more precise

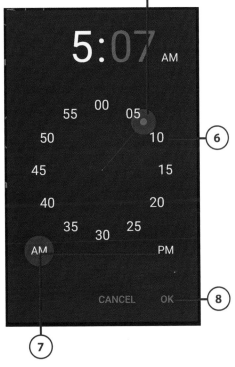

9. Tap to set a name for your alarm.

10. Tap to choose a ringtone to play when the alarm triggers.

11. Tap to choose whether you want your new alarm to be repeated. If the Repeat check box is selected, the days of the week appear below it. Select the days of the week you want your alarm to repeat.

12. Check the box if you want your phone to vibrate when the alarm triggers.

13. Tap the up arrow to save the alarm.

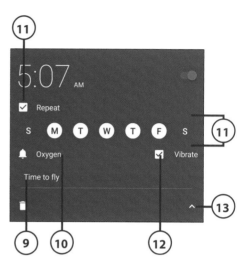

Adjust Clock Settings

Use the Settings to adjust the settings for the Clock app and control how all alarms function.

1. Tap the Menu icon.

2. Tap Settings.

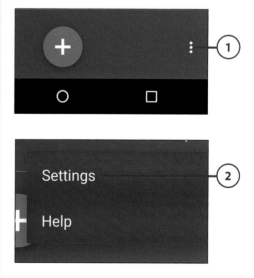

3. Tap to choose whether you want the clock style to be digital or analog.

4. Check the box if you want a new clock to be automatically added for your hometown when you travel.

5. Tap to change your home city's time zone.

6. Tap to set how long the alarm plays before it automatically silences itself. Your choices range from 5 minutes to 30 minutes; alternatively, you can set it to Never so that the alarm plays until you wake up and dismiss it.

7. Tap to set the duration of the snooze period. Your choices range between 1 and 30 minutes.

8. Tap to set the volume for all alarms.

9. Tap to set how the volume buttons behave if you press either of them when the alarm sounds. Your choices are Do Nothing, Snooze, and Dismiss.

10. Tap to save the settings and return to the main Clock screen.

⑩

← Settings ⋮

Clock

Style
Digital ③

Automatic home clock
While traveling in an area where the time is
different, add a clock for home ☑ ④

Home time zone
(GMT-5:00) Eastern Time ⑤

Alarms

Silence after
10 minutes ⑥

Snooze length
10 minutes ⑦

Alarm volume ⑧

Volume buttons
Do nothing ⑨

Using the Calendar App

The Calendar app enables you to synchronize all of your Google Calendars and calendars from other accounts like your work calendar and any personal calendars to your Android phone. You can accept appointments and create and modify appointments right on your phone. Any changes are automatically synchronized wirelessly back to each calendar service.

Get to Know the Calendar Main Screen

The main screen of the Calendar app shows a one-day, three-day, one-week, or a Schedule view of your appointments. The Calendar app also shows events from multiple calendars at the same time.

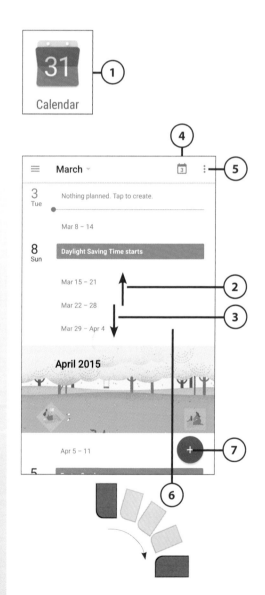

1. Tap the Calendar icon.

2. Swipe up to go backward in time.

3. Swipe down to go forward in time.

4. Tap to jump to today's date.

5. Tap to search the calendar for an event and choose the Calendar view. You can choose from the Schedule, Day, 3-Day, and Week views.

6. Rotate your phone into landscape orientation to see a seven-day week view. While in landscape orientation, you will always see a seven-day week view, no matter what view you have selected while in portrait orientation.

7. Tap to create a new calendar event.

What Is Schedule View?

Schedule view shows only your upcoming appointments/events in a list. It also shows the start of each new month, and represents each week of a month on one line. On some Android phones, the Schedule view is called the Agenda view.

Viewing the Month and Agenda Views at the Same Time

On some larger Android phones, the Calendar app also allows you to show a Month view. This shows the entire month on one screen. On Samsung phones, the Calendar app also has a view called Month and Agenda. This shows the entire month on the top half of the screen, plus the Agenda view on the bottom half of the screen. The Agenda view is the same as the Schedule view.

Month and Agenda view

Color-Coding Calendar Events

The Calendar app can display one calendar or many calendars at the same time. If you choose to display multiple calendars, events from each calendar are color-coded so that you can tell which events are from which calendar.

Adjust Calendar Settings

In this section, you find out how to tweak the Calendar app and how to choose which calendars are synchronized to your phone.

1. Swipe in from the left side of the screen to reveal the menu.

2. Tap a calendar under each account to show or hide it. When it is hidden, no events from that calendar are visible. Some account types can only have one calendar, whereas others can have many.

3. Tap Settings.

4. Tap General.

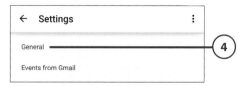

5. Tap to set the first day of your week. You can choose Saturday, Sunday, or Monday. You can also choose Locale Default so that the locale you have set in the device settings determines what the first day of the week is. See Chapter 10, "Customizing Your Android Phone," for more information on setting the device locale.

6. Tap to enable or disable using the current time zone that you and your phone are in when displaying the calendar and event times. When this is disabled, the time zone you choose in step 7 is always used instead of using the local time zone you are traveling in.

7. Tap to set the time zone you want your phone to use when you have disabled Use Device Time Zone in step 6.

8. Tap to enable or disable showing the week number. When enabled, the number of the week (between 1 and 52) is shown.

9. Tap to enable or disable showing events that you have already declined in your calendar.

10. Tap to set the default event length time when you create a new event in your Google Calendar. This setting does not affect non-Google calendars.

11. Scroll down for more settings.

← **General**   ⋮

Start of the week
Sunday   ⑤

Use device time zone   ⑥

Time zone
Eastern Standard Time GMT-5   ⑦

Show week number   ⑧

Show declined events   ⑨

Default event duration   ⑩

⑪

12. Tap to enable or disable receiving notifications for calendar events.

13. Tap to choose the ringtone to play when you are being alerted for calendar events.

14. Tap to set your Android phone to vibrate when a new calendar notification triggers.

15. Tap to edit your Quick Responses.

16. Tap the left arrow on the to of the screen (not shown) to save your changes and return to the main Settings screen.

17. Tap to choose whether you want events you receive in your Gmail account, such as flight details, concert details, or a restaurant reservation, to be automatically added to your calendar.

18. Tap to choose to whether to include birthdays from your Google account on your calendar.

19. Tap to choose whether you want to include national holidays on your calendar and to specify the country those holidays are in.

20. Tap a calendar to choose the color that it uses, and change the default notifications you want to receive when an event is coming up.

21. Tap to return to the Calendar app.

What Are Quick Responses?

Let's say that you are running late for a meeting. When the meeting reminder appears on your phone and you know that you are running late, you can choose to use a predefined Quick Response, such as "Be there in 10 minutes" or "Go ahead and start without me." When you choose a Quick Response, your phone emails that response to all meeting participants. See how to use Quick Responses in the next section.

Use Quick Responses

If you are running late to a meeting, you can send a Quick Response to all meeting participants directly from the meeting reminder.

1. Pull down the Notification panel.

2. Tap Email Guests in the event reminder.

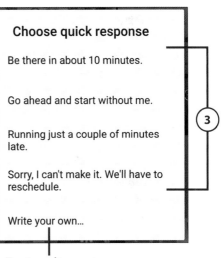

Expanding an Alert

If you do not see Email Guests, you can expand the alert by placing your two fingers on the alert and pulling down. Expanding alerts works on all kinds of alerts, including email alerts.

3. Tap one of the predefined Quick Responses to send it.

Tap to write your own custom email

Add a New Event

While you're on the road, you can add a new appointment or an event, and you can even invite people to it. Events you add synchronize to your Google and corporate calendars in real time (or when you next connect to a network).

1. Tap to add a new event. Alternatively, you can tap a day or time; then tap it again after the plus symbol appears.

2. Tap to enter the event title, people, and place where the event will take place.

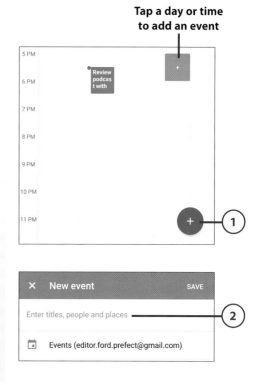

Tap a day or time to add an event

Using the Title, People, and Places Wizard

When you tap to enter title, people, and places in step 2, you are guided through the process. You start by entering the title for the event and then tap AT. This then allows you to tap previously used places or type new places. As you type the new address, your phone suggests places. When one pops up that is correct, simply tap it to add it. Finally you tap WITH. This allows you to choose previously used people from your Contacts, or you can type new names or email addresses. As you type, your phone finds matches in your Contacts, including corporate directories if you are adding a work event. Beware that the contacts you add here *are not* added as event invitees, and you need to add them as invitees later. After you are done, tap the green check mark on the bottom right of the screen.

3. Tap to change the account to use and the calendar to create the event in (if you use multiple calendars in each account).

4. Tap to mark the event as an all-day event.

5. Set the start date and time of the event.

6. Set the end date and time of the event.

7. Tap to select the time zone the meeting will be held in. This is useful if you will be traveling to the meeting in a different time zone.

8. Tap to set this as a recurring event. You can make it repeat daily, weekly, or monthly, but you can also set a meeting to repeat—for example, monthly but only every last Thursday.

9. Tap to change where the event will take place. This can be a full physical address, which is useful because most smartphones and tablets can map the address.

10. Scroll down for more event options.

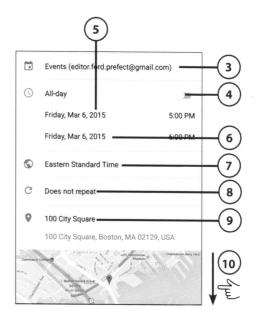

11. Tap an existing notification to edit it or remove it. You can be notified of the upcoming event on your phone as a pop-up notification, or by an email.

12. Tap to add a new notification.

13. Enter the event guests or event invitees. As you type names, your Android phone retrieves matching names from your Contacts and your corporate directory.

14. Tap to include an invitation to a Google Hangout that can be used during the event. This option is available only if you are creating an event in a Google Calendar.

15. Tap to change the color used to represent this event in your calendar.

16. Tap to add a note to the event invite.

17. Tap to add an attachment to the event invitation.

18. Tap to save the event. Any attendees you have added as invitees are automatically sent an event invitation.

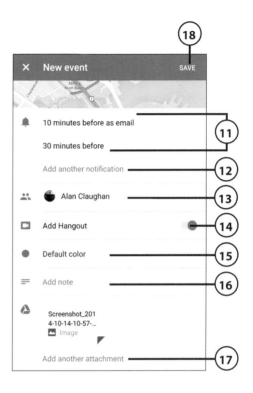

Using Additional Options for Corporate Calendars

If you are adding a new event on your corporate calendar that uses Microsoft Exchange, then you can choose whether the event is public (can be seen by anyone with permission to view your calendar) or private. You can also choose how your availability will appear during the time of the event. You can choose to display Available or Busy. When creating a new event in your corporate calendar, you cannot add a Google Hangout, and you are not able to attach files to the event invite.

Set privacy

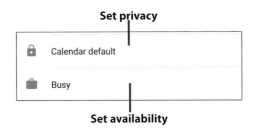

	Calendar default
	Busy

Set availability

Editing and Deleting Events

To edit or delete a calendar event, tap the event, and tap the Pencil icon to start editing it. While editing the event, you can tap Delete to delete the event, or simply make changes to the event. When you successfully delete an event that you previously accepted, the Calendar app sends an event decline notice to the event organizer. If you originally created the meeting and it has guests, a meeting cancellation notice is sent to them automatically when you delete it. Any changes you make to an event that has invitees are sent to them as an event update.

Respond to an Event Invitation

When you are invited to an event, you can choose your response right on your Android phone.

1. Tap to open the event invitation email. Any Google meeting invites are automatically moved to the Updates label in Gmail.

2. Tap Yes, Maybe, or No to indicate whether you will be attending.

3. For corporate invites, tap View In Calendar to view the meeting invite in the calendar.

Google invite

Invitation: Interview Schedule @ Wed Mar 4, 2015 6am - 7am (James Johnston) ⓘ Inbox

Craig Johnston
to me
5:30 AM View details

Interview Schedule		more details »
When	Wed Mar 4, 2015 6am – 7am Eastern Time	
Where	Starbucks 3699 McKinney Ave Dallas TX 75204 (map)	
Calendar	James Johnston	
Who	• Craig Johnston organizer	
	• James Johnston	

Going? Yes · Maybe · No   more options »

2

Corporate invite

Performance Review   Inbox ☆

C   Craig Johnston
to Ford
5:46 AM View details

Calendar invite   VIEW IN CALENDAR ─── **3**

Going?   YES   MAYBE   NO

When: Mar 4, 2015 10:00:00 AM
Where: 100 City Sq, Charlestown, MA 02129, United States

Reply   Reply all   Forward

2

Using an Alternative Event Response Method

You can also respond to event invitations directly in the Calendar app. When you receive an event invite in your Inbox, it also appears in your calendar with an outline. Tap the outlined event to open it and respond.

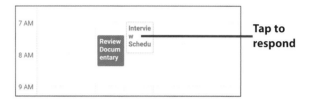

Tap to respond

It's Not All Good

What Happens to Canceled Events?

When an event organizer cancels an event, you would expect Gmail to handle it gracefully, but it doesn't. If the event you accepted was in your Google account, then the event cancellation is handled by your Google Calendar behind the scenes, you are notified that the event was canceled, and it is removed from your calendar. However, if the event you accepted was in your corporate calendar, when the event cancellation arrives, it just changes the event in your calendar by adding the word Canceled to the event title. The event is not removed and it remains on your calendar, unless you manually open it and delete it. If you don't delete it, when the time comes for the canceled meeting, your phone alerts you as if the event was still on.

Canceled Event: Interview Schedule @ Wed Mar 4, 2015 7am - 8am (James Johnston) Inbox

Craig Johnston
to me
6:00 AM View details

This event has been canceled and removed from your calendar.

Google event

10 AM
Canceled: Perfor
11 AM

Corporate event

See the top free apps

Search for apps

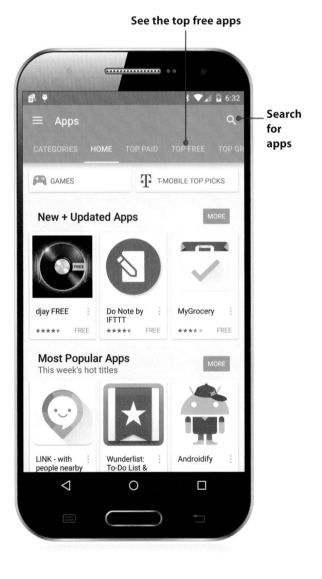

In this chapter, you find out how to purchase and use Android apps on your Android phone. Topics include the following:

→ Finding apps with Google Play
→ Purchasing apps
→ Keeping apps up to date

9

Working with Android Apps

Your Android phone comes with enough apps to make it a worthy phone. However, wouldn't it be great to use it to play games, update your Facebook and Twitter statuses, or even keep a grocery list? Well, you can use the Google Play Store to find these types of apps. Read on to discover how to find, purchase, and maintain apps.

Configuring Google Wallet

Before you start buying apps in the Google Play Store, you must first set up your Google Wallet account. If you plan to download only free apps, you do not need a Google Wallet account.

1. From a desktop computer or your Android phone, open the web browser and go to http://wallet.google.com. Sign in using the same Google account you used to set up your phone.

2. Click or tap Payment Methods.

3. Click or tap Add a Payment Method, and select either Add a Credit or Debit Card or Link a Bank Account.

4. Enter the required information to add your payment method (not shown).

Finding and Installing Apps

The Google Play Store is the place where you can search for and buy Android apps for your phone.

Navigate Google Play

1. Tap the Play Store icon.

Play Store

2. Swipe in from the left of the screen to see Google Play Store actions.

3. Tap to see any apps you have already purchased or downloaded.

4. Tap to select which Google account you want to use when you use the Google Play Store (if you have multiple Google accounts).

5. Tap to see your Wishlist. This list shows all apps, music, books, and movies that you have placed on your Wishlist.

6. Tap to see people you know on Google+ and see the apps they like.

7. Tap to redeem a Google Play Store gift card.

8. Tap to change the settings for the app. See the "Adjust Google Play Store Settings" section later in this chapter for more information.

9. Tap to manage payment methods and see your order history.

10. Tap anywhere outside the menu to return to the main screen.

11. Tap Apps to see only Android apps.

12. Swipe left and right to move between different top app lists, including Top Paid apps, Top Free apps, Top New apps, and so on.

13. Tap to search the Google Play Store. This searches everything available in the store, including apps, music, movies, and books.

14. Tap Categories to see apps organized by category.

Categories highlighted by Google

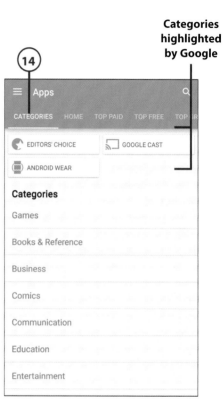

Install Free Apps

You don't have to spend money to get quality apps. Some of the best apps are free.

1. Tap the free app you want to install.

2. Scroll down to read about the app's features, reviews by other people who installed it, and information on the person or company who wrote it. Scrolling down also enables you to share a link to the app with friends.

3. Swipe left and right on the app screenshots to see all of them.

4. Tap Install to download and install the app.

5. Tap to accept the app permissions and proceed with the installation.

Beware of Permissions

Each time you download a free app or purchase an app from Google Play, you are prompted to accept the app permissions. App permissions are permissions the app wants to have to use features and functions on your Android phone, such as access to the wireless network or access to your phone log. Pay close attention to the kinds of permissions each app is requesting, and make sure they are appropriate for the type of functionality that the app provides. For example, an app that tests network speed will likely ask for permission to access your wireless network, but if it also asks to access your list of contacts, it might mean that the app is malware and just wants to steal your contacts.

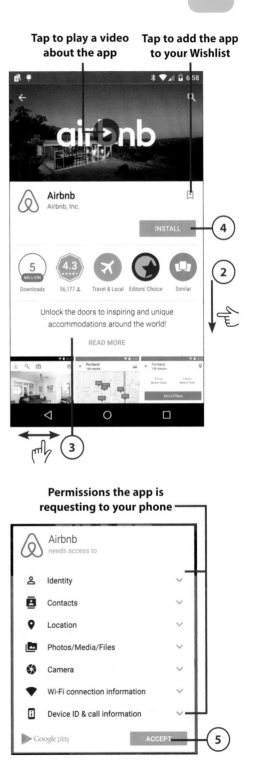

Tap to play a video about the app

Tap to add the app to your Wishlist

Permissions the app is requesting to your phone

Buy Apps

If an app is not free, the price displays next to the app icon. If you want to buy the app, remember that you need to have a Google Wallet account. See the "Configuring Google Wallet" section earlier in the chapter for more information.

1. Tap the app you want to buy.

What If the Currency Is Different?

When you browse apps in the Google Play Store, you might see apps that have prices in foreign currencies, such as in Euros. When you purchase an app, the currency is simply converted into your local currency using the exchange rate at the time of purchase.

2. Scroll down to read the app's features, reviews by other people who installed it, and information on the person or company who wrote it. Scrolling down also enables you to share a link to the app with friends.

3. Swipe left and right on the app screenshots to see all of them.

4. Tap the price to purchase the app.

Tap to add the app to your Wishlist

5. Tap to accept the app's requested permissions and proceed to the payment screen.

6. Tap Buy to purchase the app. You receive an email from the Google Play Store after you purchase an app. The email serves as your invoice.

Permissions the app is requesting to your phone

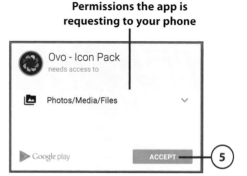

What Are In-App Purchases?

An app you install that is either free or costs little may offer extra features that you need to pay for later if you want to take advantage of them. For example, an app might provide ways to edit photos and add effects to them, but some effects are not available until you pay extra for them. This is considered an in-app purchase.

Tap to change the payment method

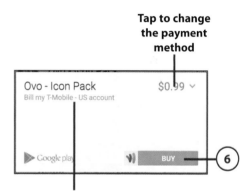

Some cellular providers allow billing your account for purchases

Manage Apps

Use the My Apps section of the Google Play Store to update apps, delete them, or install apps that you have previously purchased.

1. Swipe in from the left of the screen.

2. Tap My Apps.

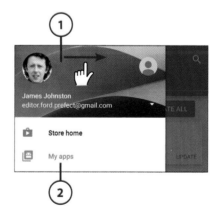

3. Tap All to see all apps that are currently installed or previously were installed on all your Android devices.

4. The word Free indicates a free app that you previously installed, but that is not installed on this phone. Tapping the app enables you to install it again for free.

5. The word Purchased indicates an app you previously purchased and installed, but that is no longer installed on this phone. Tapping the app enables you to install it again for free.

Tap to see only apps you have installed on this device

Tap to update all apps

Tap each app to update it

Allowing an App to Be Automatically Updated

When the developer of an app you have installed updates it to fix bugs or add new functionality, you are normally notified of this in the Notification panel so that you can manually update the app. However, you can choose to have the app automatically updated without your intervention. To do this, open the My Apps screen and tap the app you want to update automatically. Tap the Menu icon and make sure that Auto-Update is checked. Automatic updating is suspended if the developer of the app changes the permissions that the app requires to function. This enables you to review them and manually update the app.

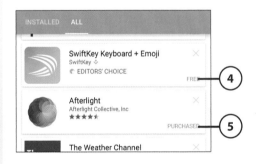

Tap to allow automatic updating

Uninstalling an App

When you uninstall an app, you remove the app and its data from your Android phone. Although the app no longer resides on your Android phone, you can reinstall it as described in steps 4 and 5 because the app remains tied to your Google account.

Tap to uninstall the app

Adjust Google Play Store Settings

1. Swipe in from the left of the screen.

2. Tap Settings.

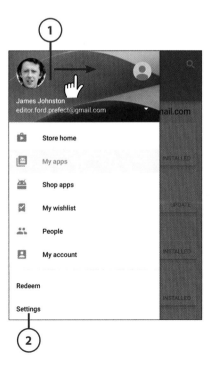

3. Check the box to enable notifications of app or game updates.

4. Tap to choose whether apps update themselves automatically, and if they do, over what networks. For example, you can set your apps to update automatically at any time, which means they will update over the cellular data network or Wi-Fi. Because cellular data charges apply, you may choose to have your apps only update over Wi-Fi.

5. Check the box to create an app shortcut icon to appear on your Home screen for each app that you install.

6. Tap to clear the Google Play search history. This removes the log of searches you have made in the Google Play Store on this device only.

7. Tap to adjust or set your content filtering level (for example, apps for everyone, or apps with medium maturity content, and so on). Use this to filter out apps, movies, music, or books that you deem to be inappropriate.

8. Tap to choose whether you want to enter your Google password for every Google Play Store purchase, or only every 30 minutes. If you choose 30 minutes, you can purchase content in the store for 30 minutes without retyping your password. After 30 minutes have elapsed, you are prompted to enter your password for your next purchase.

9. Tap the Back button to return to the main screen.

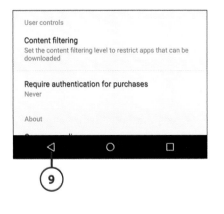

What Happens If I Accidentally Uninstall an App?

What if you accidentally uninstall an app or you uninstalled an app in the past but now decide you'd like to use it again? To get the app back, go to the My Apps view. Tap All, scroll to that app, and tap it. Tap Install to reinstall it.

Installing Apps Not from the Google Play Store

Although it is not recommended that you install Android apps not found in the Google Play Store, there is a way to do it. Open Settings, tap Security, and tap the switch next to Unknown Sources. If you use your phone for work, your company's Mobile Device Management (MDM) system will likely require this setting to be enabled so that it can push down the MDM Agent app and enable you to install your company's internal apps. Outside the requirement to install non-Google Play Store apps for your company, it is dangerous to install nonapproved apps. You open yourself up to apps that may contain malware, spyware, or viruses.

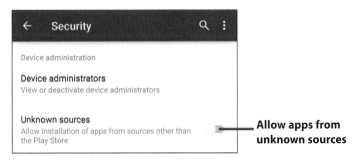

Allow apps from unknown sources

>>>Go Further
OTHER APP STORES

If you have a Samsung Galaxy phone, you will find an additional app store icon called Galaxy Apps. This is an app store run by Samsung that uses its own, separate method of billing; you cannot use your existing Google Wallet account. The Galaxy App store is separate, but it doesn't have anything that isn't already in the Google Play Store. The only difference is that apps made by Samsung may be updated more quickly in the Galaxy App store than the Google Play Store. Amazon.com has its own Android app store. Before you install it, you need to allow installing apps not from the Google Play Store (see the previous margin note). Then open the Chrome web browser and go to http://amazon.com/gp/mas/get/amazonapp. Like the Samsung app store, the Amazon.com app store has the same apps that are in the Google Play Store; however, sometimes Amazon.com offers the apps at a cheaper price than they are listed at in the Google Play Store.

See apps by category   Tap for apps and games

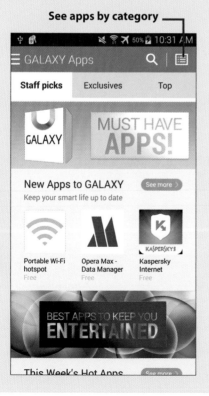

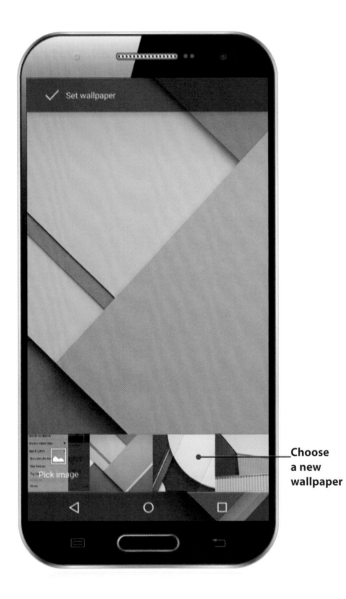

Choose
a new
wallpaper

In this chapter, you discover how to customize your Android phone to suit your needs and lifestyle. Topics include the following:

→ Using wallpapers and live wallpapers
→ Replacing the keyboard
→ Adding widgets
→ Changing sound and display settings
→ Setting region and language

Customizing Your Android Phone

Your Android phone arrives preconfigured to appeal to most buyers; however, you might want to change the way some of the features work or personalize it to fit your mood or lifestyle. Luckily, your Android phone is customizable.

Changing Your Wallpaper

Your Android phone comes preloaded with a cool wallpaper. You can install other wallpapers, use live wallpapers that animate, and even use pictures in the Photos app as your wallpaper. On most Android phones, the wallpaper you choose is used both on the Lock screen and the Home screen.

1. Touch and hold on the Home screen.

2. Tap Wallpapers. Use the steps in one of the following three sections to select your wallpaper.

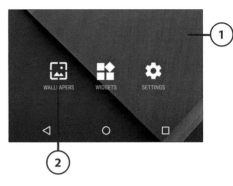

Select Wallpaper from Pictures in the Photos App

You can use any picture in your Photos app as a wallpaper.

1. Tap Pick Image. If you don't see the Pick Image box, swipe left to right over the images until it comes into view. On some phones that still use the Gallery app, this box might be labeled From Gallery.

2. Select the photo you want to use as your wallpaper.

3. Move the picture around on the screen so that it is positioned the way you want it.

4. Use the pinch-to-zoom gesture to zoom in or out of the picture.

5. Tap the check mark to set the photo as the wallpaper.

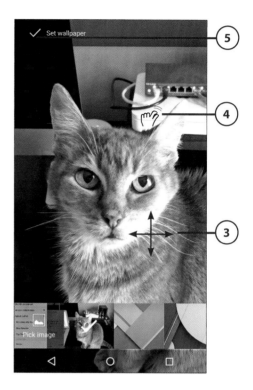

Use Live Wallpaper

Live wallpaper is wallpaper with some intelligence behind it. It can be a cool animation or even an animation that responds to things such as the music you are playing on your Android phone. Live wallpaper can also be something simple, such as the time. There are some cool live wallpapers in the Google Play Store that you can install and use, or you can stick with the selection already on your phone.

1. Swipe from right to left over the wallpaper thumbnails until you see live wallpaper thumbnails. Live wallpaper thumbnails have the wallpaper title displayed over the thumbnail.

2. Tap the live wallpaper you want to use.

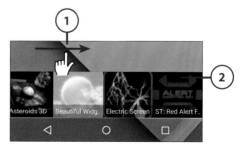

3. Tap Set Wallpaper to use the live wallpaper.

Finding More Wallpaper

You can find wallpaper or live wallpaper in the Google Play Store. Open the app using the Play Store icon and search for **wallpaper** or **live wallpaper**. Read more on how to use the Google Play Store in Chapter 9, "Working with Android Apps."

Some live wallpapers have settings

Choose Wallpaper

Unlike images from the Photos app, wallpaper images are designed to be used as wallpaper on your phone. Your phone comes preloaded with some wallpapers, but you can install more from the Google Play Store.

1. Scroll left and right to see all the wallpapers.

2. Tap a wallpaper to preview it.

3. Tap Set Wallpaper to use the wallpaper.

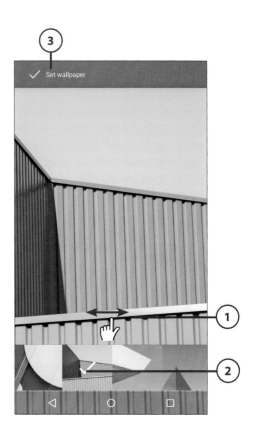

Choosing Wallpaper on the Lock Screen Versus the Home Screen

On most Android phones, when you make your wallpaper selection, it is used on the Lock screen and the Home screen. On some Android phones, such as Samsung phones, when you choose your wallpaper, you can decide whether the wallpaper you are choosing should be used on your Lock screen, Home screen, or both Lock and Home screens.

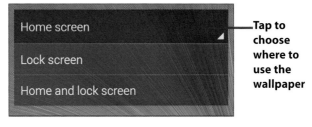

Tap to choose where to use the wallpaper

Changing Your Keyboard

If you find it hard to type on the standard Android phone keyboard, or you just want to make it look better, you can install replacement keyboards. You can download free keyboards or purchase replacement keyboards from the Google Play Store. Make sure you install a keyboard before following these steps.

Using Keyboard Setup Wizards

Most keyboards you install provide a setup wizard that walks you through the following steps, but in case the one you chose does not, you can use the following steps. You can also follow these steps to simply switch between already installed keyboards.

Choose a New Keyboard

Follow these steps to manually choose a new keyboard.

1. Tap Settings.

2. Tap Language & Input in the Personal section.

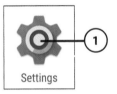
Settings

3. Tap Current Keyboard.

4. Tap Choose Keyboards.

5. Tap the On/Off slider next to a keyboard you have previously installed (SwiftKey, in this case) to enable that keyboard.

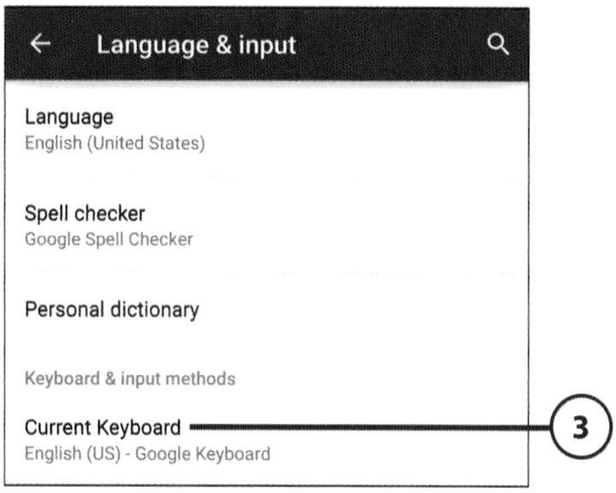

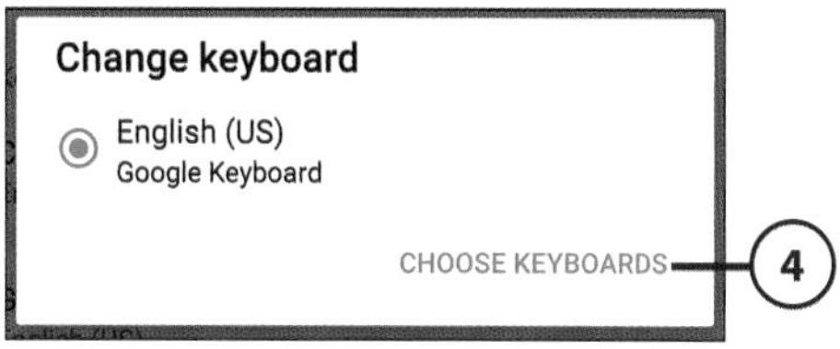

← **Language & input** 🔍

Language
English (United States)

Spell checker
Google Spell Checker

Personal dictionary

Keyboard & input methods

Current Keyboard ————————— ③
English (US) - Google Keyboard

Change keyboard

⊙ English (US)
 Google Keyboard

CHOOSE KEYBOARDS ———— ④

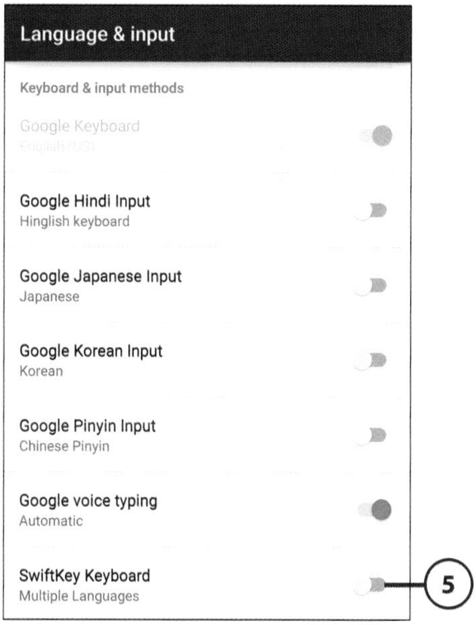

Language & input

Keyboard & input methods

Google Keyboard
English (US)

Google Hindi Input
Hinglish keyboard

Google Japanese Input
Japanese

Google Korean Input
Korean

Google Pinyin Input
Chinese Pinyin

Google voice typing
Automatic

SwiftKey Keyboard ———————— ⑤
Multiple Languages

6. Tap OK to change the input method and tap the Back button to return to the previous screen.

Researching Keyboards

When you choose a different keyboard in step 5, the Android phone gives you a warning telling you that nonstandard keyboards have the potential for capturing everything you type. Do your research on any keyboards before you download and install them.

7. Tap Current Keyboard again to change the default keyboard to the one you have just enabled.

8. Tap the name of your new keyboard to select it.

What Can You Do with Your New Keyboard?

Keyboards you buy in the Google Play Store can do many things. They can change the key layout, change the color and style of the keys, offer different methods of text input, and even enable you to use a T9 predictive input keyboard that you may have become used to when using an old "dumb phone" that had only a numeric keypad.

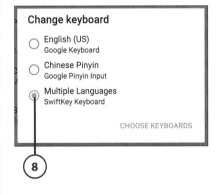

Attention

This input method may be able to collect all the text you type, including personal data like passwords and credit card numbers. It comes from the app SwiftKey Keyboard. Use this input method?

CANCEL   OK — ⑥

←   **Language & input**   🔍

Language
English (United States)

Spell checker
Google Spell Checker

Personal dictionary

Keyboard & input methods

Current Keyboard ——————— ⑦
English (US) - Google Keyboard

Change keyboard

○ English (US)
   Google Keyboard

○ Chinese Pinyin
   Google Pinyin Input

◉ Multiple Languages
   SwiftKey Keyboard

CHOOSE KEYBOARDS

⑧

Adding Widgets to Your Home Screens

Some apps that you install come with widgets that you can place on your Home screen. These widgets normally display real-time information, such as stocks, weather, time, and Facebook feeds. Your Android phone also comes preinstalled with some widgets. This section shows how to add and manage widgets.

Add a Widget

Your Android phone should come preinstalled with some widgets, but you might also have some extra ones that were added when you installed other apps. Here is how to add those widgets to your Home screen.

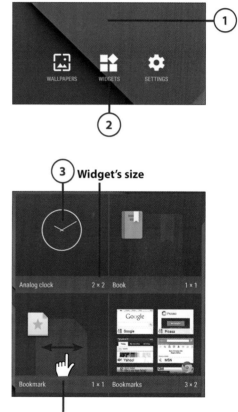

1. Touch and hold an empty area on the Home screen.

2. Tap Widgets.

3. Touch and hold a widget to move it to the Home screen. Keep holding the widget as you move to step 4.

Widget's size

Scroll left and right to see all widgets

4. Position the widget where you want it on the Home screen.

5. Drag the widget between panes of the Home screen.

6. Release your finger to place the widget. Some widgets require extra setup, so when you release them they may prompt you for more information.

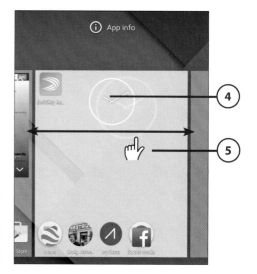

How Many Widgets Can Fit on a Home Screen Pane?

Each pane of the Home screen is divided into four blocks across and four blocks down. Notice that each widget shown in the figure for step 3 shows its size in blocks across and down. From that, you can judge whether a widget is going to fit on the Home screen pane you want it to be on, and the information also helps you position the widget in step 4. If the widget won't fit on a Home screen pane, simply drag it onto another pane, or if all panes are full, drag the widget to the right-most pane to create a new Home screen pane.

Remove and Move a Widget

Sometimes you want to remove a widget, resize it, or move it around.

1. Touch and hold the widget until you see a faint shadow of the widget, but continue to hold the widget.

2. Drag the widget to the word Remove to remove it.

3. Drag the widget around the screen, or drag it between the Home screen panes to reposition it.

4. Release the widget.

Resizing Widgets

Some widgets can be resized. To resize a widget, touch and hold the widget until you see a blue shadow and then release it. If the widget can be resized, you see the resizing borders. Drag them to resize the widget. Tap anywhere on the screen to stop resizing.

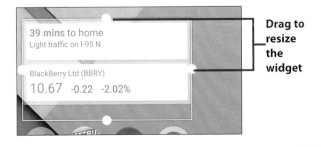

Drag to resize the widget

Customizing Language

If you move to another country or want to change the language used by your Android phone, you can do so with a few taps.

Choose a Different Language

Follow these steps to choose a new language on your phone.

1. Tap Settings.

2. Tap Language & Input in the Personal section.

3. Tap Language.

4. Tap the language you want to switch to.

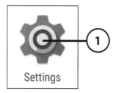

Settings

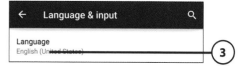

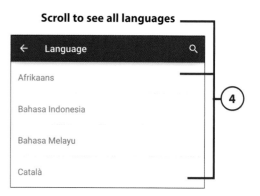

Adjusting Accessibility Settings

Your Android phone includes built-in settings to assist people who might otherwise have difficulty using some features of the device. The Android phone has the capability to provide alternative feedback such as vibration, sound, and even spoken feedback.

Manage Accessibility Settings

Follow these steps to manage your Accessibility settings.

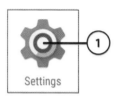

1. Tap Settings.

2. Tap Accessibility in the System section.

3. Tap to enable or disable TalkBack. When enabled, TalkBack speaks everything, including menus.

4. Tap to enable or disable Switch Access.

5. Tap to enable or disable captions and their appearance.

6. Tap to enable or disable the magnification gestures. When enabled, you can zoom any screen by triple-tapping the screen. When zoomed, you can pan around with your fingers.

7. Tap to enable or disable large text. When enabled, all text displayed appears in a larger size.

8. Tap to enable or disable High Contrast Text. This feature is experimental right now, but it makes text easier to read. For example, any white text automatically gets a black outline to make it easier to read.

9. Tap to enable a feature that allows you to press your phone's Power button to end calls.

10. Tap to enable automatic screen rotation. When disabled, the screen does not rotate between Portrait and Landscape modes.

11. Scroll down for more settings.

What Is Switch Access?

Switch Access is designed for people with limited mobility. After you connect your external switch hardware via Bluetooth, you can enable and configure the Switch Access feature. You can teach Android to do certain things based on switch combinations. Read more about Switch Access at https://support.google.com/accessibility/android/answer/6122836?hl=en.

12. Tap to enable or disable the feature that causes your phone to speak your passwords as you type them.

13. Tap to enable or disable a shortcut that allows you to enable accessibility features using two gestures.

14. Tap to choose which text-to-speech service to use and what language it uses. If you don't want to use the Google service, you first need to install additional text-to-speech apps from the Google Play Store before attempting to select them here.

15. Tap to change how long you have to hold when you perform a touch and hold on the screen.

16. Tap to enable color inversion. When enabled, your phone uses the negative of each color, which can help people with vision disabilities.

17. Tap to enable or disable color space correction for color blindness. After enabling this feature, you can choose the color blindness correction mode to use.

18. Tap to save your settings and return to the previous screen.

(18)

← **Accessibility**

High contrast text
(Experimental)

Power button ends call

Auto-rotate screen

Speak passwords — (12)

Accessibility shortcut — (13)
Off

Text-to-speech output — (14)

Touch & hold delay — (15)
Short

Display

Color inversion — (16)
(Experimental) May affect performance

Color correction — (17)
Off

Managing Text-to-Speech

By default, your Android phone uses the Google Text-to-Speech service to speak any text that you need to read. You can install other text-to-speech software by searching for it in the Google Play Store. When it's installed, it shows as a choice for text-to-speech output.

Extra text-to-speech service installed from the Google Play Store

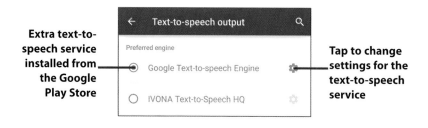

Tap to change settings for the text-to-speech service

Modifying Sound and Notification Settings

You can change the volume for games, ringtones, and alarms; change the default ringtone and notification sound; and control what system sounds are used.

Modify Sound and Notification Settings

Follow these steps to manage your sound and notification settings.

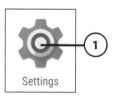

1. Tap Settings.

2. Tap Sound & Notification in the Device section.

3. Move the slider to adjust the volume for games and media, such as videos and music.

4. Move the slider to adjust the volume for alarms.

5. Move the slider to adjust the volume of the ringtone that plays when you receive incoming calls.

6. Tap to vibrate your phone when there is an incoming call, in addition to playing the ringtone.

7. Tap to manage your interruptions from notifications like messages, calls, and events, and whether you always want to be notified or only during specific hours.

8. Tap to choose what ringtone plays when you receive incoming calls.

9. Tap to choose the default ringtone that plays when you receive a new notification.

10. Tap to manage whether to play sounds when you lock your phone or if you want your phone to play the dialpad keys sounds when using the phone. You can also choose whether you want it to play a sound when you touch the screen or vibrate when you touch it.

11. Scroll down for Notification settings.

12. Tap to manage whether notifications are displayed on the Lock screen.

13. Tap to manage whether notifications are displayed on a per-app basis, and choose whether an app can send notifications when your phone is set to receive priority notifications only.

14. Tap to manage which apps have access to the notifications. Some apps may need to have access to notifications so they can pass them along to external devices like smartwatches.

15. Tap to save your changes and return to the previous screen.

←   Sound & notification   🔍

15

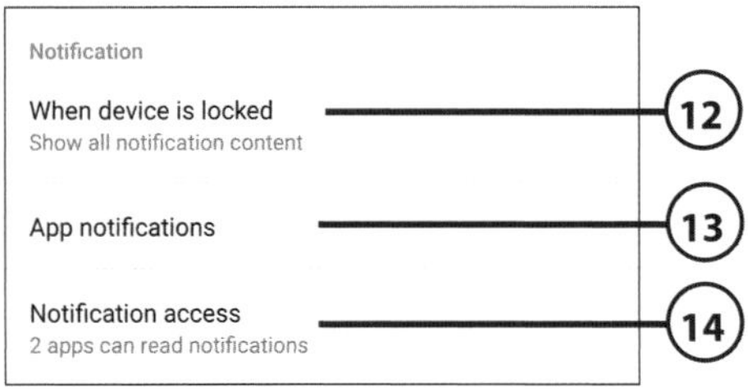

Notification

When device is locked — 12
Show all notification content

App notifications — 13

Notification access — 14
2 apps can read notifications

Managing Interruptions

You can manage how you are interrupted by notifications by tapping When Calls and Notifications Arrive and choosing either Always Interrupt, Priority Only, or Never. This enables you to manually set when you are notified. If you choose Priority Only, you can choose what types of notifications you want to receive and even who you want to receive calls from. Finally, you can set your downtime, which is normally while you are asleep. When you set your downtime, your phone automatically switches to receiving only priority notifications during that time. This is great for when you go to sleep at night; your phone will silence all notifications except for calls from certain people and messages, events, and reminders if you have them enabled.

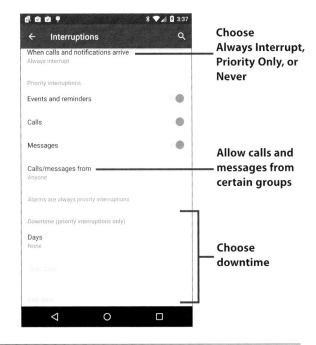

Choose Always Interrupt, Priority Only, or Never

Allow calls and messages from certain groups

Choose downtime

Changing Display Settings

You can change the screen brightness or set it to automatic, change the wallpaper, change how long to wait before your Android phone goes to sleep, change the size of the font used, and change whether to use the Pulse notification light.

1. Tap Settings.

2. Tap Display in the Device section.

3. Tap to manually change the screen brightness.

4. Tap to enable adaptive brightness. When enabled, your Android phone uses the built-in light sensor to adjust the brightness based on the light levels in the room.

5. Tap to change the wallpaper. See more about how to change the wallpaper earlier in this chapter.

6. Tap to choose how many minutes of inactivity must pass before your Android phone puts the screen to sleep.

7. Tap to enable Daydream mode and choose what happens when your phone daydreams. It can show the clock, cycle through colors, or show pictures from the Photos app.

8. Tap to enable or disable Ambient Display. When enabled, your phone shows a dimly lit monochrome screen when new notifications arrive, or when you pick it up and there are waiting notifications.

9. Tap to choose the font size of all text used.

10. Tap to choose whether the contents of the screen rotate when you rotate your phone.

11. Tap to use Miracast to mirror your phone's screen on a TV or other device that has the Chromecast dongle or Nexus Player attached.

12. Tap to save your changes and return to the previous screen.

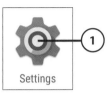

Settings

Settings

Device

Display 2

12

Display 3

Brightness level 3

Adaptive brightness 4
Optimize brightness level for available light

Wallpaper 5

Sleep 6
After 2 minutes of inactivity

Daydream 7
Clock

Ambient display 8
Wake screen when device picked up or notifications arrive

Font size 9
Normal

When device is rotated 10
Rotate the contents of the screen

Cast screen 11

Using the Cast Screen

If you own a Google Chromecast or a Google Nexus Player (or are in an area where there is a Chromecast or Nexus Player), then you can use the Cast Screen feature to mirror your phone's screen on the TV. Your phone must be on the same Wi-Fi network as the Chromecast or Nexus Player for this feature to work. On some devices—such as those from HTC—the Cast Screen section is under Settings, Wireless & Networks, Media Output. On some devices—such as those from Samsung—Cast Screen sometimes doesn't work.

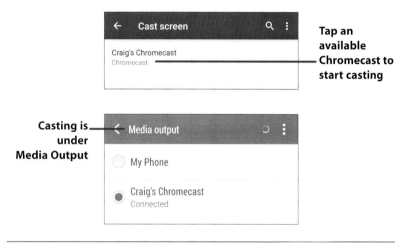

Tap an available Chromecast to start casting

Casting is under Media Output

Changing Security Settings

The security of the data on your phone is important. You may opt to set a device lock password or even encrypt the data that resides on your phone.

1. Tap Settings.

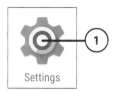

2. Tap Security in the Personal section.

3. Tap to set how your phone is unlocked. Your can choose Swipe (which simply requires that you swipe across the screen), Pattern Lock (which uses an onscreen pattern instead of a passcode), PIN (which is a numeric passcode), or Password (which is a password made up of all types of characters).

4. Tap to choose how long after your phone goes to sleep (when the screen goes blank) it will lock.

5. Tap to choose whether pressing the Power button immediately locks your phone.

6. Tap to choose whether you want your owner information displayed on your phone's Lock screen, and what information to show.

7. Tap to enable and manage the Smart Lock feature that allows you to keep your phone unlocked when it detects a particular Bluetooth or NFC device, when it detects that it is in a specific location, or when it sees your face.

8. Tap to encrypt the data on your phone. When you encrypt, unless you have a Samsung phone, the encryption is irreversible. After your phone's data is encrypted, any time you power down your phone and power it up again, you need to enter a decryption passcode.

9. Scroll down for more settings.

Settings

Personal

Location

Security — ②

Screen security

Screen lock
PIN — ③

Automatically lock
5 seconds after sleep, except when kept unlocked by Smart Lock — ④

Power button instantly locks
Except when kept unlocked by Smart Lock — ⑤

Owner info — ⑥

Smart Lock — ⑦

Encryption

Encrypt phone — ⑧
Encrypted

⑨

Using Your Fingerprint

Some Android phones, such as those sold by Samsung, include a physical fingerprint reader. You can register one or more fingerprints and then choose to use them to unlock your phone, pay for things on PayPal, and log in to websites instead of typing unlock codes or login names and passwords.

< Finger Scanner

SETTINGS

Fingerprint manager ——————— **Register**
1 fingerprint is registered. **fingerprints**

Change backup password

FEATURES

Screen lock
Swipe

Web sign-in **Choose**
Off **when to**
use them
Verify Samsung account
Off

Pay with PayPal

---

10. Tap to set or manage a lock on your phone's SIM card. Use this if you want to lock the SIM card in case it is ever stolen out of your phone.

11. Tap to make passwords visible onscreen as you type them.

12. Tap to manage device administrators.

13. Tap to allow your phone to accept apps not found in the Google Play Store.

14. Scroll down for more settings.

SIM card lock

Set up SIM card lock ———————— ⑩

Passwords

Make passwords visible ● ⑪

Device administration

Device administrators ———————— ⑫
View or deactivate device administrators

Unknown sources
Allow installation of apps from sources other than ● ⑬
the Play Store

Credential storage

Storage type ⑭
Hardware-backed

15. The Storage Type item is strictly informational. It indicates whether your phone supports storing your private encryption keys in the hardware (hardware-backed) or in software only.

16. Trusted Credentials allows you to view and select or deselect Trusted Credentials that the Android system uses, and the ones you may be using.

17. Tap to install certificates from your phone's storage. This assumes you previously saved the certificate to storage.

18. Tap to enable or disable Trust Agents. Today, there is only one Trust Agent called Smart Lock, but in the future there could be other options created by other software vendors.

19. Tap to enable or disable Screen Pinning, which allows you to "pin" an app so that the person using it cannot exit the app.

20. Tap to manage which apps running on your phone are allowed to collect app usage information about all apps you have installed. This usage information includes how often each app is run, how long it sits in the foreground (active on your screen), and how long it sits in the background (still running but not visible).

21. Tap to save your changes and return to the main Settings screen.

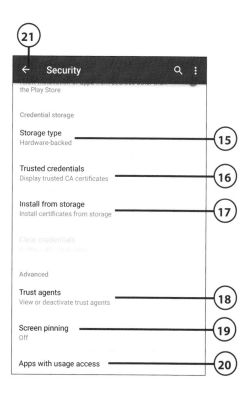

What Is a Device Administrator?

Device administrators are apps that you have given permission to administer your phone. One of the device administrators is the Android Device Manager. This enables you to log in to www.google.com/android/devicemanager on a desktop computer and reset your device password or erase all your device's data if it has been stolen. If you enroll your phone in your company's Enterprise Mobile Management (EMM) system, like those made by AirWatch or MobileIron, those systems also add a device administrator.

UNDERSTANDING SMART LOCK

Your phone allows trust agents. Trust agents are services that you and your phone trust are safe and are allowed to perform functions that override regular Android functionality. Today, there is only one trust agent called Smart Lock. Smart Lock overrides your phone's screen-lock functionality as long as it detects that you have a Bluetooth or NFC device close (for example, it detects your smartwatch or your car's Bluetooth), you are in a specific geographic location, or it is able to recognize your face using the front-facing camera when you pick up the phone. To set up Smart Lock, tap Smart Lock, as shown in step 7, and follow the steps to configure either a trusted Bluetooth or NFC device, a trusted geographic location, a trusted face, or a combination of these things to keep your phone unlocked.

← Trusted devices

Gear Live 10C9
Connected

+ Add trusted device ———— **Add a trusted device**

>>>Go Further

PINNING APPS

When you enable screen pinning in step 19, you are enabling a feature that allows you to "pin" an app to the screen. When an app is pinned to the screen, you cannot exit the app, go back to the Home screen, pull down the Notification panel or Quick Settings Bar, or do anything other than interact with the app. When you pin an app, you are asked whether you want to require a passcode to unpin the app. You can only pin the last app you ran; you can't select just any app. To pin an app to the screen, first run the app so that it is the most recently used app. Tap the Overview button, and slide the app up so that you can see the Pin icon. Tap the Pin icon to pin the app to the screen. To exit Pinned mode, touch and hold the Back and Overview buttons at the same time. Pinning an app to the screen is a quick way to allow someone to use your phone without letting them access anything other than the app they should be using.

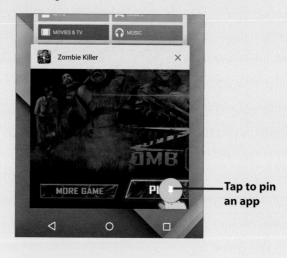

Tap to pin an app

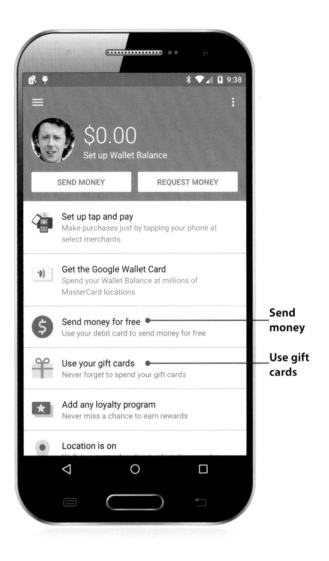

Send money

Use gift cards

In this chapter, you find out how to set up
Google Wallet on your phone. Topics include
the following:

→ Setting up Google Wallet
→ Using Google Wallet

Google Wallet

Your Android phone has a built-in Near Field Communications (NFC)
radio, which, among other things, enables you to pay for things
such as groceries by holding your phone close to the reader at the
checkout counter. Currently in the United States you can use Google
Wallet to pay for anything in stores where MasterCard® PayPass™ is
accepted.

Downloading Google Wallet

Your Android phone might not come preinstalled with Google Wallet.
If it isn't, search for Google Wallet in the Google Play Store and install
it. See Chapter 9, "Working with Android Apps," for more information
on installing Android apps.

Install
Google Wallet

Setting Up Google Wallet

Before using Google Wallet on your phone, you need to set a PIN to secure it.

1. Tap to launch Google Wallet. Google Wallet launches and starts the setup using the primary Google account on your phone.

2. Type a four-digit PIN to secure the Google Wallet app on your phone. After typing a four-digit PIN, the screen automatically advances.

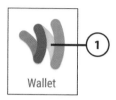

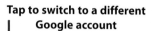

Tap to switch to a different Google account

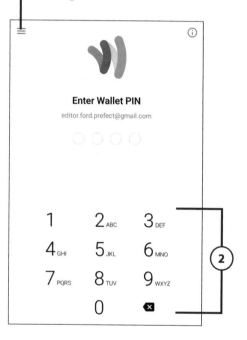

Adding Methods of Payment

Before you can use Google Wallet to wirelessly pay for items at the checkout counter, you need to set it up and select methods of payment. You may have already set up payment methods in Google Wallet if you have purchased items in the Google Play Store. If you have, those payment methods are already available in the Google Wallet app.

Add a Credit Card or Checking Account

Perform these steps from the main Google Wallet screen to add a credit card or debit card as a method of payment.

1. Swipe in from the left of the screen.

2. Tap Cards & Accounts.

3. Tap an existing payment method to edit it.

4. Tap to link a checking account to your Google Wallet.

5. Tap to add a new credit or debit card to your Google Wallet.

6. Tap to save your payment methods and return to the main Google Wallet screen.

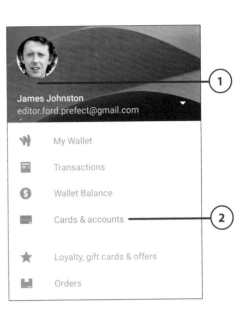

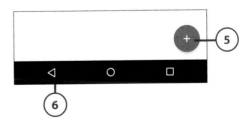

Setting Up Tap and Pay

Now that you have added your credit, debit, and checking accounts as methods of payment, you need to set up Tap and Pay, which makes it possible for you to tap your phone at the checkout to pay for items. To enable Tap and Pay, swipe in from the left of the screen and tap Settings. Select Tap and Pay. Google Wallet does one last check on your payment methods and then you're set. See the "Using Google Wallet" section later in the chapter to learn how to use Tap and Pay.

← **Settings**

Google Wallet Card
Order the Google Wallet Card

Set up Tap
and Pay

Tap and Pay
Setup tap and pay

Using Loyalty and Gift Cards

Instead of carrying around your loyalty and gift cards, you can add them to Google Wallet. After a card is in Google Wallet, you can bring up the card at the checkout counter and the cashier can scan the onscreen bar code.

Add an Existing Gift Card

When you add gift cards to Google Wallet, you take pictures of the front and back of your gift cards, enter the merchant information, and enter your balance. This enables you to leave the physical cards at home. When a gift card is added, you get notifications when you are near a location where you can use it.

1. Swipe in from the left of the screen.

2. Tap Loyalty, Gift Cards & Offers.

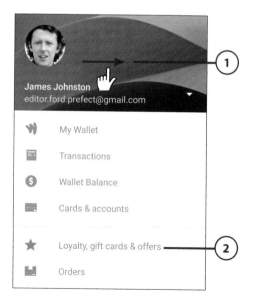

James Johnston
editor.ford.prefect@gmail.com

My Wallet

Transactions

Wallet Balance

Cards & accounts

Loyalty, gift cards & offers

Orders

3. Tap the plus symbol to add cards.

4. Tap Add Gift Card to add a new gift card. Google Wallet walks you through the steps of taking a picture of the front and back of the gift card, typing in your current balance, entering the merchant name, and entering your gift card account number.

Using Gift Cards

To use your gift cards, open Google Wallet and open Loyalty, Gift Cards & Offers. Tap a gift card to use. Google Wallet sets the brightness level on the screen very high and displays the card information—including a bar code for the account number—so that the store clerk can scan the bar code. If that option is not available, the clerk can simply read the information about your gift card on the screen.

Featured loyalty programs

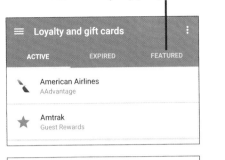

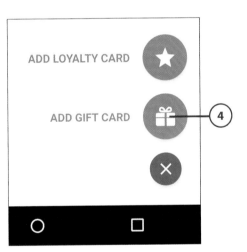

Add an Existing Loyalty Card

You can add your store loyalty cards to Google Wallet so that you can use them at the store without having to carry around the actual physical reward card. After you add a loyalty program card, you can be alerted when you are near a location where the card can be used, and in some cases your points balance can be automatically updated in Google Wallet.

1. Swipe in from the left of the screen.

2. Tap Loyalty, Gift Cards & Offers.

3. Tap the plus symbol.

4. Tap Add Loyalty Card.

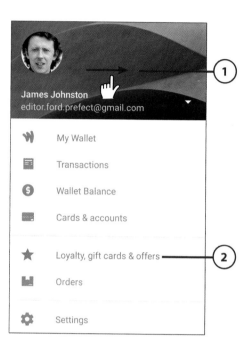

See loyalty programs
you may want to join

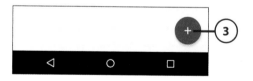

5. Take a photo of the back of your loyalty card. The screen automatically advances after you align the camera angle and position so that the card is directly below and the edges are close to the corners of the photo area. Each edge turns blue when the card is correctly aligned.

Why Skip the Card Photos?

Although it is good to have photos of the front and back of your loyalty card, it is not required, and this is why you can tap Skip Photos. The one required piece of information is your loyalty card number.

6. Take a photo of the front of your loyalty card. The screen automatically advances after you align the camera angle and position so that the card is directly below and the edges are close to the corners of the photo area. Each edge turns blue when the card is correctly aligned.

Blue indicates this edge is correctly aligned

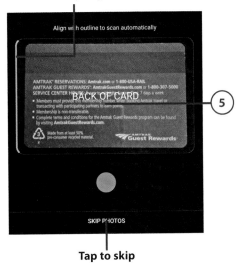

Tap to skip

Tap to skip

7. Tap Next to continue if the captured front and back of your loyalty card look good; otherwise, tap the Back button to take another photo of the card.

8. Start typing the name of the company that the loyalty program is with. When you see the company's name in the list, tap the name to add it. The screen automatically advances. This example uses an Amtrak Guest Rewards card, so the company is Amtrak.

9. Enter the name of the loyalty program if it hasn't been automatically filled in for you. This example uses the Amtrak Guest Rewards program, so type **Guest Rewards**.

10. Enter your loyalty program account number.

11. Tap if there is a barcode on your loyalty card. When you scan the barcode, the account number is automatically filled in.

12. Check this box if the loyalty card you are adding belongs to someone else.

13. Tap to save your loyalty card.

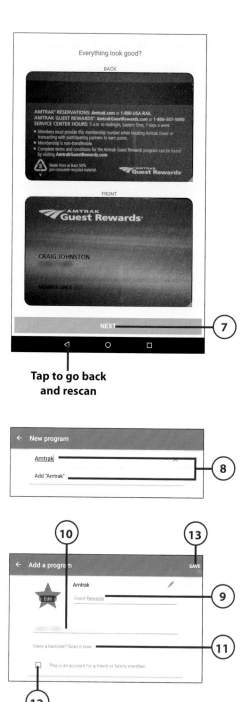

Tap to go back and rescan

Using Google Wallet

After you have Google Wallet set up on your Android phone, you can use it to pay for items at the checkout counter.

1. First make sure that you can use Google Wallet at the checkout counter by looking for the symbols shown in the figure.

2. When it is time to pay, press the Power button on the side of your phone to wake it up. Some phones do not require that you first press the Power button to wake them up; these phones wake up when they detect the signal from the reader when you perform step 3.

3. Tap your phone on the reader that has the symbols shown in the figure for step 1.

4. You might be prompted to enter your Google Wallet PIN.

5. Remove your phone from the reader after you hear the confirmation tone.

Changing Google Wallet Settings

You can tweak the way Google Wallet behaves on your phone.

1. Swipe in from the left of the screen.

2. Tap Settings.

3. Tap to order a physical Google credit card from Google. This credit card allows you to use your Google Wallet Balance in the real world by just swiping your card.

4. Tap to set up Tap and Pay. You need to set up Tap and Pay before you can use Google Wallet at the checkout counter. Setting up Tap and Pay is simply choosing which method(s) of payment you want to use when you check out.

5. Tap to manage notifications from Google Wallet. You can choose to be notified when you are near a merchant where you can use one of your gift or loyalty cards, when there is an update to one of your gift or loyalty cards, or when someone sends you money.

6. Tap to choose whether you want to receive email updates from Google Wallet.

7. Tap to change your Google Wallet PIN and select how often you are required to enter the PIN. You can set the PIN timeout to 15 minutes, 1 day, or never. Setting it to 1 day or never is more convenient but may also be unsafe if your phone is lost.

8. Tap to show real-time order information for items you have purchased with Google Wallet.

9. Tap to view your monthly Google Wallet statements.

10. Tap to save your changes and return to the main Google Wallet screen.

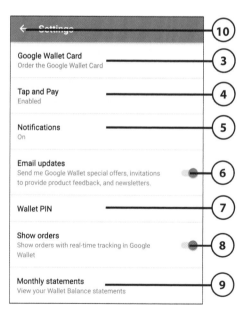

What Is Google Wallet Balance?

Your Google Wallet Balance goes hand in hand with your Google Wallet Card. When you order a Google Wallet Card or you tap your Google Balance, you are asked to verify your identity. After the verification, you receive a physical credit card that is tied to the Google Wallet Balance. You can add to the Google Wallet Balance by transferring money from your existing bank accounts or by accepting money sent to you via Google Wallet.

Sending and Receiving Money

Use your Google Wallet to send money to friends and family. You can also request money from others.

Send Money

1. Tap Send Money.

2. Start typing the person's name. If a matching name appears, tap it to select it and continue.

3. Type the amount to send.

4. Type a short message to the person you are sending the money to.

5. Tap Review.

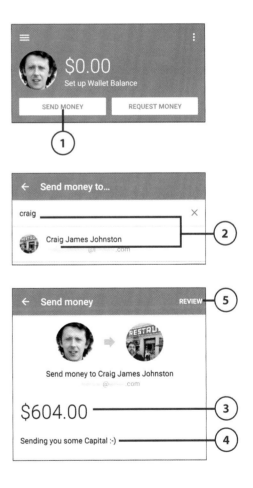

6. Tap to change the credit card or checking account being used to send the money from.

7. Tap Send.

Sending and Receiving Money

When you have a positive Google Balance, you can send money to your friends and family using Google Wallet. If the person you are sending money to does not have a Google Wallet account, the person first needs to set one up to receive the money. You can either use the Google Wallet app to send money, or, if you use Gmail in a desktop web browser, you can attach money just like you would attach a picture. If someone owes you money, you can request that they send you money. Again, if the other person does not have a Google Wallet account, he or she needs to set one up before sending you the money.

Request Money

1. Tap Request Money.

2. Start typing the person's name. If a matching name appears, tap it to select it and continue.

3. Type the amount that you are requesting.

4. Type a short message to the person you are requesting the money from.

5. Tap Send to send the money request.

Both Parties Need Google Wallet

When you have a positive Google Balance, you can send money to your friends and family using Google Wallet. If the person you are sending money to does not have a Google Wallet account, the person first needs to set one up to receive the money. You can either use the Google Wallet app to send money, or, if you use Gmail in a desktop web browser, you can attach money just like you would attach a picture. If someone owes you money, you can request that they send you money. Again, if the person does not have a Google Wallet account, he or she needs to set one up before sending you the money.

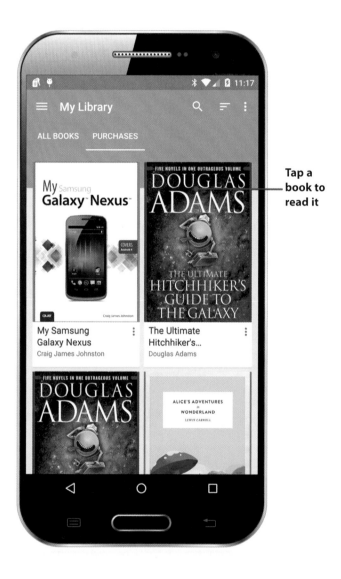

Tap a book to read it

In this chapter, you find out how to buy books, read books, and subscribe to your favorite magazines. Topics include the following:

→ Buying books
→ Reading books
→ Buying magazine subscriptions

12

Books and Magazines

This chapter covers how you can use your Android phone for reading books and magazine subscriptions.

Purchasing Books

The Google Play Store has a section that enables you to purchase (and in some cases get free) books in e-book form. After you have an e-book, you can read it at your leisure and even bookmark your favorite pages.

Navigate the Play Books App

The Play Books app enables you to read your books, bookmark pages, and find and purchase more books.

1. Tap to launch Play Books. You see the Read Now screen that shows books you have recently opened and books that Google recommends you read.

2. Swipe in from the left of the screen.

3. Tap Shop to find and purchase more books.

4. Tap My Library to see books already in your library.

5. Tap to change the Play Books app settings.

6. Tap the switch to see only books that have been physically downloaded to your phone as opposed to all books you have purchased, some of which may still be stored in the Google Cloud.

7. Tap to return to the Read Now screen.

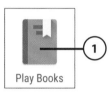

Play Books

Buy Books

The procedure is the same for down-loading a free book and buying a book. The only difference is a free book shows a price of zero.

1. Swipe in from the left of the screen.

2. Tap Shop to open the Google Play Store to the Books section. Bear in mind that at this point you are exiting the Google Books app and opening the Google Play Store.

3. Tap a book to open it.

James Johnston
editor.ford.prefect@gmail.com

Read Now

My Library

Shop

Downloaded Only

Settings

Help & feedback

Books

1. Chariots of the Gods
Erich Von Daniken
★★★★✦
$7.99 $6.59

Searching for a Book

Finding books in the Google Play Store is easy. You can swipe left and right in the blue area at the top of the screen to switch between different groupings of books—for example, Top Selling books, New Releases in Fiction, Top Free books, and so on. If you tap Categories, you see books listed by categories such as Art & Entertainment, Education, Engineering, and so on. You can also use the Search icon to find books. When you choose to search, remember that you can also speak your searches. One drawback of searching is that your search is done across all stores, so you see related results for apps, movies, TV shows, and books.

Browse books by category

Books

CATEGORIES   HOME   TOP SELLING   DEALS   NEW R

Search for books

4. Scroll down to read reviews on the book.

5. Tap to read a free sample of the book before you purchase it.

6. Tap to purchase the book.

7. Tap to change the method of payment if you need to.

8. Tap to buy the book. The book immediately starts downloading to your phone and appears in the Read Now screen.

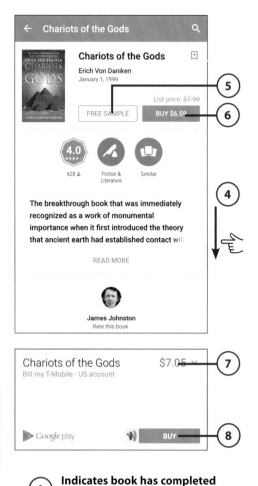

Reading Books

As you read a book, you can bookmark certain pages, jump to different chapters, and even change the font size.

1. Tap a book to open it.

Indicates book has completed downloading

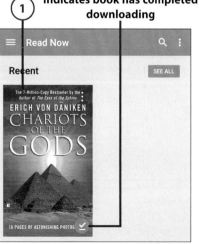

2. Swipe left and right across the screen to flip forward and backward through the book.

3. Tap near the middle of the screen to reveal the formatting controls and controls for quickly moving to specific pages.

4. Swipe down from the top of the screen or swipe up from the bottom of the screen to reveal only the formatting and other controls.

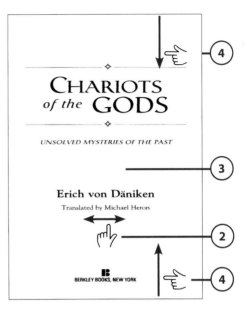

Jump to Pages Quickly

After you tap the middle of the screen, you can quickly move to specific pages in the book.

1. Drag left and right to quickly jump to a specific page.

2. Swipe left and right to skim through the pages.

3. Tap a page to return to the Reading view.

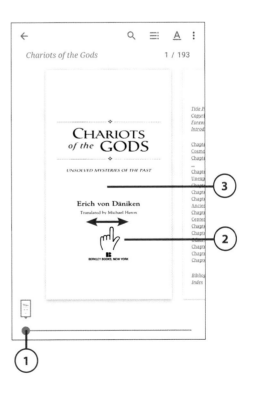

Adjust Formatting and Other Controls

After you tap the middle of the screen, swipe down from the top of the screen, or swipe up from the bottom of the screen, to control the way the book is presented on the screen.

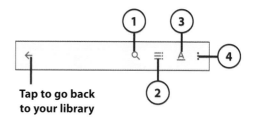

Tap to go back to your library

1. Tap to search the entire book for a word or phrase.

2. Tap to list all the chapters in the book and jump to them, see notes you may have taken, and view bookmarks that you previously set.

3. Tap the Font icon to change the way the book appears on your screen.

4. Tap the Menu icon to see more options.

Controlling the Visuals

Tap the Font icon to reveal ways to control how the book appears on your screen. You can choose black text on a white background (typically used during the day), white text on a black background (typically used at night), or a simulation of real book paper color. If you are viewing the book using the Flowing Text mode, you can also change the typeface, text alignment, brightness, line height, and font size. Read more about Flowing Text in the margin note titled "What Are Original Pages?"

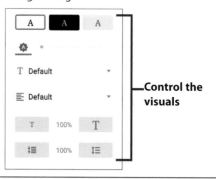

Control the visuals

5. Tap to switch between Original Pages and Flowing Text (if the book supports it).

6. Tap to share a link to the book you are reading via social media, email, and other methods.

7. Tap to add or remove a bookmark.

8. Tap to change the settings for the app.

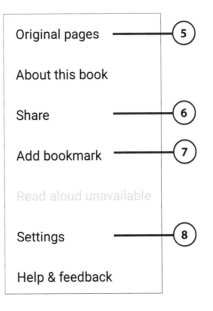

What Are Original Pages?

When you read a book on your phone, the app defaults to showing the book using Flowing Text. This means that the text of the book is all there, but it's not structured in its original format per page. When viewing the book using Flowing Text, you are able to change the font, font size, alignment, and other properties. Some books allow you to switch to Original Pages, which makes it possible for you to page through the book as it was originally laid out, using the original typeface and alignment.

>>>Go Further

TRANSLATING TEXT AND TAKING NOTES

As you read through your book, you might need a translation of some foreign text, or you might want to highlight some text and make notes about it. To do either thing, touch and hold the text you want to translate or make a note on, and then drag the markers left and right until you have selected all the text you want. Tap the appropriate icon in the toolbar.

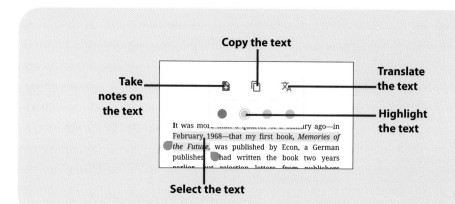

Copy the text

Take notes on the text

Translate the text

Highlight the text

Select the text

> It was more than a quarter of a century ago—in February, 1968—that my first book, *Memories of the Future*, was published by Econ, a German publisher. I had written the book two years earlier, but rejection letters from publishers

>>>*Go Further*

READING BOOKS WHERE THERE IS NO INTERNET ACCESS

When you buy and read a book, it is downloaded to your phone and stays there while you are reading it. If you know that you will be reading more than one book in an area with no Internet access (such as on a plane), you should first manually download any books you think you will be reading so that they are available. On the My Library screen, tap the Menu icon under the cover image of each book you want to download, and then tap Download. A downloaded book is indicated by a blue check mark.

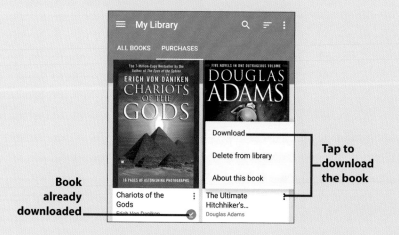

Tap to download the book

Book already downloaded

Purchasing Magazines and Newspapers

You can subscribe to magazines and newspapers on your phone and have them delivered in electronic form to read anytime. The Play Newsstand app enables you to subscribe to and read your magazines.

Installing Google Play Newsstand

The Newsstand app may not come preinstalled on your Android phone. Before continuing with the following steps, please first install the app from the Google Play Store. See Chapter 9, "Working with Android Apps," for more information on installing apps.

1. Tap to launch the Play Newsstand app. The first screen you see is the Read Now screen. This screen shows stories from different publications that you can read without subscribing to those publications.

2. Tap a highlight to read it.

3. Scroll down to see more highlights.

4. Tap to search for magazines and newspapers to subscribe to.

5. Swipe left and right to scroll through the categories of stories. Highlights are a mixture of stories from all categories; all the other categories only show stories relevant to that category.

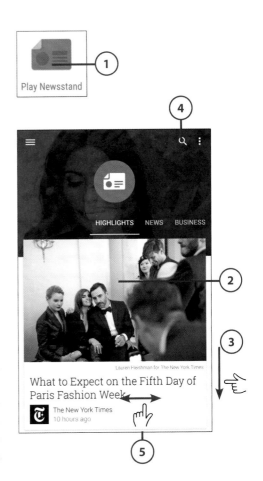

Purchase or Subscribe to Publications

You can subscribe to publications or just purchase a single edition.

1. Swipe in from the left of the screen.

2. Tap Explore.

3. Tap a category. This example uses the Automotive category.

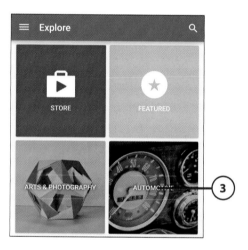

4. Tap a publication.

5. Tap Buy to buy only the latest edition of the magazine, or tap Subscribe to buy a subscription to the magazine.

6. Tap Subscribe to complete the transaction. If you chose to just buy the latest issue, the button is labeled Buy.

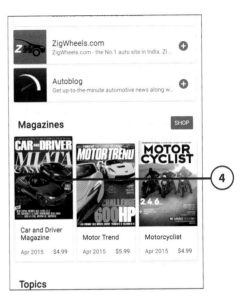

Add the magazine to your Wishlist

Read a Publication

1. Swipe in from the left of the screen.

2. Tap My Library.

Why Would I Download a Magazine?

When you open and read magazines, they are temporarily downloaded to your phone, but you are still required to be connected to the Internet before you read them. If you are going to be in an area with no Internet access (such as on a plane) and you want to read a magazine, you need to manually download it while you are still connected to the Internet. Tap the Menu icon under the magazine's cover and then tap Download. The downloaded magazine is indicated by a blue check mark.

3. Tap the appropriate tab for the type of publication. This example uses a purchased magazine, which is on the Magazines tab.

4. Tap the publication to open it.

Indicates magazine has been downloaded

5. Scroll down to see all of the magazine's articles.

6. Tap the magazine cover to open the magazine at the cover, or tap one of the articles to open it.

Switch between Page view and Article view

6

5

ARTICLE VIEW VERSUS PAGE VIEW

If you tap the blue icon in the top right of the screen, you can switch between viewing the magazine as it is laid out in the print version—page by page—or in Article view, which reformats the magazine so that you can move between the articles. When in Page view, if you tap a page to jump to it, you can then continue to swipe left and right to page back and forth through the magazine. When in Article view, if you tap an article, you must scroll up and down to scroll through the article, and when you swipe left and right, you can switch between articles.

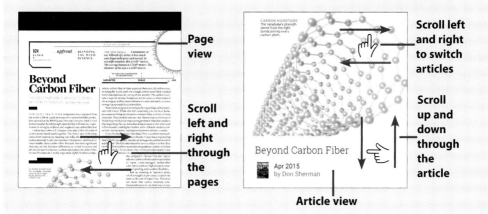

Page view

Scroll left and right through the pages

Scroll left and right to switch articles

Scroll up and down through the article

Article view

See your battery usage trends

In this chapter, you find out how to maintain your Android phone and solve problems. Topics include the following:

→ Updating Android
→ Optimizing battery life
→ Identifying battery-hungry apps
→ Caring for your Android phone

Maintaining Your Android Phone and Solving Problems

Every so often, Google releases new versions of Android that have bug fixes and new features. In this chapter, you find out how to upgrade your Android phone to a new version of Android and how to tackle common problem-solving issues and general maintenance of your phone.

Updating Android

New releases of Android are always exciting because they add new features, fix bugs, and tweak the user interface. Here is how to update your Android phone.

Updating Information

Updates to Android are not delivered on a set schedule. The update messages appear as you turn on your Android phone, and they remain in the Notification panel until you install the update. If you tap Install Later, your Android phone reminds you every 30 minutes that there's an update. Sometimes, people like to wait to see if there are any bugs that need to be worked out before they update, so when you choose to update is up to you.

1. Tap Download.

2. Tap Download to download the Android update to your phone.

3. Tap Restart and Install. Your Android phone reboots and applies the update, showing you the status of its progress. When the update is complete, you see the Lock screen and you can use your phone normally.

Manually Checking for Updates

If you think there should be an update for your Android phone, but you have not yet received the onscreen notification, you can check manually by tapping Settings, About Phone, and System Updates. If there are updates, they are listed on this screen. If not, tap Check For Update to check manually.

System update available
Android 5.0.1 System Update

LATER   ✓ DOWNLOAD — 1

Tap to install later

Android 5.0.1 System Update

Requires a restart · 72.8 MB

This software update will upgrade your Nexus 6 to Android 5.0.1, which improves performance and stability and fixes bugs. Downloading via Wi-Fi is recommended. Downloading over a mobile network or while roaming may cause additional charges.

Download — 2

Restart & install — 3

Optimizing Battery Life

The battery in your Android phone is a lithium-ion battery that provides good battery life when you take care of it. Changing the way you use your Android phone helps prolong the battery's life, which gives you more hours in a day to use it.

Look After the Battery

There are specific actions you can take to correctly care for the battery in your Android phone. Caring for your battery helps it last longer.

- Try to avoid discharging the battery completely. Fully discharging the battery too frequently harms the battery. Instead, try to keep it partially charged at all times (except as described in the next step).

- To avoid a false battery-level indication on your Android phone, let the battery fully discharge about every 30 charges. Lithium-ion batteries do not have "memory" like older battery technologies; the battery meter gives a false reading if you don't fully discharge the battery every 30 charges.

- Do not leave your Android phone in a hot car or out in the sun anywhere, including on the beach, because this can damage the battery and make it lose its charge quickly. Leaving your Android phone lying in the snow or in extreme cold also damages the battery.

- Consider having multiple chargers. For example, you could have one at home, one at work, and maybe one at a client's site. This enables you to always keep your Android phone charged.

Determine What Is Using the Battery

Your Android phone enables you to see exactly what apps and system processes are using your battery. Having access to this information can help you alter your usage patterns and reduce the battery drain.

1. Tap Settings.

2. Tap Battery in the Device section.

3. Tap to manually refresh the display.

4. Tap an app or Android service to see more details about it, including how much time it has been active, how much processor (CPU) time it has used, and how much data it has sent and received (if applicable).

5. Tap the battery history graph for more details on the battery history and how it relates to GPS, Wi-Fi, cellular data, and screen-on time.

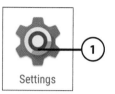

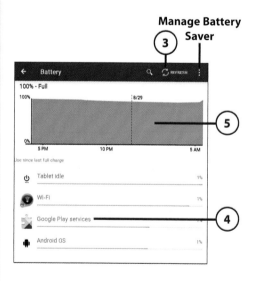

6. Cellular Network Signal indicates when the cellular radio was being used and the signal strength through the graph's time span.

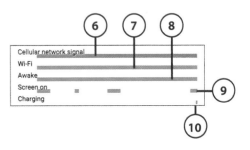

7. Wi-Fi indicates when the Wi-Fi radio was used through the battery graph's time span.

8. Awake indicates when your Android phone was awake through the time span.

9. Screen On indicates when your phone's screen was on through the battery graph's time span.

10. Charging indicates when your phone was charging through the battery graph's time span.

What Is Battery Saver?

When Battery Saver is enabled, your phone severely limits its functionality in order to keep the battery alive as long as possible. Your phone reduces its performance, turns off Ambient Display, stops synchronizing data in the background, and stops vibrating for notifications. All these steps help increase the battery discharge rate, but of course your phone's usefulness is much more limited than normal. You can either manually activate Battery Saver or set your phone to automatically activate it when the remaining battery charge reaches 5% or 15%. From the Battery screen, tap the Menu icon. Tap the On/Off switch to manually activate Battery Saver. To leave Battery Saver off, but set it to automatically activate when the remaining charge reaches a certain level, tap on Turn On Automatically, and choose either 5% or 15%.

Controlling Apps and Memory

Android phone apps run in a specific memory space that is limited to between 1-3 GB. (This number varies by phone manufacturer.) Although Android tries to do a good job of managing this memory, sometimes you have to close an app that is consuming too much memory.

1. Tap Settings.

2. Tap Apps in the Device section.

3. Tap Running to see only apps that are currently running.

4. The graph shows you how much memory is being used by the system (Android), apps that are currently running, and how much free memory there is available.

5. Tap an app to see more information about it.

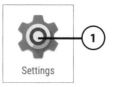

Settings

Device	
🔅	Display
🔔	Sound & notification
🗄	Storage
🔋	Battery
🤖	Apps

← **Apps**   🔍 ⋮

DOWNLOADED   RUNNING   ALL

Device memory

System	243MB of RAM
Apps	605MB of RAM
Free	2.1GB of RAM

App RAM usage

⚙	Settings 1 process and 0 services	185MB
T	T-Mobile My Account 1 process and 3 services	32MB 11:57
ⓟ	Path 1 process and 1 service	11MB 12:06
f	Facebook 1 process and 1 service	83MB 01:46

Apps memory footprint

6. Tap Stop if you believe the app is misbehaving.

7. Tap to report an app to Google. You might want to do this if it is misbehaving, using up too many resources, or you suspect it is stealing data.

Indicates the processes that are used by this app

When Should I Manually Stop an App?

After you have been using your Android phone for a while, you'll become familiar with how long it takes to do certain tasks, such as typing, navigating menus, and so on. If you notice your phone becoming slow or not behaving the way you think it should, the culprit could be a new app you recently installed. Because Android never quits apps on its own, that new app continues running in the background and may be causing your phone to slow down. This is when it is useful to manually stop an app.

>>>Go Further

MOVING AN APP TO EXTERNAL MEMORY

If your Android phone has a slot for external memory, you can move part of an app to that external memory, thereby freeing up some space in your phone's main memory. Typically, the external memory is a Micro SD (Micro Secure Digital) card. Not all apps support being run from external memory, so you might not be able to move all or part of the app. To move an app to the SD card, go to Settings, tap Apps, and tap the Downloaded tab. Next, tap the app you want to move. If it can be moved, tap the Move to SD Card button.

App info	
P Path Version 4.0.4	
Force stop	Uninstall
✓ Show notifications	
STORAGE	
Total	29.36MB
Application	29.36MB
SD card app	0.00B
Data	0.00B
SD card data	0.00B
Move to SD card → Move to SD card	Clear data

Checking and Controlling Data Usage

You might want to see how each app consumes data while it runs in the foreground or in the background. You might also want to limit an app's data consumption when it runs in the background. Finally, you can set your cellular billing cycle and a data limit to let your phone warn when you are getting close to your limit.

1. Tap Settings.

2. Tap Data Usage.

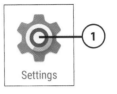

Showing Cellular and Wi-Fi Usage

Because Wi-Fi is free and doesn't count toward your cellular data plan, many people are only interested in seeing their data usage, what apps are using how much cellular data, and setting cellular data limits. However, you can also show your phone's Wi-Fi usage by tapping the Menu icon and choosing Show Wi-Fi. You then see two tabs: one for cellular and one for Wi-Fi.

Total data usage for the period

How much data each app has used

Set a Data Usage Warning

You might want to let your phone warn you when you reach a certain amount of cellular data usage each month.

1. Tap the date range.

2. Tap Change Cycle.

3. Choose the first day of your cellular billing cycle.

4. Tap Set.

5. Drag the data warning bar left and right to choose at what point of cellular data usage you want to be warned.

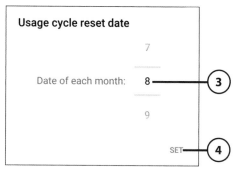

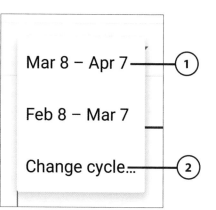

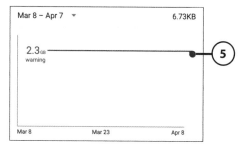

Set a Data Usage Limit

You might want to let your phone limit your data usage after it reaches your cellular data plan limit. If you use this feature, when your cellular data usage reaches the limit you set, your phone stops using cellular data; however, it continues to use Wi-Fi data.

1. Tap the date range.

2. Tap Change Cycle.

3. Choose the first day of your cellular billing cycle.

4. Tap Set.

5. Tap the On/Off switch next to Set Cellular Data Limit to enable setting a cellular data limit.

6. Drag the data limit bar left and right to choose the maximum amount of cellular data you want your phone to use before it stops using cellular data altogether.

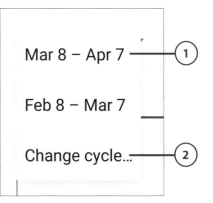

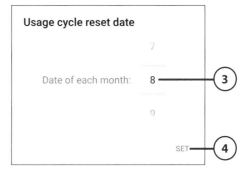

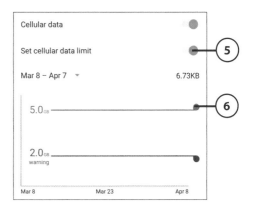

Caring for the Android Phone's Exterior

Because you need to touch your Android phone's screen to use it, it picks up oils and other residue from your hands. You also might get dirt on other parts of the phone. Here is how to clean your Android phone.

1. Wipe the screen with a microfiber cloth. You can purchase these in most electronics stores, or you can use the one that came with your sunglasses.

2. To clean dirt off other parts of your phone, wipe it with a damp cloth. Never use soap or chemicals on your Android phone because they can damage it.

3. When inserting the Micro-USB connector, try not to force it in the wrong way. If you damage the pins inside your Android phone, you cannot charge it.

Getting Help with Your Android Phone

Many resources are on the Internet where you can get help with your Android phone.

1. Visit the Official Google website at http://www.android.com.

2. Check out some Android blogs:

   - Android Central at http://www.androidcentral.com/

   - Android Guys at http://www.androidguys.com/

   - Androinica at http://androinica.com/

3. Contact me. I don't mind answering your questions, so visit my official *My Android Phone* book site at http://www.CraigsBooks.info.

Take
panoramas

In this chapter, you find out how to take pictures with your Android phone, how to store them, and how to share them with friends. Topics include the following:

→ Using the camera
→ Taking panoramic pictures
→ Taking Photo Sphere pictures
→ Synchronizing pictures
→ Viewing pictures

Taking and Managing Pictures

Most Android phones have both front- and rear-facing cameras. The rear-facing camera is normally quite good, so taking pictures is not a disappointing experience. After you take those great pictures, you can share them with friends. You can also synchronize the pictures directly with your computer using Google Photos in the cloud.

Using the Camera

Before you start taking photos, you should become familiar with the Camera app.

Why Does My Camera App Look Different?

This chapter covers the stock Google Camera app, but some phones from certain manufacturers replace the stock Google Camera app with their own camera app. In many cases, the camera apps have similar features, so you should be able to follow along. However, if you prefer, you can get the stock Google Camera app from the Google Play Store. Search for "Google Camera" and install it.

1. Tap to launch the Camera.

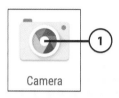

2. Swipe in from the left of the screen to change the camera mode between still camera, panoramic camera, Lens Blur, Photo Sphere, and video camera. (These modes are covered in more detail later in the chapter.)

3. Tap to change the camera settings. (See the next section for more information about the camera settings.)

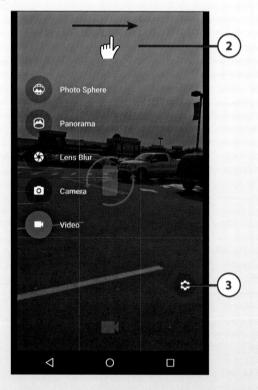

4. Tap anywhere in the frame to make the camera focus specifically in the area.

5. Tap to switch between the front-facing and rear-facing cameras, overlay a grid pattern on the screen, or manually adjust the exposure setting.

6. Tap to take a picture.

It's Not All Good

Zooming In—Is It Worth It?

Before you snap your picture or record a video (and also while you're recording a video), you can zoom in on the frame. To zoom in, place your thumb and forefinger on the screen and move them apart. To zoom out, move your thumb and forefinger back together. This is commonly called *pinch to zoom*.

When you slide your thumb and forefinger apart to zoom in, the Camera app is faking the zoom. Although the image appears to get larger, what is actually happening is the image is simply manipulated to appear like it's zooming in. This is commonly called *digital zoom*. Optical zoom is when the camera actually zooms using a lens movement, which is something that this camera cannot do.

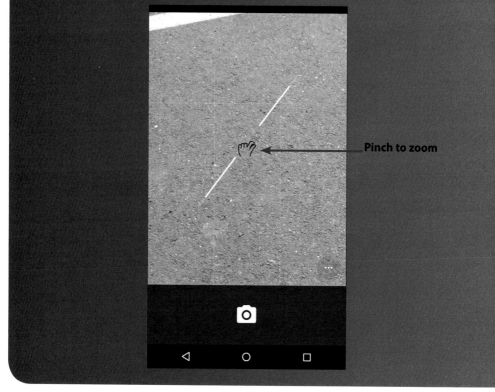

Pinch to zoom

Adjust Camera Settings

Using camera settings, you can change things such as the resolution of each picture, picture review time, filters, Scene mode, white balance, and more. The settings that are not available when you're in Video mode are noted in the steps.

1. Swipe in from the left of the screen.

2. Tap to see Settings.

3. Tap to enable or disable embedding your GPS coordinates into pictures you take.

4. Tap to enable or disable showing the manual exposure setting on the main camera screen.

5. Tap Resolution & Quality.

6. Tap to adjust the resolution and format of the pictures taken with the rear-facing camera. Your choices range from a 13 megapixel 4:3 ratio image to a 2.1 megapixel 16:9 ratio image. The exact range of resolution and aspect ratio depends on your phone's camera capabilities.

7. Tap to adjust the resolution and format of the pictures taken with the front-facing camera. Your choices range from a 2.1 megapixel 16:9 ratio image to a 0.1 megapixel 4:3 ratio image. The exact range of resolution and aspect ratio depends on your phone's camera capabilities.

8. Tap to adjust the format of the video taken with the rear-facing camera. Your choices are Ultra High Definition (UHD) 4K, High Definition (HD) 1080p, HD 720p, and SD 480p. The exact range of resolution depends on your phone's camera capabilities.

9. Tap to adjust the format of the video taken with the front-facing camera. Your choices are HD 1080p, HD 720p, SD 480p, and CIF. The exact range of resolution depends on your phone's camera capabilities.

10. Tap to adjust the quality of the images taken with the rear-facing camera when shooting panoramas. Your choices are High, Normal, and Low. The higher the image quality you choose, the slower your camera is to take panoramas.

11. Tap to adjust the quality of the images taken with the rear-facing camera when shooting Lens Blur pictures. Your choices are Normal and Low. The higher the image quality you choose, the slower your camera is to take Lens Blur pictures.

12. Tap to save your changes and return to the main Settings screen.

13. Tap to save your changes and return to the main Camera screen.

Reading More About Recording Video

If you want to read more about using the Camera app to record video, go to Chapter 3, "Audio, Video, and Movies."

Take Regular Pictures

Now that you have the settings the way you want them, take a few pictures. You can jump to step 5 and take the picture, but you might want to first set up your shot.

1. Tap the Camera icon.

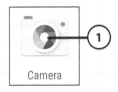

2. Swipe in from the left of the screen to change the camera mode.

3. Tap to select regular Camera mode.

4. Tap the area of the frame you want to focus on specifically. When you release your finger, the camera adjusts its focus.

5. Tap to take the picture.

Focusing on Part of a Picture

You can actually focus on a certain part of a scene. By tapping the part of the picture you want in focus, you see that the rest of the picture goes out of focus. Using this trick enables you to create depth in your photos.

Take Panoramic Pictures

Your Android phone can take panoramic pictures. Panoramic pictures are achieved by taking multiple pictures from left to right or right to left and stitching them together in one long picture. Luckily your Android phone does all that work for you.

1. Tap the Camera icon.

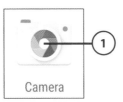

2. Swipe in from the left of the screen.

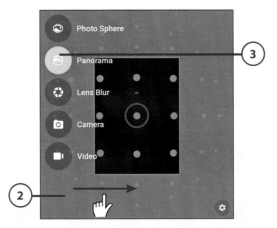

3. Tap to select Panorama.

4. Tap to select the type of panorama you want to take.

5. Tap to shoot a horizontal panorama (left to right or right to left).

6. Tap to shoot a vertical panorama (up/down or down/up).

7. Tap to shoot a wide angle panorama.

8. Tap to shoot a fish-eye panorama.

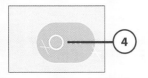

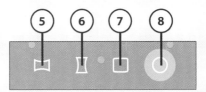

9. Tap to start the panorama.

10. Move your phone until the circle is over the closest white dot. This is your starting point. After the dot turns blue, more dots appear to guide you.

11. Slowly move your phone around and guide the circle over the blue dots. Each time you line them up, another image is captured for your panorama.

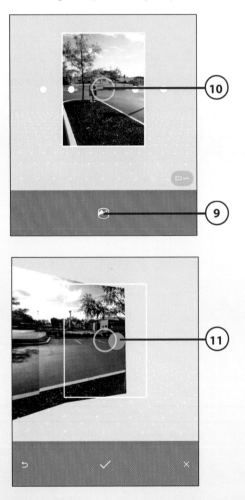

12. After you capture all the images necessary for the type of panorama you chose, the camera automatically stitches the pictures together into a panorama and saves it.

Can You Change the Width of the Panorama?

To create shorter horizontal or vertical panoramas, instead of rotating all the way from left to right, or up or down, you can tap the check mark to immediately stop the panorama process and save it as is.

Moving Too Fast

When you take panoramic pictures, you have to rotate slowly. If you start moving too fast, the camera indicates this to you. Slow down when this happens; otherwise the panorama will not look good.

Take Photo Sphere (360 Panoramic) Pictures

Your phone can take 360-degree panoramic pictures—or, as Google calls them, Photo Spheres. Photo Sphere pictures are achieved by taking multiple pictures in all directions around you and stitching them together in one large sphere image.

1. Tap the Camera icon.

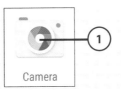

2. Swipe in from the left of the screen.

3. Tap Photo Sphere.

4. Move your phone until the circle is over the blue dot. After you have done that, wait until you see other white dots appear.

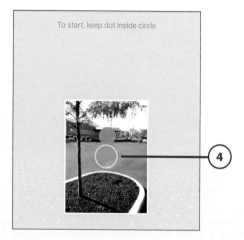

5. Slowly move your phone around and guide the circle over the blue dots. Each time you line them up, another image is captured for your Photo Sphere.

6. Tap the check mark when you have captured enough images. The images are stitched together in the background. You can view your Photo Sphere using the Photos app, which is covered later in this chapter.

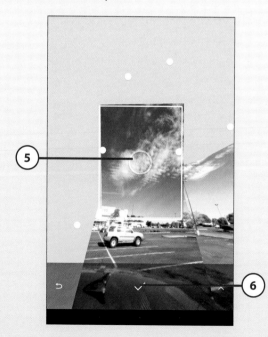

Take Lens Blur Pictures

When you take a Lens Blur picture, you can change the focus of the picture after the fact.

1. Tap the Camera icon.

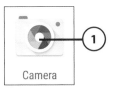

2. Swipe in from the left of the screen.

3. Tap Lens Blur.

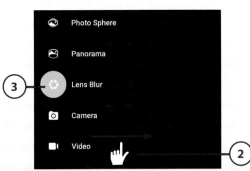

4. Tap to start the Lens Blur capture.

5. Slowly move your phone up as indicated by the arrow.

6. After the picture has completed, swipe in from the right of the screen to see the image and adjust the blur.

7. Tap to edit the blur.

8. Tap the picture where you want it to be the clearest.

9. Drag the slider to change how blurry the rest of the picture appears.

10. Tap Done to save your changes.

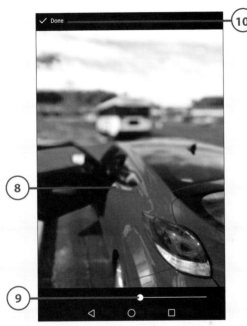

USING SAMSUNG CAMERAS

Samsung phones ship with a different Camera app that fits into their unique look and feel plus has some additional features. The Camera app on Samsung phones also lets you download additional functionality from Samsung. Tap the Mode icon to see the available camera modes. The built-in camera modes include similar features found on other Android phone cameras, such as Panorama mode and Lens Blur (although Samsung calls it Selective Focus). Tap the Download icon to get more camera modes from Samsung. Some modes are not free.

Manage which modes appear in the list

Download new camera modes from Samsung

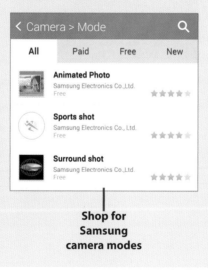

Shop for Samsung camera modes

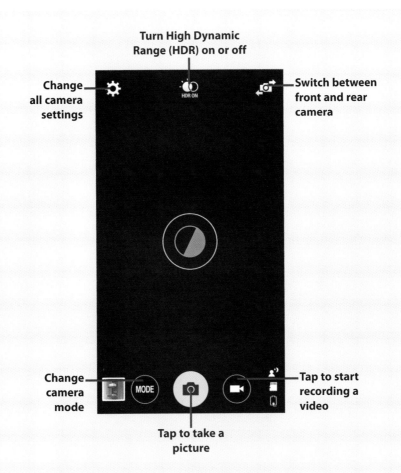

Turn High Dynamic Range (HDR) on or off

Change all camera settings

Switch between front and rear camera

Change camera mode

Tap to start recording a video

Tap to take a picture

USING HTC CAMERAS AND ZOE

HTC has also modified Android on its phones, including the Camera app. The HTC Camera app has a special mode called Zoe. When you put the camera into Zoe mode, you can take pictures and videos one after the other, and when you're done, you can run the Zoe app to create a new Zoe. A Zoe is a compilation of the pictures and videos you took that has been set to music. The Zoe app allows you to discover other HTC users' Zoes and share yours online.

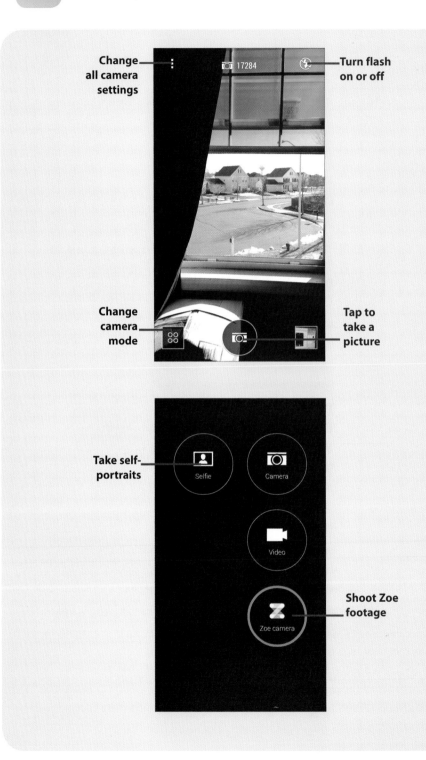

Change all camera settings

Turn flash on or off

Change camera mode

Tap to take a picture

Take self-portraits

Shoot Zoe footage

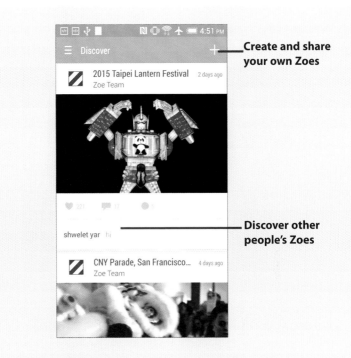

Create and share your own Zoes

Discover other people's Zoes

Viewing and Managing Your Photos

This section covers the photo-specific activities of the Photos app, such as viewing a Photo Sphere and editing photos. For more details about using the Photos app, read Chapter 3, "Audio, Video, and Movies."

Navigate Photos

1. Tap to launch the Photos app. If this is the first time you are running the Photos app, you may be prompted to enable Auto-Back, which is a feature that makes a backup of all of your photos to your Google Cloud account.

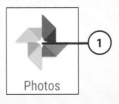

Photos

2. Tap to open a photo.

3. Tap to open a Photo Sphere.

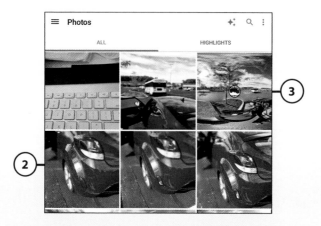

Where Are All My Photos and Videos Stored?

When you open the Photos app, in addition to allowing you to view photos and videos on your device, it shows you a lot of other options, so what are they? If you tap Google+, you see your Google+ profile. If you tap Photos, you see all photos and videos on your device and also ones that have previously been copied to your Google+ Cloud account from this and all other devices you own. If you tap Stories, you access a feature of Google+ that creates stories from photos and videos that have previously been copied to your Google+ Cloud account. Tapping Albums shows you all albums on your device and in the Google+ Cloud. Tapping Auto Awesome shows you any photos and videos that have been automatically backed up to your Google+ Cloud account and turned into little movies. (You can also manually create them.) Tapping Videos shows you only videos on your device and in your Google+ Cloud account. Tapping Photos of You displays only photos in which you have been tagged on Google+. Tapping Trash shows photos that you have recently deleted and gives you the opportunity to undelete them.

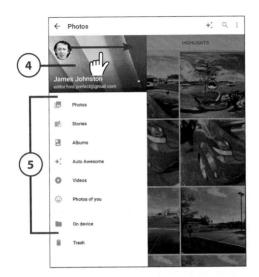

4. Swipe in from the left of the screen.

5. Select where you want to look for your photos, or tap On Device to see only photos and videos you have recorded on this Android phone.

Delete Photo Albums

You can delete one or many photo albums but only if they were created on your Android phone. You cannot delete albums created on your desktop computer that you can also see on your phone.

1. While you have an album open, tap the Menu icon.

2. Tap Delete Album. Bear in mind that deleting an album is permanent and all the photos in that album will be lost.

Review and Share Pictures

After you open a photo, you can review it and share it with your friends.

1. With a photo open, double-tap the picture to zoom in to the maximum zoom level. Double-tap again to zoom all the way back to 100 percent.

2. Use the pinch gesture to have a more controlled zoom in and zoom out.

3. Scroll left and right to see all the photos in the album.

4. Tap to share the picture with friends using Facebook, Twitter, Gmail, Email, Google+, Picasa (Google Photos), and more.

5. Tap the method you want to use to share the picture.

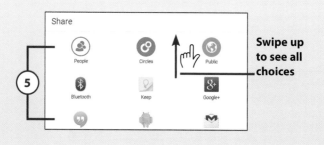

Using a Photo as Wallpaper or Contact Picture

While viewing a photo, tap the Menu icon, and choose Set As. You can choose to use the photo as a contact picture for one of your contacts, or use it as the wallpaper on the Home screen.

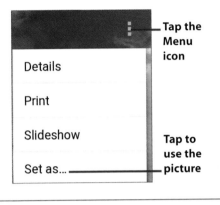

Tap the Menu icon

Tap to use the picture

Can I Share a Photo Sphere?

You can share a Photo Sphere in one of two ways: as an interactive Photo Sphere, where the viewer can move around your sphere interactively, or as a static image. Google+ is currently the only place that supports interactive Photo Sphere uploads. All other photo-sharing services and social networks, such as Facebook and Twitter, support only static images.

Edit Pictures

You can edit a picture by adding filters to it, enhancing it, or cropping it. These steps apply to still pictures, panoramic pictures, and Photo Sphere pictures.

1. With a photo open, tap the Edit icon.

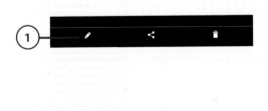

2. Tap to let the Photos app automatically enhance your picture using changes it thinks will work best.

3. Tap to the crop the picture. When cropping, you can crop freely by dragging the crop box in any direction, choose to keep the original picture's aspect ratio as you drag the cropping box, or crop the picture always as a square image.

4. Tap to rotate the picture. When rotating the picture, you can rotate it freely using your fingers to make slight adjustments, or use icons to rotate it left or right.

5. Tap to add a filter to the picture.

6. Tap to fine-tune your picture by adjusting brightness, contrast, saturation, shadows, and so on.

7. Tap to do selective image tuning. This allows you to adjust selective parts of the image.

8. Tap to adjust the structure and sharpness of your picture.

9. Swipe right to see more picture adjustments.

10. Tap to make your picture look vintage.

11. Tap to add drama to your picture.

12. Tap to turn your picture into a black-and-white image.

13. Tap to enhance your picture to look like a High Dynamic Range (HDR) landscape.

14. Tap to enhance your picture using the Retrolux enhancement, which makes your photos look like they were taken with old camera equipment, complete with light streaks and scratches.

15. Tap to force focus on the center of your picture.

16. Tap to apply the Tilt Shift enhancement, which makes the objects in your picture look like they are miniature.

17. Swipe right to choose frames for your picture.

18. Tap Done at the top left of the screen to save your edited photo.

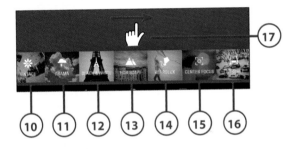

Getting the Original Back

Even after you modify and save the picture, you can get the original picture back. To do this, edit the picture you want to get the original back for, tap the Menu icon, and choose Revert. The original version of the picture is loaded and the modified version is removed permanently.

Change the Look of Pictures (Filters)

You can apply filters to your picture to change the way it looks.

1. Scroll left and right to see all the available filters (or looks).

2. Tap a look to preview how it changes your picture.

3. Tap the check mark to save your changes to the picture.

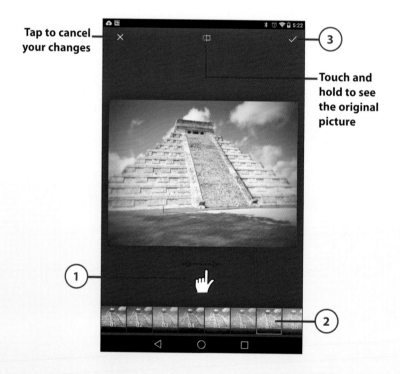

Tap to cancel your changes

Touch and hold to see the original picture

Tune Image

You can fine-tune the image by adjusting brightness, saturation, and contrast.

1. Touch and hold on the picture and swipe up and down to see the different settings. Release when you see the setting you want to change.

2. Swipe left and right over the setting value area to adjust the setting.

3. Tap the check mark to save your changes to the picture.

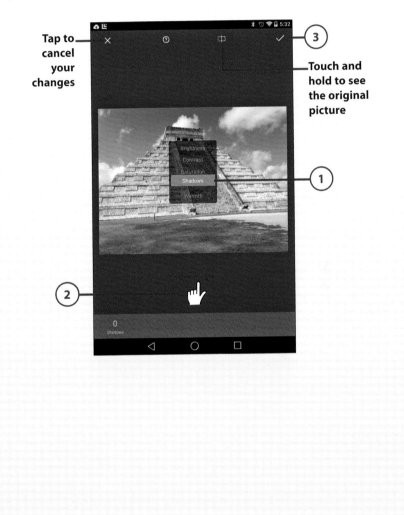

Tap to cancel your changes

Touch and hold to see the original picture

Selectively Tune Image

You can fine-tune different parts of your image instead of the entire image at once.

1. Tap the Add button to add a tune point.

2. Drag the tune point to the part of your image you want to fine-tune. The tune point appears as a blue dot.

3. Touch and hold on the picture and swipe up and down to see the different settings. Release when you see the setting you want to change.

4. Swipe left and right over the setting value area to adjust the setting.

5. Tap the check mark to save your changes to the picture.

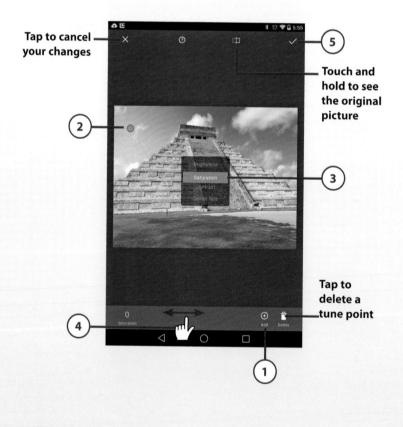

Tap to cancel your changes

Touch and hold to see the original picture

Tap to delete a tune point

Adjust Structure and Sharpness (Details)

1. Touch and hold on the picture and swipe up and down to see the different settings. Release when you see the setting you want to change.

2. Swipe left and right over the setting value area to adjust the setting.

3. Tap the check mark to save your changes to the picture.

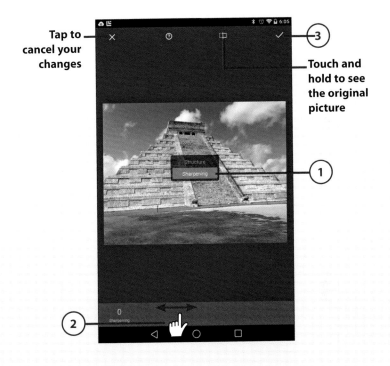

Tap to cancel your changes

Touch and hold to see the original picture

Adjusting Structure and Sharpness

To read more about the differences between the Structure and Sharpness enhancements, visit http://blog.phaseone.com/how-to-enhance-details-with-structure/.

Make Your Picture Look Aged Using Vintage Styles

1. Tap Style to choose a style of aging you want to apply.

2. Tap Blur if you want to make your picture look blurry.

3. Touch and hold on the picture and swipe up and down to see the different settings. Release when you see the setting you want to change.

4. Swipe left and right over the setting value area to adjust the setting.

5. Tap the check mark to save your changes to the picture.

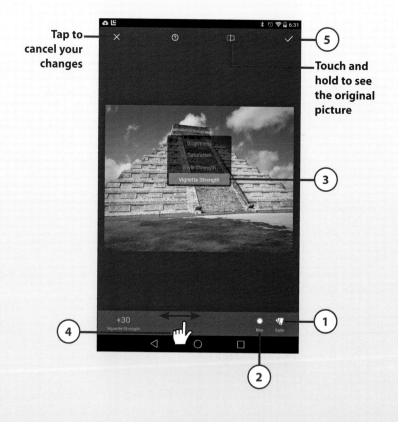

Tap to cancel your changes

Touch and hold to see the original picture

Style Pictures with Drama

1. Tap Style to choose a style you want to apply.

2. Touch and hold on the picture and swipe up and down to see the different settings. Release when you see the setting you want to change.

3. Swipe left and right over the setting value area to adjust the setting.

4. Tap the check mark to save your changes to the picture.

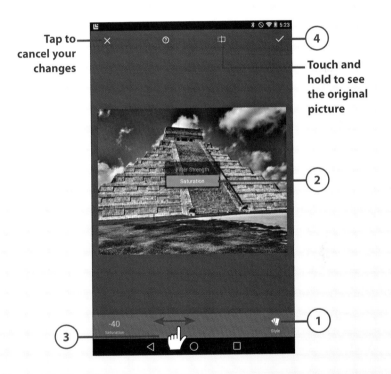

Tap to cancel your changes

Touch and hold to see the original picture

Style Pictures as Black-and-White Pictures

1. Tap Style to choose the Black & White style.

2. Touch and hold on the picture and swipe up and down to see the different settings. Release when you see the setting you want to change.

3. Swipe left and right over the setting value area to adjust the setting.

4. Tap the check mark to save your changes to the picture.

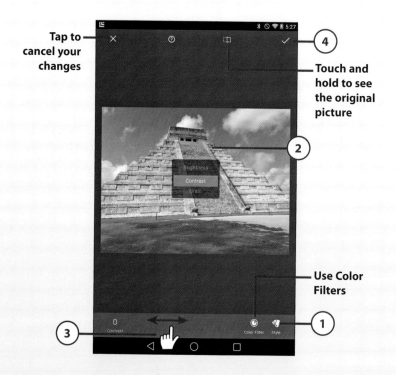

Tap to cancel your changes

4

Touch and hold to see the original picture

2

Use Color Filters

1

3

Using Color Filters and Black-and-White Pictures

Because some colors look the same when converted to black and white, you can use color filters to correct this. Tap the check mark to save your changes. Read more about using color filters for black-and-white pictures at http://www. photographymad.com/pages/view/using-coloured-filters-in-black-and-white-photography.

Enhance Your Pictures with HDR Landscape

If your picture is of a landscape, you might want to enhance it using High Dynamic Range (HDR) processing.

1. Tap Style to choose a style you want to apply (for example, whether your picture has people in it or not).

2. Touch and hold on the picture and swipe up and down to see the different settings. Release when you see the setting you want to change.

3. Swipe left and right over the setting value area to adjust the setting.

4. Tap the check mark to save your changes to the picture.

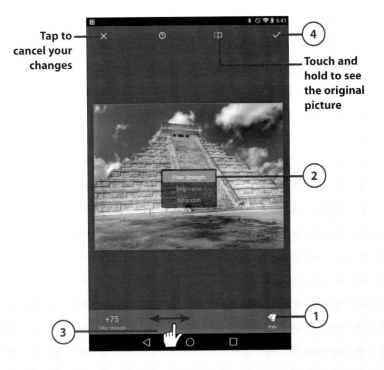

Tap to cancel your changes

Touch and hold to see the original picture

Learning about HDR Landscape Pictures

Read more about using HDR landscape processing at http://www.lightstalking. com/getting-started-in-hdr-landscape-photography/.

Style Pictures as Retrolux Pictures

Give your picture the appearance of being from film that has been damaged.

1. Tap Style to choose the Retrolux style. Tap the style multiple times to cycle through where in your picture the simulated defects should be added.

2. Touch and hold on the picture and swipe up and down to see the different settings. Release when you see the setting you want to change.

3. Swipe left and right over the setting value area to adjust the setting.

4. Tap the check mark to save your changes to the picture.

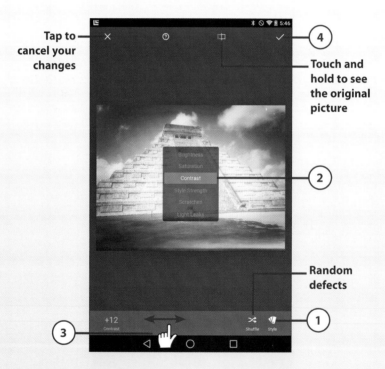

Use a Center Focus

Give your picture the appearance of being focused only at the center.

1. Tap Style and choose the Center Focus style.

2. Tap Blur to choose whether the blur is weak or strong.

3. Touch and hold on the picture and swipe up and down to see the different settings. Release when you see the setting you want to change.

4. Swipe left and right over the setting value area to adjust the setting.

5. Tap the check mark to save your changes to the picture.

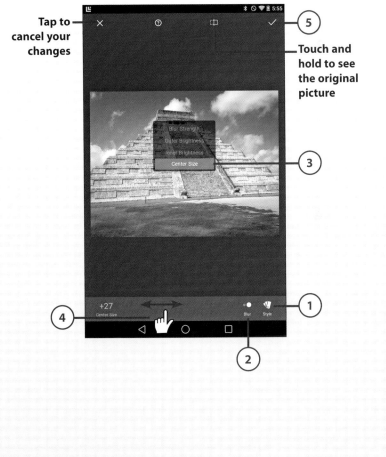

Style Pictures as Tilt Shift Pictures

The Tilt Shift effect makes the objects in your picture look like they are miniatures.

1. Tap Style and choose the Tilt Shift style.

2. Drag the blue dot to where you want the Blur Tilt effect to be applied.

3. Touch and hold on the picture and swipe up and down to see the different settings. Release when you see the setting you want to change.

4. Swipe left and right over the setting value area to adjust the setting.

5. Tap the check mark to save your changes to the picture.

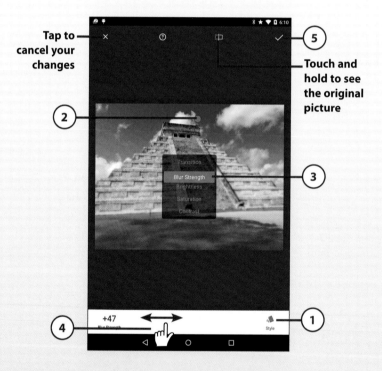

Tap to cancel your changes

Touch and hold to see the original picture

Learning about Tilt Shift Pictures

To read more about the Tilt Shift effect, visit http://www.tiltshiftphotography. net.

USING THE GALLERY APP

Some Android phones do not ship with the Photos app (although you can always download it from the Google Play Store). Those phones instead come with an app called Gallery. Many of them do this because the manufacturers have heavily modified Android and need to keep the Gallery app around to handle device-specific features. The Gallery app has its own editing capabilities, which are similar to what is found in the Photos app, but they are sometimes not as good.

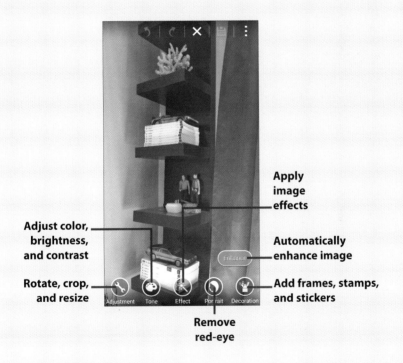

Apply image effects

Adjust color, brightness, and contrast

Automatically enhance image

Rotate, crop, and resize

Add frames, stamps, and stickers

Remove red-eye

Modify Photos App Settings

1. Tap the Menu icon.

2. Tap Settings.

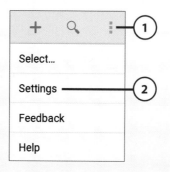

3. Tap to manage automatically backing up your pictures and videos to your Google+ account.

4. Tap an account to edit settings for that specific Google account.

5. Check the box to see in Google Photos the photos and videos you have stored in your Google Drive Cloud account.

6. Check the box to show the location of where photos and videos were taken.

7. Tap to manage how Google handles location settings for this Google account.

8. Tap to let Google automatically enhance your pictures when they are uploaded.

9. Check the box to let Google create "Auto Awesome" images, movies, and stories from your photos and videos. Read more about "Auto Awesome" in Chapter 3.

10. Check the box to allow your phone to do the Auto Awesome processing.

11. Check the box to let Google recognize your face in photos uploaded to Google+ by your friends, and prompt them to tag you.

12. Tap to save your changes and return to the previous screen.

Managing Photos with Your Computer

When you connect your Android phone to a computer, you can move pictures back and forth manually by using software such as Android File Transfer. If you have not yet installed Android File Transfer, follow the installation steps in the Prologue earlier in this book.

Manually Manage Pictures

This section covers moving pictures using the Android File Transfer app if you use a Mac or the media transfer functionality if you use Windows.

1. Plug your phone into your computer using the supplied USB cable.

2. Pull down the Notification panel to reveal the USB Connected notification.

3. Tap the Connected As a Media Device notification.

4. Tap to check the box next to Media Device (MTP) if it is not already checked.

Move Pictures (Mac OS X)

After your phone is connected to your Mac, the Android File Transfer app automatically launches, so you can browse the files on your phone as well as move or copy files between your Mac and your phone.

1. Browse your phone to locate the pictures using the Android File Transfer app.

Where Are the Pictures?

Pictures taken with the phone's camera are in the DCIM\Camera folder. All other pictures are in a Pictures folder.

---

2. Save folders from your phone to your Mac by dragging one or more pictures from your phone to a folder on your Mac.

3. Create a new photo album on your phone by dragging one or more pictures, or a folder filled with pictures, on your Mac to the Pictures folder on your phone.

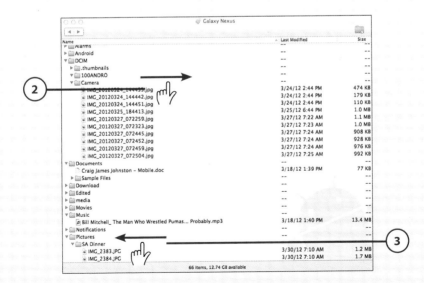

Move Pictures (Windows)

After your phone is connected to your Windows computer and mounted, you can browse the phone just like any other drive on your computer.

1. Click if you want to import the pictures automatically.

2. Click to open an Explorer view and see the files on your phone.

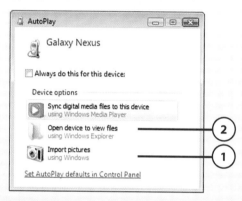

3. Save pictures from your phone to your PC by dragging one or more pictures from your phone to a folder on your PC.

4. Create a new photo album on your phone by dragging one or more pictures, or a folder filled with pictures, on your PC to the Pictures folder on your phone (not shown).

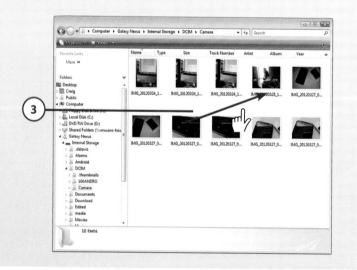

Where Are the Pictures?

Pictures taken with the phone's camera are in the DCIM\Camera folder. All other pictures are in the Pictures folder.

Automatically Manage Pictures on a Mac

By setting your phone to connect as a Camera, your Mac automatically opens the Photos app.

1. Plug your phone into your computer using the supplied USB cable.

2. Pull down the Notification panel to reveal the USB Connected notification.

3. Tap the Connected As a Media Device notification.

4. Tap to check the box next to Camera (PTP), if it is not already checked.

5. Your phone appears in the Photos app under Import so that you can import photos like you would with any other digital camera. In this example, the phone is a Nexus 6.

Synchronizing Pictures Using Your Google Cloud

You can synchronize pictures to your phone from your computer without connecting your phone to your computer. Just use your Google account's built-in Cloud service. All photo albums that you create in the Cloud are automatically synchronized to your phone.

1. Log in to Google with your computer. Hover your mouse over the menu, and click Photos.

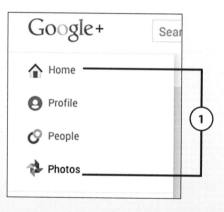

2. Download all photos from a specific day by clicking the down arrow to the right of the date and selecting Download.

3. Download a specific photo by opening the photo, clicking the More menu, and selecting Download Photo.

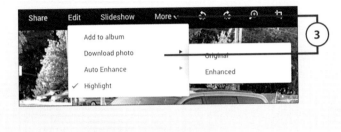

Using HTC Synchronization Software

If you have an HTC Android phone, you can use the HTC Sync Manager software to move images between your HTC phone and your desktop computer. You can also automate the synchronization of data between your computer and phone any time you plug it into your computer. When you plug your HTC phone into your computer, you should see a link to download HTC Sync Manager. If you don't, go to this link: http://www.htc.com/us/software/htc-sync-manager/.

Change synchronization settings

Using Samsung Synchronization Software

If you have a Samsung Android phone, you can use the Samsung Kies software to move images between your Samsung phone and your desktop computer. You can also automate the synchronization of data between your computer and phone anytime you plug it into your computer. You can download Samsung Kies from http://www.samsung.com/us/kies/.

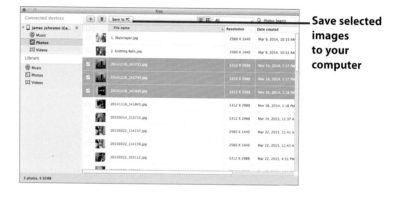

Save selected images to your computer

Swipe up
to read

In this chapter, you discover how to set up your Android Wear smartwatch and use it with your Android phone. Topics include the following:

→ Setting up your Android Wear watch
→ Choosing settings and installing apps
→ Navigating the Android Wear watch's interface
→ Using the Android Wear watch's apps

Using Your Android Phone with an Android Wear Smartwatch

To get the most out of your Android phone, you can link it to an Android Wear smartwatch. Android Wear watches are sold by vendors such as Samsung, LG, and Motorola, and they act as a companion for any Android smartphone. The Android Wear watch enables you to display essential information, make phone calls, and have simple interactions with apps without taking your Android phone out of your pocket.

Setting Up Your Android Wear Watch

To set up the Android Wear watch, you need to use your Android phone.

1. Unpack the Android Wear watch and identify its components: the Android Wear watch itself, a charging dock/clip, and the charger.

2. Fully charge your Android Wear watch.

3. Turn the Android Wear watch on by pressing and holding its button for a moment. The button is on the right side of the Android Wear watch.

4. Tap to choose your preferred language on the watch screen.

5. When you see a screen on your watch telling you to install the Android Wear app on your phone, switch to your Android phone for steps 6–14.

6. Search the Google Play Store for the Android Wear app. When you find it, tap Install.

7. Tap Accept to accept the permissions that the Android Wear app needs to run correctly. After the app installs, run it to start setting up your watch.

8. Tap the right arrow to start setting up your watch.

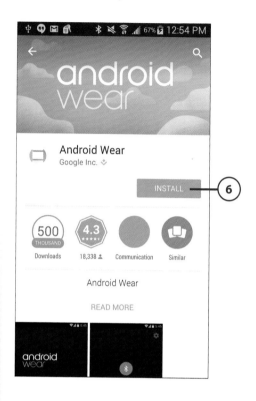

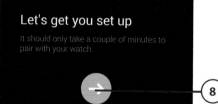

9. Tap Accept to accept that the Android Wear app will synchronize data between your watch and your Android phone.

10. Tap the name of the watch you want to use. In this example, it is a Samsung Gear Live, listed as "Gear Live 10C9."

11. When prompted, accept the Bluetooth Pairing PIN on both your Android phone and your watch. The PIN should be the same on both devices.

12. When your watch and Android phone are paired over Bluetooth, you see a screen preparing you to configure Android to allow the Android Wear app to have access to notifications. Tap Notification Settings.

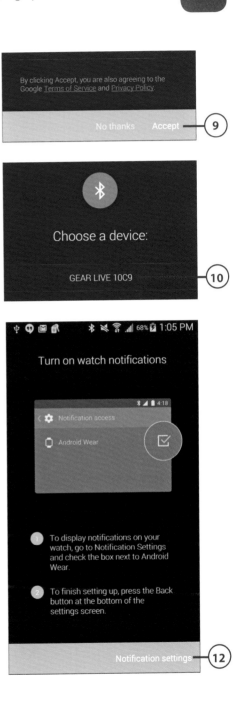

13. Check the box to allow the Android Wear app to receive access to Android notifications.

14. Tap OK to verify that you want the Android Wear app to have access to all Android notifications.

Notification access

☐ Android Wear — (13)

Allow Android Wear

Android Wear will be able to read all the notifications you receive, which may include personal information such as contact names and messages sent to you. It will also be able to dismiss these notifications or select actions related to them.

Cancel   OK — (14)

Explaining Android Wear Smartwatches

Android Wear is a framework that Google created to support smartwatches connecting to Android devices. This enables different vendors to create and sell smartwatches that have their own unique look and build quality but can all be compatible with any Android device as long as the owner installs the Android Wear app. Smartwatches that use the Android Wear framework can have square or round faces. Examples of Android Wear watches that have a round face are the Motorola Moto 360 and the LG G Watch R. Examples of Android Wear watches that have a square face are the Asus ZenWatch, Sony SmartWatch 3, Samsung Gear Live, and the LG G Watch. No matter whom you buy your Android Wear–based smartwatch from, and regardless of whether it has a square or round face, the instructions and guidance in this chapter are relevant.

Choosing Settings for Your Android Wear Watch

After pairing your Android Wear watch with your Android phone, you'll probably want to spend some time customizing the Android Wear watch. You can use the Android Wear app on your Android phone to configure overall settings for the Android Wear watch, as explained in this section. To configure other settings, you use the Settings app on the Android Wear watch itself, as discussed in the following section.

Navigate the Android Wear App

The Android Wear app gives you access to features and settings for configuring and managing your Android Wear watch.

1. Tap to launch the Android Wear app.

2. Tap a watch face to change it on your watch.

3. Tap to see all watch faces you have installed and find more.

4. Scroll down to see all voice actions and what apps are launched when the voice action triggers.

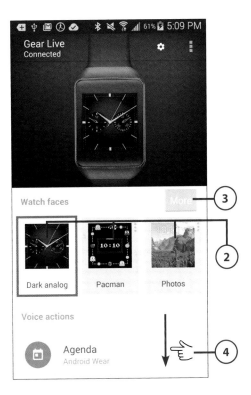

Set Voice Actions

Voice actions are voice commands you speak to your watch. Based on what you say, your watch either launches an app or takes an action, or it tells your Android phone to launch an app. Some voice actions can be customized to make use of third-party watch apps that you install.

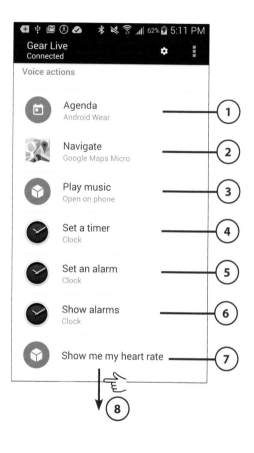

1. Shows your agenda.

2. Launches the Google Maps Micro watch app, which enables you to get turn-by-turn directions. The Google Maps Micro watch app also launches the Google Maps app on your Android phone, which actually provides the navigation to your watch.

3. Opens the Google Play Music app on your Android phone and plays music.

4. Sets a timer on your watch.

5. Sets an alarm on your watch.

6. Shows the alarms set on your watch.

7. Shows your heart rate. Tap to choose which watch app launches to show your heart rate.

8. Scroll down for more voice actions.

9. Shows how many steps you have walked with your watch on.

10. Starts a stopwatch on your watch. Tap to select which watch app launches to start the stopwatch.

Why Is the Icon Gray?

In the following steps, each of the voice actions shown in the figure has a gray Google Play icon next to it. That icon indicates that there is currently no app installed to handle the function provided by the voice action. After you install an appropriate app on your Android phone, these actions will be available.

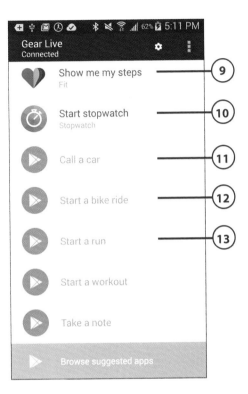

11. Calls a car to pick you up. Install an app such as Lyft to make this voice action available. If you have two apps installed that both handle this function, tap Call a Car to choose the app you prefer to use.

12. Launches an app to start a bike ride. Install an app such as RunKeeper to make this voice action available. If you have two apps installed that both handle this function, tap Start a Bike Ride to choose the app you prefer to use.

13. Launches an app to start a run. Install an app such as RunKeeper to make this voice action available. If you have two apps installed that both handle this function, tap Start a Run to choose the app you prefer to use.

14. Launches an app to start a workout. Install an app such as RunKeeper to make this voice action available. If you have two apps installed that both handle this function, tap Start a Workout to choose the app you prefer to use.

15. Launches an app in which you can take a note. If you do not install an app to handle this voice action, when you use this feature, the note you dictate is emailed to your Gmail address. Installing an app such as Chaos Control allows this voice action to launch your favorite note-taking app.

16. Tap to browse the Google Play Store for watch apps to handle voice actions and standalone watch apps that provide additional functionality.

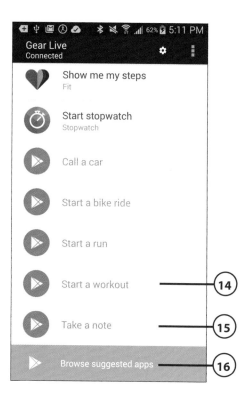

Handling Riding, Running, and Workouts

Start a Bike Ride, Start a Run, and Start a Workout are functions that will not work until you install an app on your Android phone to handle them. It is your choice which apps you want to install to handle these functions. The one used for this chapter was RunKeeper. It just so happens that RunKeeper handles all three functions; however, that does not mean that you need to use just one app for all three functions. You can install three different apps to handle each of the three functions separately. Your favorite apps that you already use for tracking bike rides, for example, might already support Android Wear. If that is the case, select that app to support the bike-ride function. If you have two apps installed that handle one or more of the functions, tap the function to choose which app you want to use. For example, to change what app handles Start a Bike Ride, tap Start a Bike Ride and choose the app.

Choose a Watch Face

Your watch comes with some pre-installed watch faces, and you can use the Android Wear app to choose which one you want to use. You can also browse the Google Play Store for more. Some are free; some you must purchase.

1. From the main Android Wear app screen, tap one of the three most recent watch faces to set your watch to use it.

2. Tap More to see all watch faces you have installed.

3. Select a watch face to use.

4. Scroll down to the bottom of the screen and tap Get More Watch Faces to find more watch faces in the Google Play Store.

5. Tap to install a watch face. After your new watch face has been installed, it automatically downloads to your watch and is visible in the Android Wear app.

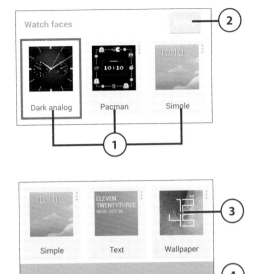

Some watch faces cost money

6. Tap the watch face in the Android Wear app to make your watch start using it.

7. Some watch faces have configuration options. If the watch face has settings that you can change that affect the way it works, the Settings icon displays over the watch face. Tap it to adjust the watch face's settings.

8. Tap to return to the main Android Wear app screen.

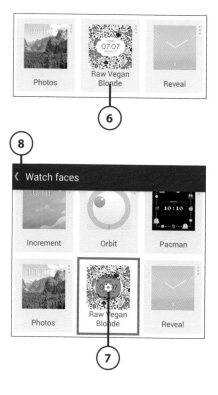

Adjust the Android Wear App's Settings

The Android Wear app does allow for some configuration, and it also offers you ways to view your watch's battery life and available memory.

1. From the main Android Wear app screen, tap the gear icon to see the settings.

2. Tap to choose apps that you no longer want to receive notifications for on your watch. By default, every notification from every app is sent to your watch. Use this setting to select which notifications you really care about.

3. Check the box to set your watch to keep a low-resolution monochrome version of the screen on at all times, even when it goes to sleep.

4. Check the box to set your watch to wake up when it detects that you have tilted your wrist.

5. Tap to see how your watch's battery is performing and how much power each app is taking. Using this screen can help you identify apps that are draining the battery.

6. Tap to see your watch's memory usage and how much memory each app is using.

7. Check the box to allow a preview of an alert to be displayed on the bottom of the watch screen. If you uncheck this box, there will be no alert previews; however, you can still swipe up to view alerts.

8. Check the box to mute any alerts, notifications, or any other interruptions on your Android phone while it is connected to the watch. Having this enabled helps cut down having alerts vibrate your Android phone and your watch at the same time.

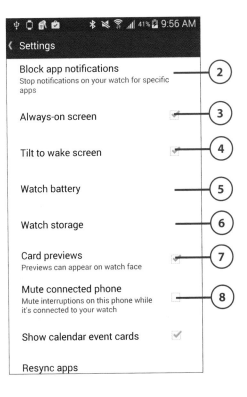

9. Check the box to show calendar events on your watch in the form of a card.

10. Tap to resynchronize apps between your Android phone and your watch. You don't normally need to do this, but if you suspect that an app you recently installed on your Android phone has not installed a mini-app on your watch, you can tap here.

11. Tap to return to the previous screen.

11

⟨ Settings

Block app notifications
Stop notifications on your watch for specific apps

Always-on screen ☑

Tilt to wake screen ☑

Watch battery

Watch storage

Card previews ☑
Previews can appear on watch face

Mute connected phone ☐
Mute interruptions on this phone while it's connected to your watch

Show calendar event cards ☑ **9**

Resync apps **10**

Viewing Your Watch Battery Usage

Viewing your watch's battery performance can help to determine how much longer your watch will last on its current charge based on current usage. You can also see which apps and watch faces are using the most battery time. Watch faces with a lot of animation can use a lot of battery charge. If you see a watch face or watch app that is using a lot of battery charge, you may choose to uninstall the app or stop using the watch face to help your watch last longer on a single charge.

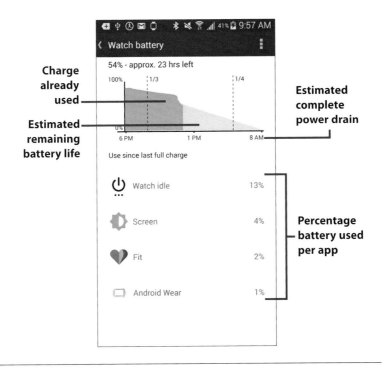

Charge already used

Estimated remaining battery life

Estimated complete power drain

Percentage battery used per app

Viewing Your Watch Memory Usage

Viewing your watch's memory usage can help you see if your watch is running out of space, and if it is, which apps and watch faces are using the most memory.

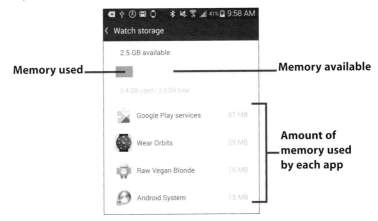

Memory used

Memory available

Amount of memory used by each app

Install Apps on the Android Wear Watch

Some apps installed on your Android phone automatically install an app on your watch that helps you interact with the app from your watch. There are also dedicated watch apps that you can install from the Google Play Store.

1. In the Android Wear app, scroll down to the bottom of the screen and tap Browse Suggested Apps.

2. Scroll down to see all of the categories of watch apps. The categories are Watch Faces, New Year, Tools, Social, Productivity, Communication, Health & Fitness, Entertainment, Travel & Local, and Games.

3. Tap More to see more apps in a specific category.

4. Tap an app you want to download. Some apps cost money. This example uses Reversi for Wear.

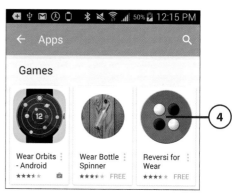

5. Tap Install.

6. Tap Accept to accept any device or information permission the app needs to run. In this example, the app does not need any permissions.

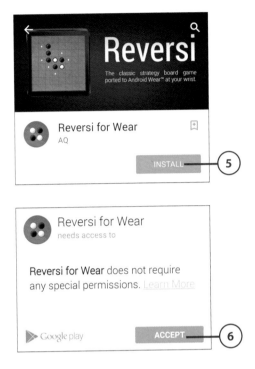

Using Your Android Wear Watch

After you have set up your watch via the Android Wear app, and you've installed some watch faces and apps, you can start using the watch itself.

Exploring Watch Features

Your Android Wear watch actually runs on the Android operating system. As of the writing of this book, the version of Android running on Android Wear watches is Android 5.01 (Lollipop). Your watch either has a round or square face, and includes an accelerometer to detect movement, a capacitive touch screen so you can perform gestures such as tapping and swiping, and a microphone to listen for voice commands. Your watch probably also has a sensor to monitor your heart rate and a pedometer to measure your activity. Your watch relies on your Android phone for the majority of its functions, including voice commands, so you must always have your Android phone close by to use your watch. Although most Android Wear watches include a physical button, some do not.

Navigate Your Watch

Your watch responds to taps and swipes that allow you to navigate the interface, run apps, and see and respond to onscreen information.

1. While your watch is not being used, the screen becomes low resolution, monochrome, and dimmed to save energy.

2. Lift your arm to view your watch, and the screen turns to full color.

3. Swipe notifications up to read them and, in some cases, take actions on them. If you have more than one notification, swipe up repeatedly to read all of them.

4. Tap the preview of the notification to show more of it, and scroll down to read all of it.

5. Swipe the notification to the left to see any actions that you can take on the notification. This includes an option to block the app so that you don't see notifications from it again.

6. Swipe the notification to the right to dismiss it. To dismiss most apps while using them on your watch, swipe to the right.

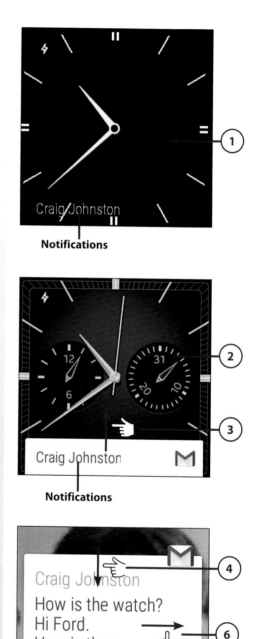

7. After you dismiss a notification, if you change your mind, you can quickly swipe up from the bottom of the screen to see a dismiss timer. Tap the timer to undo the dismiss before it runs out.

8. Swipe down from the top of the screen to see options and settings.

9. Tap to toggle mute on or off. When muted, your watch stops vibrating when alerts appear.

10. Swipe left to see more options.

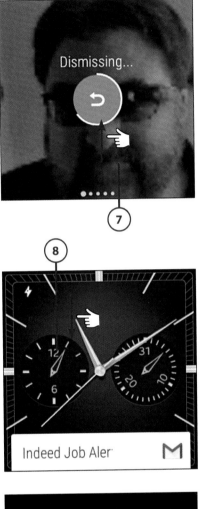

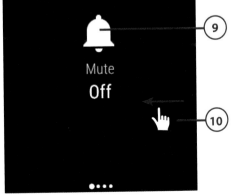

11. Tap to put your watch in Theater Mode. When in Theater Mode, the screen remains blank, you receive no notifications, and the action of lifting your arm to look at your watch is deactivated. Press the watch button to exit Theater Mode. If your watch doesn't have a button, double-tap the screen and then swipe down to turn off Theater Mode.

12. Swipe left to see more options.

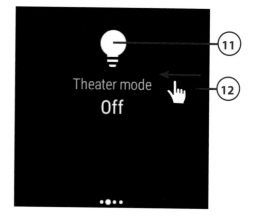

Using an Alternative Method of Activating Theater Mode

If you double-press your watch's button, you will set it to Theater Mode. Double-pressing the button makes the watch exit Theater Mode.

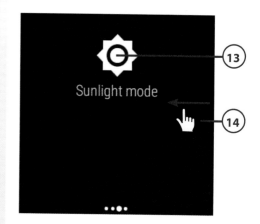

13. Tap to set your watch to Sunlight Mode for five seconds. Sunlight Mode sets the screen brightness to the maximum for five seconds to help with bright sunlight.

14. Swipe left to see more options.

Using an Alternative Method of Activating Sunlight Mode

If you triple-press your watch's button, Sunlight Mode is engaged for five seconds.

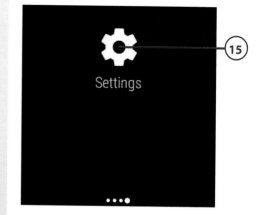

15. Tap to change your watch's settings. See the next section for a description of all settings.

Adjust Your Watch's Settings

Use this section to adjust your watch's settings. To enter your watch's settings, you can either swipe down from the top of the screen and swipe left until you see the Settings icon, or tap your watch screen and scroll down to Settings.

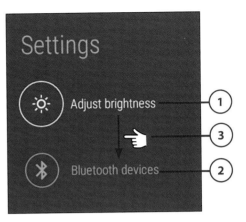

1. Tap to manually adjust the brightness of your watch's screen.

2. Tap to pair your watch with Bluetooth devices, such as Bluetooth speakers.

3. Scroll down for more settings.

4. Tap to toggle Always-On Screen on or off. When this is off, your watch screen no longer switches to the low-resolution mode when it goes to sleep; instead, it turns off completely. Some watches call this setting Ambient Screen.

5. Tap to toggle Airplane Mode on or off. When in Airplane Mode, your watch is not able to communicate using Bluetooth to your Android phone.

6. Tap to power off your watch.

7. Scroll down for more settings.

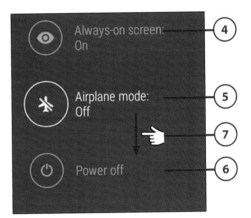

8. Tap to restart your watch. All your information remains untouched; your watch just restarts.

9. Tap to reset your watch. This puts the watch back to the way it came out of the box, and all your saved information will be lost.

10. Tap to change your watch face.

11. Scroll down for more settings.

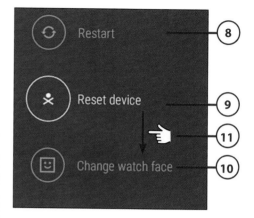

Choosing a New Watch Face

To change your watch face, swipe left and right to see all your installed watch faces and then tap the one you want to use.

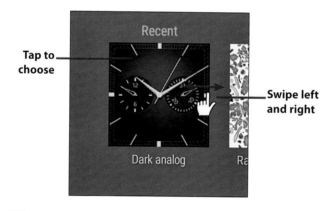

Tap to choose

Swipe left and right

12. Tap to change the size of the font used on your watch.

13. Tap to see information about your watch, as well as whether there is an update for it.

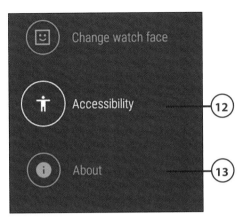

Use Your Watch and Run Watch Apps

Your watch was designed to be controlled by your voice. However, you can also manually select functions and apps by tapping and swiping on the screen.

1. Wake up your watch by lifting your arm. Alternatively, you can tap your watch's screen to wake it up.

2. After your watch wakes up and the screen turns to full color, say "OK Google." Alternatively, you can tap the watch screen.

3. Your watch is now listening for a command. Say a command to perform an action or start an app. Use the next section to learn how to use each command and launch watch apps.

Use Watch Functions and Watch Apps

Your watch is designed for voice commands. However, if you don't speak, your watch stops listening so you can select functions and run apps using the touch screen. It is your choice how you want to perform the following functions—either by speaking or by touching.

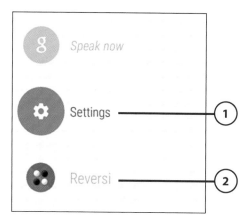

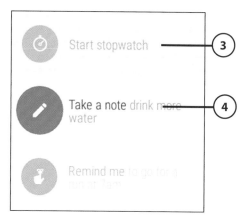

1. Say "Settings," or tap to see the Settings screen.

2. Say "Start Reversi" to start the Reversi app installed earlier in this chapter, or tap the Reversi icon to start it. Remember that Reversi is a watch app, so you must say "Start." You can also start watch apps by saying "Run" (for example, "Run Reversi").

3. Say "Start Stopwatch," or tap to start the Stopwatch watch app.

4. Say "Take a note," or tap and speak the text of the note, to take a note. For example, you can say "Take a note to drink more water," and a new note is created with the text "Drink more water." If you have previously installed an app that handles notes, the note is saved to that app. Otherwise, your note is emailed to your Gmail account.

5. Say "Remind me," or tap and speak the reminder to add. For example, you can say "Remind me to go for a run at 7:00 a.m." and a new reminder is created labeled "Go for a run" set for 7:00 a.m. the next day. You can also set recurring reminders. For example, you can say "Remind me to make coffee at 8:00 a.m. every weekday."

6. Say "Start a run," or tap to launch the app you installed to handle your runs. Start running and use the watch app you installed to monitor your run.

7. Say "Show me my steps," or tap to show how many steps you have walked. Your watch uses its built-in pedometer to keep track of your steps.

8. Say "Show me my heart rate," or tap to activate your watch's heart rate monitor. Follow the instructions to allow your watch to take your heart rate.

9. Say "Send text," or tap and speak the name of the recipient and the text message to send a text message to someone. For example, you can say "Send a text to Jim, see you later" and a new text message is created addressed to Jim with the text "See you later." If the contact has more than one phone number, you need to say the phone number to use, for example "Send a text to Jim mobile."

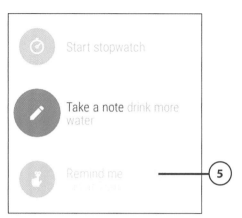

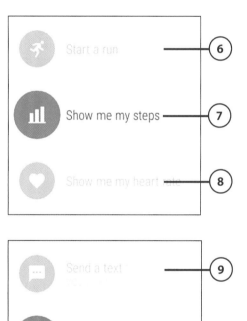

Enabling Contact Recognition

You must enable contact recognition for the "send a text" and "send an email" functions to work. To do this, on your Android phone, tap Settings, Accounts, Google, Accounts & Privacy, and check the box next to Contact Recognition.

10. Say "Email," or tap and speak the name of the recipient and message. For example, you can say "Email Jim, you free on Friday?" and a new email is created addressed to Jim with the body of the message set to "You free on Friday?" If you have more than one person with the same name, and you are not specific, you are prompted to say the person's full name. If the person has more than one email address, you are prompted to say the one to use (for example, Home or Work).

11. Say "Agenda" or tap to see your agenda for today.

12. Say "Navigate," or tap and speak the desired destination to start turn-by-turn directions from your current location to your desired destination. You can say things like "to a pizza place nearby" or "home" or "work," or you can speak an address. Turn-by-turn directions start on your Android phone, with a mini version of them being displayed on your watch.

13. Say "Set a timer," or tap and speak the time the timer must use. For example, you can say "Set a timer for 45 minutes." The timer starts on your watch.

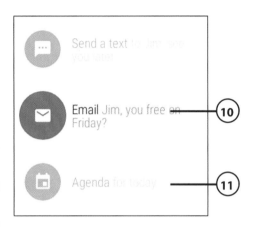

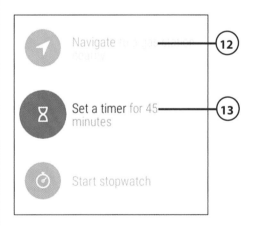

14. Say "Start stopwatch," or tap to start the stopwatch app on your watch.

15. Say "Set an alarm," or tap and speak the time for which the alarm must be set. For example, you can say "Set an alarm for 6 this evening." The alarm is created. Before the alarm is finished being created, you can tap Edit to edit the alarm and even make it recurring by selecting certain days of the week when it must trigger.

16. Say "Show alarms," or tap to show the alarms that have been set on your watch. You can edit or remove individual alarms by using the touch screen.

17. Say "Call a car," or tap to launch the car pickup service you installed on your Android phone that supports Android Wear, such as Lyft.

18. Say "Play music," or tap to start playing an "I'm feeling lucky" mix on your Android phone. You can also say "Play Depeche Mode" to start playing all songs by Depeche Mode on your Android phone. See the "Playing Music from Your Watch" sidebar at the end of this chapter for more information.

19. Say "Settings," or tap to see your watch's settings.

20. Say "Start," or tap and say the name of a watch app you have installed. For example, if you installed an app called Eat24, you would say "Start Eat24."

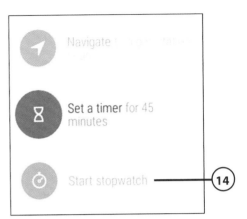

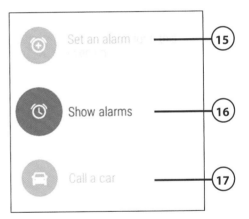

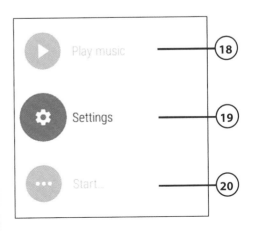

Replying to an Email Using Your Voice

When you receive a new email notification on your watch, you can reply to the email using your voice. To do this, swipe up the email notification. Swipe the notification to the left twice and tap Reply. Speak your reply. When you stop speaking, your watch sends the reply using the message you dictated.

Tap to reply

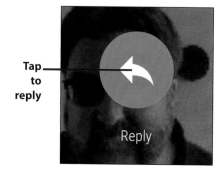

Reply

Reply

Speak your reply

Reply

I'm replying to the email using my voice

UNDERSTANDING NOTIFICATIONS

If there is more than one notification from an app (this is common for email notifications), you see a plus (+) symbol and a number indicating how many more notifications there are from this app. Tap the number to see all the notifications. Tap the one you want to interact with.

M

Digg

This Week's Best Videos: A Ruthless Dart-Throwing Man, North Carolina's

+3 more

Tap to see all notifications from the app

Some notifications you see come from apps that do not provide any way to interact with them. Your only choice is to have your watch tell your Android phone to open the corresponding app. You can then continue interacting with the app on your Android phone. To do this, swipe the notification to the left and tap Open on Phone.

Tap to open the corresponding app on your Android phone

Open on phone

PLAYING MUSIC FROM YOUR WATCH

It's easy to command your watch to play music that is stored on your Android phone; however, you can also store music on your watch. To do this, open the Google Play Music app, open Settings, and check the box next to Download to Android Wear to download to your Android Wear watch a copy of any music that you choose. To switch to playing music from your Android phone to your watch, after you say "OK Google, Play music," tap the blue X and tap Android Wear. This then allows you to play only music that is stored on your watch. To hear the music, you need to have a Bluetooth speaker paired with your watch. To switch back to playing music on your Android phone, say "OK Google, Play music," tap the blue X, and tap Phone.

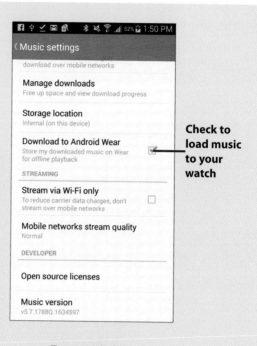

Check to load music to your watch

Tap to switch to playing music from your watch

Play on phone

When you choose to play music from your watch, swipe up and down to scroll through the albums. When you find an album you want to play, swipe left to choose to shuffle the songs on the album. Swipe left again to see the songs on the album. Scroll through the songs and tap one to start playing it. If you try to play music from your watch before you have paired a Bluetooth device capable of receiving the audio, you are prompted to complete the pairing process.

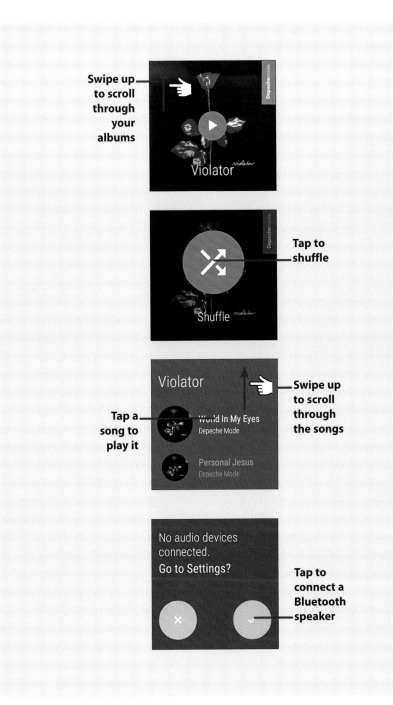

Swipe up to scroll through your albums

Tap to shuffle

Tap a song to play it

Swipe up to scroll through the songs

Tap to connect a Bluetooth speaker

Index

R

Radio Frequency Identification (RFID), 184

radios, 7-8, 95

Radio Stations. *See* Instant Mixes

Reader View in Internet browser, 243

reading
books, 340-341
email
determining important emails, 214
with Gmail app, 211-213
free book samples, 340
publications, 348-349
reviews (books), 340

read reports, 75

rear-facing camera, 7

receiving
calls
accepting calls, 62
missed calls, 65-66
rejecting calls, 64
sending Quick Responses, 64-65
text messages, 79-80

Recent Apps button, 5, 21

Recents tab, dialing calls, 56

recording video, 131-132

recurring events, creating, 275

redeeming gift cards in Google Wallet app, 326-327

Reduce Data Usage, 242

refreshing websites in Chrome, 226

re-installing apps, 291

rejecting calls, 64

reminders, creating on Android Wear watches, 435

Remote Security Administration, 87

removing. *See* deleting

renaming
Bluetooth devices, 171
bookmarks in Chrome, 234

renting movies, 143-146

repeating music, 124

replying to email
on Android Wear watches, 438
with Gmail app, 212

repositioning shortcuts, 106

requesting money via Google Wallet, 334-335

resizing
text in Chrome, 240
widgets, 305

resolution, changing in Camera app, 370

responding to Gmail event invitations, 277-279

restoring deleted video, 139

restricted profiles, creating, 42

Retrolux style (photos), 398

Return key, 23

reverse pairing Bluetooth devices, 170

Reversi app, 434

reverting to original photo, 389

reviews (books), reading via Play Books app, 340

rewinding/fast forwarding music, 124

RFID (Radio Frequency Identification), NFC as, 184

ringtones
Calendar app, 272
changing, 68
choosing, 311

roaming
enabling/disabling, 190
selecting network operators manually, 191

rotating
photos, 388
screen, 22

RTF (Rich Text Formatting) in email, 211

RunKeeper app, 420

runs, starting on Android Wear watches, 419-420, 435

S

S Beam
enabling, 186
troubleshooting beaming files, 188

S Pen (Samsung phones), 28

Samsung Kies, 49
synchronizing photos with, 410

Samsung phones
camera modes, 379-381
Contacts app, 91
extra features during calls, 63
Flipboard, 21
Galaxy Apps store, 292
handwriting mode, 28
Kies, 49, 410
Month and Agenda view (Calendar app), 269
multi-window mode, 32-38
My Files app, 51
one-handed keyboard, 26
Phone app variations, 58
Quick Settings gestures, 18
S Beam, enabling, 186
Service Loading feature, 74
TouchWiz, 12
troubleshooting beaming files, 188
unlocking, 13
wallpaper, 299

saturation of photos, 391-392